The Burdens
of Formality

The Burdens of Formality

EDITED BY SYDNEY LEA

Essays on the Poetry of Anthony Hecht

THE UNIVERSITY OF GEORGIA PRESS   *Athens and London*

Paperback edition, 2012
© 1989 by the University of Georgia Press
Athens, Georgia 30602
www.ugapress.org
All rights reserved
Designed by Debby Jay
Set in Linotron 202 10/12 ½ Trump Mediaeval
Printed digitally in the United States of America

The Library of Congress has cataloged the hardcover edition
of this book as follows:

The Burdens of formality: essays on the poetry
of Anthony Hecht / edited by Sydney Lea.
xvi, 212 p. ; 24 cm.
Bibliography: p. 207–210.
ISBN 0-8203-1091-3 (alk. paper)
1. Hecht, Anthony, 1923–2004—Criticism and interpretation.
I. Lea, Sydney, 1942–
PS3558.E28 Z58   1989
811'.54—dc19   88-17519

Paperback ISBN-13: 978-0-8203-4161-3
ISBN-10: 0-8203-4161-4

British Library Cataloging-in-Publication Data available

For Laurence Lieberman
    —poet, critic, editor, friend

Contents

Acknowledgments ix
Introduction: Something More Than Elegance xi
   SYDNEY LEA

Part I: Contexts

Poet for a Dark Age 3
   BRAD LEITHAUSER
The Poetry of Anthony Hecht 10
   ASHLEY BROWN
Poetic Devises: Anthony Hecht as a Student and Teacher of Writing 26
   NORMAN WILLIAMS
Our Common Lot 42
   DANIEL HOFFMAN
Anthony Hecht and the Art of Poetry 49
   JOSEPH BRODSKY

Part II: Texts

Comedy and Hardship 53
   EDWARD HIRSCH
Anthony Hecht's "Rites and Ceremonies": Reading *The Hard Hours* 62
   PETER SACKS
Millions of Strange Shadows: Anthony Hecht as Gentile and Jew 97
   ALICIA OSTRIKER

Pastiche and Pain: After Anthony Hecht's
Translation of Voltaire   106
 LINDA ORR

"The Venetian Vespers": Drenched in Fine
Particulars   120
 JOHN FREDERICK NIMS

Part III: Anatomies

Horatian Hecht   145
 WILLIAM MATTHEWS

Anthony Hecht and the Imagination of Rage   159
 KENNETH GROSS

Anatomies of Melancholy   186
 J. D. MCCLATCHY

Appendix   205
Bibliography   207
Contributors   211

Acknowledgments

The editor and publisher thank the following for permission to use materials in this book:

© 1984, "Joseph Brodsky Introduces Anthony Hecht," *Envoy* (fall/winter 1981–82), published by The Academy of American Poets, Inc.

"The Poetry of Anthony Hecht," by Ashley Brown, first appeared in *Ploughshares*. © 1978 by Ashley Brown.

Selections from *The Seven Deadly Sins* and *Aesopic*, by Anthony Hecht, reprinted by permission of Gehenna Press.

"Our Common Lot," by Daniel Hoffman, first appeared in *The Harvard Guide to Contemporary American Writing*, ed. Daniel Hoffman (Harvard University Press). © 1979 by the President and Fellows of Harvard College, reprinted by permission.

"Poet for a Dark Age," by Brad Leithauser, reprinted with permission from *The New York Review of Books*. © 1986 Nyrev, Inc.

"Anatomies of Melancholy," © 1986 by J. D. McClatchy and Grand Street Publications, Inc., reprinted by permission.

"*Millions of Strange Shadows*: Anthony Hecht as Gentile and Jew," by Alicia Ostriker, first appeared in *Canto* (spring 1978).

Sydney Lea

Introduction: Something More Than Elegance

This project owes its birth of course to my admiration for Anthony Hecht's work; yet it is prompted as well by a kind of itch I have long felt when expressing that admiration to fellow poets and poetry readers—a mild irritation that even those sharing my esteem should resort so automatically to the word *elegant*. The term creeps into conversation about Hecht as inevitably as *passionate* into comment, say, on Jeffers.

Needless to say, there is no blunder in speaking of elegance in this author's work; but the appeal to that quality, I have sometimes imagined, may substitute for the further reflection the writer deserves, his poems being, to my mind, among the most ambitious, bold, and penetrating of our time.

I don't in the least wish to be strident, nor to point fingers, nor to tar even Hecht's admirers with the brush of intellectual laziness. For one thing, I too easily understand the very response I have disparaged. I recall my earliest encounters with *The Hard Hours* and how dazzling in and of itself seemed Hecht's technique; the craft alone enough to cow me, how might I dare push further on, into "subject matter" (a matter freighted, moreover, with all that daunting erudition and immense *literacy*)?

Happily, the writers for this volume are a wiser and maturer lot than I was when I initially came across Hecht's verse. To begin with, none surmises such a division (perhaps supremely wrongheaded in consideration of Anthony Hecht) between matter and manner. More than one will rigorously examine how the very "elegance" of Hecht's presentation is immutably bound to the themes and issues that obsess him. Kenneth Gross observes that Hecht's "work is often praised for its verbal beauty and formal mastery," but "praised thus with little clear thought about what burdens such beauty and mastery might impose." Gross, along with his fellows here convened, understands that the poet in his very devotion to craftedness implies an uneasiness with it. (Compare William Matthews's cautionary essay on Hecht in respect of another great writer, Horace, so often sentimentalized as one who finds consolation in artifice.) There is in Hecht's vision, to say it too simply, a taut and demanding relation between formality and fate; for Hecht, the artist is in a sense *reduced* to formal expression by destiny (versions of the Fall persist from *A Summoning of Stones* through the most recent of his writings), yet formality is token of whatever redemption he may find. As another critic, Peter Sacks, asserts, "empowerment exists only in tension with a kind of submission"—and, we may add, vice versa.

Even a careless preliminary reading of a Hecht passage, therefore, may lead one to think of Robert Frost's famous and eminently lapsarian judgment on the poem's function as "a momentary stay against confusion"; whatever their relations otherwise, surely there is at least an oblique association between these two masters' aims in composing verse at all. It is, though, worth noting that Hecht is inclined to study evil and violence more directly than his celebrated senior, and to take them on in their macrocosmic shapes. Poems like the chilling "Rites and Ceremonies" or "More Light! More Light!" may leap to mind at first, but in fact there are myriad others.

Even as we note the immanence of the death camps and all they represent in Hecht's work, however, we should be conscious that the author seeks, in the words of Edward Hirsch, "to write a civic poetry after Buchenwald and Auschwitz." This is the kind of thing that the Buckaroo School will instantly turn on its head, the very notion of the *civic* leading to rote charges of archaism, of insufficient "honesty" or "authenticity," these virtues for that school's academicians residing in unadornment, personalism, directness, what have you? (The litany is familiar, I think.) I do not suggest that there are no splendid practitioners of such preachment, but to many of their partisans it is scarcely imaginable that a man could have seen combat against the Nazis, for example, and not subsequently rendered the experience as "confessionally" or "nakedly" as possible.

Where, such critics must demand, is the "I" in these poems, the "I" not as persona but as autobiographer? That kind of question overlooks Hecht's aims—maybe especially worthy in our moment—to engage a universe that supersedes the self in importance and at the same time to wonder how (or whether) the legions of separate selves may find some principle of social cohesiveness. While I flatly reject any claim that Hecht is short on passion, the plain fact is that he understands how concentration on one's own fragile lot can skew his or her appreciation of much larger issues (such self-absorption, when it does arise in a Hecht poem, being usually an object of irony). It is not that Hecht shies away from his own unmediated responses to evil (or joy) or cruelty (or love), but that he conceives of these responses as subordinate to the general human circumstances occasioned by such powers. For him, one might say, thinking of a poem like "More Light! More Light!," it is less important that someone named *I* might have suffered in face of unexampled wickedness than that such wickedness should exist in the first place, and that it should affect so many. Whatever the wrought quality of his writing (whether "elegant" or plain style, for we shouldn't forget Hecht's thorough command of both idioms), it is simply wrong to accuse Hecht of being deflective or, in the ungainly locution of our day, "tight-assed." It is instead, in Daniel Hoffman's apt formulation, that he "characteristically makes of private tensions statements of the human condition rather than revelations of his own anxiety." I for one regard this propensity as the opposite of stinting; it is a mode of generosity and is typical of Anthony Hecht as poet and as person. (I am one of many less acclaimed writers who can testify to this; see, for example, Norman Williams's reminiscence here on Hecht as teacher.)

Thus my principal motive in assembling this anthology was perhaps less after all to confute the notion of Anthony Hecht as elegant author than to push the implications of that notion into deeper and more thoughtful enterprises. To that extent, I sought only secondarily to make the volume in any way exhaustive. I assigned my writers no topics—even if by some hectoring I may have influenced the execution of an essay or two. Rather, I looked for commentators whose intelligence and imagination had impressed me in the past and, proceeding on the faith that each person's individuality would make redundancy (at least of point of view) highly unlikely, gave them free rein. My further faith in such laissez-faire was that it would make for a ranginess greater than plotting would have produced. Peter Sacks has rightly claimed that his reading of *The Hard*

Hours "should suggest an approach to the work at large," and I think that the claim will hold for each of the following writers, even when, as for instance in Linda Orr's discussion of a single translation, the titular topic of a given article may initially appear rather narrow.

Readers who favor what the French call a well-made book may, therefore, be somewhat disappointed by the overall shape (or its lack) of *The Burdens of Formality*. They may find, say, too much emphasis on *The Hard Hours*, not enough on *Millions of Strange Shadows*, or Hecht's criticism, or whatever. Would it not, they may ask, have been well to balance the associative musings—characteristically vivid, witty, and learned as they are—of John Frederick Nims on Hecht's longest poem with a more scholarly treatment of "The Venetian Vespers"? Don't a disproportionate number of contributors inspect the same few poems from the four volumes? (To which last question one might answer that these are, arguably, the works that have lodged themselves most securely in the minds of contemporary readers as Hecht's "masterpieces.")

I can imagine these and multiple other challenges without great unease, for I simply sought a book that would be as readable as possible and as varied, though the grounds for variety would consist in the diversity of critical sensibilities who joined me in the endeavor, not in some preordained plan to touch all aspects of the writer we celebrate. To quote from our poet himself, I was after a kind of "controlled disorder." I make no claim, for instance, that William Matthews has here said all that will at length need saying about Hecht's relations to classical literature, a subject that might need a volume of its own. I sought from Matthews as from the other essayists—a great many of them poets themselves—responses exemplary of their own distinctiveness of mind, and worthy, to that extent, of the poet's own spiritual distinction. This seemed among other things a finer tribute to Hecht than more conventional strategies might have permitted.

So much for my method of selection, to name it honorifically. In its very non-methodicalness, it has made for significant difficulties in subsequent organization, for Alicia Ostriker's commentary on *Millions of Strange Shadows*, merely to cite a single example, could scarcely fit into some monographic niche. Like its companion pieces, it spills over in important and compelling ways, is in a sense an "overview" as much as those studies—by Gross or McClatchy, by Hoffman, Leithauser, or Brown—whose very aim is summary.

I begin with five essays, four of which, unlike the far larger part of the rest, have been published. Some of these are "dated" (though each is as cogent today as originally), but by including them I intend to show both consistency and variation in the views acute readers have held of Hecht in his artistic, social, and historical contexts. Thereafter, I offer a collation that is roughly chronological with regard to Anthony Hecht's own publishing career. At the end I make room for articles that can find no place in this or any quasi-temporal scheme. (I have also—though I'll leave their discovery to the reader—now and then juxtaposed essays that seem to coruscate brightly with one another.)

As the mere editor of other people's work, perhaps I may speak not only of my own motives, aims and methods, for which I am accountable, but also for the accomplishments of this book, for which after all I am not, its being nearly serendipitous that my commentators have achieved what I hoped for in the collection. Underneath, or in, the craft and polish of Anthony Hecht's verse—and these are, to use a lately ruined word, awesome, to my mind matchless in contemporary American literature—they have found a restive, profound, at times even a cranky psyche, one strain of which may be likened, as Linda Orr demonstrates, to Voltaire's: suffused with classical discipline and enormous learning yet streetwise and capable of breathtaking imaginative leaps into the bargain. For those who, reading without pause for reflection, would dismiss Hecht's eloquence and elegance as signs of emotional aridity or academic calm, there is Kenneth Gross's study of the poet's rage. For those who see only a kind of grim stoicism in the lapidary quality of the craft, there is Edward Hirsch's convincing case for a comic sense (however grim itself at times) in *The Hard Hours*. For those who resist the frequent bleakness of Hecht's world view, there is Brad Leithauser's emphasis on his peripeteia , also frequent, into wonder and affirmation. And so on. In short, this collection of essays itself is a kind of proof that Anthony Hecht is vividly and resoundingly himself, but also that that self is a multifarious and unflaggingly inquisitive one.

I should like, finally, to thank not only Anthony Hecht himself, who showed extraordinary goodwill in face of my plentiful nitpicking queries, but also all of the essayists whose work appears on the following pages; they suffered my slow redaction with a patience for which I am lastingly grateful. I wish also to express my obligations to Charlotte Younger for her assistance in preparing the manuscript;

to my spouse Robin Barone, whose capacity to chide me out of self-doubt and frustration was more than normally taxed on this round; and especially to J. D. McClatchy, whose advice so often put this project back on course: he is accountable for many of the book's virtues.

Part I: Contexts

Brad Leithauser

Poet for a Dark Age

Even while we are hoping that Elizabeth Bishop was wrong in evaluating ours as the "worst century so far," and that future historians will look more gently upon the scrambling lives we lived under the gathering clouds of the third millennium, hers is a judgment that many of us—and perhaps most writers—share. How obvious it sounds, and how complex it makes our existence; we perceive ourselves as the inhabitants of a dark age. Future literary historians may well begin their analyses of us with this perception. Of course no one can say which of our literary judgments these historians, peering down at us with that clarity which time alone can bring, will eventually corroborate, and which will be deemed confused or shortsighted. But whether or not our age *looks* as dark to them as it does to us, surely they will regard as central to our literature this perception of gathering darkness. To read Thomas Hardy near the end of his life defending himself from the accusation that his last volume was "gloomy and pessimistic" (quite the contrary, he insisted: "I had been, as I thought, rather too liberal in admitting flippant, not to say farcical pieces into the collection") is instantly to perceive how much has changed in our literary climate since the first decades of the century. In recent years it is the poet of celebration, like Marianne Moore or Richard Wilbur, who may feel a need to defend his or her work against a charge of optimism or, worse, lightheartedness. In a century that has witnessed two global wars and a steady, incremental amassing of weaponry that would seem designed to ensure that the next conflict finally "gets the job done" by expunging humankind from the planet, the poet almost inevitably defines himself against what, in a more religious time, might have been called the forces of darkness.

Not surprisingly, that process of definition is often provisional and complex. Responses run deep and in many directions. Some poets will turn to polemical protest or to raw documentation. Others will simply turn tail and run. There will be poets who take a queer glee in their own impotence, the utter inability of any verse to influence the times, and there will be poets who regard the world's evils as some subset and manifestation of their own ego, and in a struggle both quixotically noble and distressingly laughable will set out to subdue them. Even Marianne Moore, one of the sanest and calmest voices of the century, may have turned shrill and incoherent when seeking to deal with world warfare. A number of critics, anyway, including Randall Jarrell, have found fault with Moore's "In Distrust of Merits," particularly the lines, "They are fighting that I / may recover from the dread disease, my self." Much depends in this poem on how the "I" is interpreted, whether it springs from unintended self-aggrandizement or a vision of universal shortcomings. One might plausibly regard the poem not as egotistical but as a ferocious attack on egotism, a touching—the more so given this poet's patent honor and probity—upwelling of self-revulsion. But in any case, the poem highlights the difficulties attendant on any attempt to grapple with compromise. It raises the question of how the contemporary poet may plausibly find some practicable way to come to terms with the times.

Through the four decades of his literary career, Anthony Hecht has shown himself to belong not only to that small group of contemporary American poets whose work is truly accomplished but also to that still smaller group whose members have discovered some individual, rewarding way to dwell upon the special horrors of the age. Hecht's approach in poem after poem has been measured and thoughtful, avoiding the reciprocal temptations of self-pity and (the more dangerous because the less frequently condemned) of self-congratulation at his own toughness. But if he comes at his subject directly, he does not do so lightly armed. Most of his work is "formal" in both senses—elevated and patterned. He is probably the grandest of our contemporary poets in tone and dignity. With his ramified syntax, his amplitudinous, Latinate vocabulary, and his readiness to retrieve words and constructions that verge on archaism, he presents a voice of unexampled refinement. It is not the sort of voice one would expect to hear dealing with torture (as he does in "Behold the Lilies of the Field") or mayhem ("The Venetian Vespers," "More Light! More Light!"). Much of the power of his work derives in fact from the incongruous tension that results when the most civilized of voices confronts civilization's most gruesome barbarities.

One might conveniently, and I hope without too much distortion, divide into two groups those poets who make some successful attempt to portray the evil forces loose in the world. On the one side would be those whose hells have fury as their source; on the other, to which Anthony Hecht belongs, are those whose hells are built on cruelty. Violence and pain abound in either hell, but in the former they generally arise out of the heat of anger; in the latter, out of the coldness of malice. The former would represent the triumph of emotion over reason; the latter, the poisoning of reason itself. Cruelty—cool, collected sadism—turns up like a recurrent nightmare in Hecht's books, often to be met by a stunned disbelief. Both the victims and the mere bystanders in his poems simply cannot compass the vastness of man's inhumanity to man—a vision so dismaying that it can drive the innocent or weak into mental dissolution ("The Venetian Vespers," "Third Avenue in Sunlight").

The very innocence of so many of these personae gives Hecht's work an additional driving tension. Those same formal aspects that contrast so powerfully with his violent subject matter—the sophistication of tone and language, the intricacy of metrical and rhyme schemes—here serve to enhance innocence and render it somewhat ironic. These formal techniques distance poet from subject even while a restrained, clear, suffusing sympathy suggests deep levels of identification. Our "distant" author begins to look like a former innocent whose knowledge has been painfully achieved.

There is often something appealingly childlike about Hecht's innocents, and one may gradually come to discern the figure of a wide-eyed child at the very heart of his work. This young boy—perhaps the core archetype in Hecht's imagination—watches in a kind of frozen hypnotic horror as the evil of the world, and the desolation of death itself, unfolds. What this child perhaps finds hardest to absorb is the *thoroughness* of human cruelty—the devious and ingenious ways in which men contrive to hurt each other. In its most intimate form, this revelation finds its prototype in one man's physical torture of another; on the largest social scale, in the totality of Nazi Germany.

While Hecht's innocents are apt to buckle in the moment of horrific vision, the poet who stands behind them seems resolute in his desire to complete his examination, as though seeking to master evil as much as possible through the mind's powers of understanding and categorization. (An early poem in the out-of-print *A Summoning of Stones* was entitled "The Place of Pain in the Universe.") This effort is seen in its most ambitious and impassioned form in "Rites and Ceremonies," a poem that calls on, among other sources, the King James Bible in its sweeping locutions, Eliot of "The Waste Land" in its structure and subtitles (for example, "The Fire Sermon"), and Herbert in its paradoxical tone of intricate, ingenious simplicity (the poem quotes from, and gives a twist to, "Denial"). Yet the largest single presence, in design if not in language, may be Hopkins, especially the poet who wrote "The Wreck of the Deutschland." Like Hopkins, Hecht seeks desperately to reconcile earthly woe with heavenly well-being and at times addresses the Lord contentiously. The quest for harmony between the actual and the ideal, between evil and goodness, is left unfulfilled in "Rites and Ceremonies," although there is an implicit sense that the natural blessings of the world ("the soft light on the barn at dawn," "the perfect treasuries of the snow") stand in some sort of impenetrable causal equilibrium with the atrocities the poem so memorably recounts.

This sense of a dynamic, causal balancing of good and evil finds its most explicit formulation in Hecht's "The Deodand." An author's note explains that a deodand is a "personal chattel which, having been the immediate occasion of the death of a human being, was given to God as an expiatory offering." The poem, a meditation on a Renoir painting entitled *Parisians Dressed in Algerian Costume*, is perhaps the most brutal that Hecht has written. It contains a passage as harrowing as is to be found anywhere:

> In the final months of the Algerian war
> They captured a very young French Legionnaire.
> They shaved his head, decked him in a blonde wig,
> Carmined his lips grotesquely, fitted him out
> With long, theatrical false eyelashes
> And a bright, loose-fitting skirt of calico,
> And cut off all the fingers of both hands.
> He had to eat from a fork held by his captors.

Anyone who meets the poem first and the painting only later will likely be struck by an unanticipated innocence in the latter. One would not have expected this pretty canvas to yield a vision of such terror.

Renoir's women are in the midst of a sort of children's game of "dressing up." Their charade takes place in someone's living room, away from the eyes of the world—notably from the eyes of men, though it is a man who has depicted them. They are got up in opulent Arab finery, and what could be a more innocent pastime than this? Yet the poem very quickly begins to tinge their play with menace. The poet sees in the brass ornaments at wrist and ankle a form of sexual fetters (to be linked, some sixty lines later, to those that bind the young Legionnaire). Kohl eyeliner produces "dark savage allurements." These women are playing with the trappings of French imperialism's spoils, and under the law that the poem invokes (the reader now recalls that "deodand" is a legal term), their game of appropriation demands some eventual restitution.

This law, or balancing, is nothing so simple as "Bad must follow good" or "Innocence is doomed." The poem is a complex deliberation on the intertwined fates of innocence and evil. What these women are guilty of is an inattentiveness to the past—a failure to perceive the networks of complicity and cruelty that pervade their lives. Who would have supposed these networks capable of penetrating even here, into this shrouded luxurious livingroom that no men can see? But it turns out that their haven is no haven. Even here, there is no such thing as a private act. One might have thought their "crime" minor enough, and much of the poem's horror stems from the ferocity of the punishment, which falls on someone worlds and years away. And one notes that the Legionnaire is "very young"—which is to say a boy.

The "innocence" of childhood seems in Hecht's work a dangerously vulnerable state, an unpredictable Eden from which one may at any moment be calamitously expelled. Safety—as much as is to be found—lies in an informed adulthood, an attendance to those monstrous lessons of history that wait so eagerly to repeat themselves. While there is pathos in any good poem's portrayal of the loss of Eden, in Hecht's verse this is a poignance enriched by a bitter irony: one leaves Eden, in part, out of a need for self-protection.

If a sense of menace pervades most of Hecht's work, especially *The Venetian Vespers*—the most recent and the bleakest of his books—one meets here and there a lovely benignity as well. That child who stares in rapt incomprehension at evil has a sunny, blessed counterpart: the child or innocent who stands in sudden hushed incredulity before a vision of the undeserved bounty and goodness of life. The beauties of this world, often linked in Hecht's poetry to rainfall, have a way of taking the poet and his personae by a surprise that is vast and mystical and transformative. This state is—to assign a word to the ineffable—transcendent. One gets hints of its nature at the conclusion of "The Lull," in the moments before a cloudburst:

> Some shadowless, unfocussed light
> In which all things come into their own right,
> Pebble and weed and leaf
> Distinct, refreshed, and cleanly self-defined,
> Rapt in a trance of stillness, in a brief
> Mood of serenity, as if designed
> To be here now, and manifest
> The deep, unvexed composure of the blessed.

and in the middle section of "After the Rain":

> How even and pure this light!
> All things stand on their own,
> Equal and shadowless,
> In a world gone pale and neuter,
> Yet riddled with fresh delight.
> The heart of every stone
> Conceals a toad, and the grass
> Shines with a douse of pewter.

It finds perhaps its loveliest expression in "Peripeteia," a poem that draws on what is possibly the most haunting account of unexpected bounty and beauty ever written ("O brave new world"), Shakespeare's *The Tempest*.

"Peripeteia" opens with fragments that function like stage directions to a poem that is itself about the theater. The reader is introduced to an anonymous man—the "I" of the poem—who has come alone to a Broadway theater. If this man is a sort of Everyman spectator, the play is a kind of Everyplay; not until the poem's last few lines is the drama unfolding on the stage identified. The poem lovingly recounts that sweet anticipation, with its inexhaustible promise of release, which we feel whenever the houselights dim and the curtain rises. *This* time, we in the audience once more find ourselves believing, something extraordinary will happen.

And this time, something extraordinary does occur. The queer dreamlike world of the theater, the looser world of sleep and dreams, and the "real world" of the paying Broadway audience all are momentarily united when

> even she,
> Miraculous Miranda, steps from the stage,
> Moves up the aisle to my seat, where she stops,
> Smiles gently, seriously, and takes my hand
> And leads me out of the theatre, into a night
> As luminous as noon, more deeply real,
> Simply because of her hand, than any dream
> Shakespeare or I or anyone ever dreamed.

The poem's ending could hardly be bolder—in a sense, it rewrites Shakespeare—or more satisfying. Only now does the reader grasp the full poetic benefit of having the performance be not only "something by Shakespeare" (as the poem's "I" first identifies it) but the most magical play ever written. No, not even *The Tempest* can recreate the transportive splendor of this moment when our anonymous spectator meets his dream woman in the flesh. That reckless juxtaposition in the last line—"Shakespeare or I"—begins to look perfectly justified. No human achievement or conception can match the actual, tactile plenty of the world. Our Everyman in the audience has met something that feels like first love, and what string of mere words can stand up to that? It's as though that archetypal girl Miranda, who has no memories of human treachery, and that archetype of Hecht's verse, the boy who has encountered some desolating trauma, are united at last. No wonder, then, that they drift out "into a night as luminous as noon." Theirs is a moment far more enchanting than any poem's, though it's a poem that must attempt—again and again over the centuries—to do it, and the two of them, justice.

Ashley Brown

The Poetry of Anthony Hecht

> *What is it to be free? The unconfined*
> *Lose purpose, strength, and at the last, mind.*
> —Hecht, "The Nightingale"

The American poets who were born during the 1920s have come into their full powers and fame well before now, though the contours of some careers have emerged rather slowly. Most of them were presented in Richard Howard's brilliant commmentaries in *Alone with America*. Howard didn't mean to write literary history, and indeed he avoided the issue and perhaps emphasized his forty-one subjects' aloneness by arranging them in alphabetical order. But there is something to be said for a sense of period; in recollection one thinks of the common urgencies and possibilities in the literary scene of a generation ago: the enveloping action, as it were, that the craft of poetry would make actual. As a contemporary, born in the same year as Anthony Hecht, Louis Simpson, Denise Levertov, Daniel Hoffman, Alan Dugan, and James Dickey (not a bad year), I can hardly pretend to be disinterested about poets whose work I have watched for decades.

In the late 1940s those I read most immediately were Hecht, James Merrill, and Edgar Bowers, the latter in my opinion the most neglected member of his generation—neglected, that is, by almost everybody outside the circle created by Yvor Winters, his teacher and champion. These three came together in one number of the *Hudson Review* in 1949, I remember. They were precocious in their different ways. They had been in the army during the war and had much to write about amidst the ruins of Europe, but I think that only Bowers had got hold of his subject at that time. His special focus of experience comes out in the conclusion of "The Stoic," which is addressed to a German friend:

> You must, with so much known, have been afraid
> And chosen such a mind of constant will,
>
> Which, though all time corrode with constant hurt,
> Remains, until it occupies no space,
> That which it is; and passionless, inert,
> Becomes at last no meaning and no place.

Earlier in the same poem he evokes

> Eternal Venice sinking by degrees
> Into the very water that she lights;
>
> Reflected in canals, the lucid dome
> Of Maria dell' Salute at your feet,
> Her triple spires disfigured by the foam.

Venice, after the war, became a kind of *mise en scène* for various states of mind (Bowers returns to it in the second of his beautiful "Italian Guide-Book" poems), just as it was the place for important premieres and exhibitions. But who could have foreseen then that Merrill, with his dazzling verbal gift, would eventually perfect the comedy of manners in our generation and bring us, in the climactic sections of "The Book of Ephraim," the grandeurs and trivia of Venice as we know it? Or that Hecht would write "The Venetian Vespers," a great meditation on the tragic displacements of our century?

I have tended to put Hecht somewhere between Bowers and Merrill all these years, just as a way of defining his special poetic qualities. He partakes of the moral penetration of the one and the wit of the other, to my way of thinking. But this is too easily said, just as these qualities are too easily named, and Anthony Hecht was his own man from the beginning. He is a New Yorker, born the day before Saint Anthony's Day in January, and he took his degrees at Bard College and Columbia. After Bard he went to the war in Europe and Japan as an infantry rifleman for three years—an experience that has deeply affected his poetry. Then he turned to John Crowe Ransom at Kenyon College, like several others of his generation, and his first poems that I read came out in the *Kenyon Review* for spring 1947, where he was Tony Hecht. These early pieces have not been reprinted, but they are entirely competent and Hecht should certainly put them in a future edition of his collected poems. They are called "Once Removed" and "To a Soldier Killed in Germany." Looking back at them from the vantage point of the later Hecht, one is inclined to say that they are very direct treatments of their subjects—quite understandably the work of a twenty-three-year-old recently under fire. The second poem begins with characteristic strength of feeling keyed up by a formal stanza:

> On a small town, twitching with life and death,
> The sun pours his consuming acid down
> On broken monuments, the shattered fist
> Of Hitler's figure, stoney carrion kissed
> By the devouring light, and near this town
> They stitched your lips and cut away your breath.

A recurring image in the poems, early and late, is "stone" or some variant of it, nature inert and shattered: "this broken landscape tied by the wind together." In retrospect this seems to point toward Hecht's first book, *A Summoning of Stones* (1954), which takes its title from a phrase by Santayana implying that the poet's duty is "to call the stones themselves to their ideal places, and enchant the very substance and skeleton of the world." (Hecht uses it as his epigraph.) Someone studying the poems might explore the imagery at length and observe its permutations, but just the titles of the first three collections suggest a kind of progression: *A Summoning of Stones*, *The Hard Hours*, and *Millions of Strange Shadows*.

By autumn of 1947 Hecht was Anthony in the *Kenyon Review*, and he had moved on to the University of Iowa, another literary mecca of the period. I suppose it was his Kenyon year that left traces of Ransom in a few of the early poems and perhaps gentled them. "A Valentine," for instance:

> Surely the frost will gain
> Upon its essence, and execute
> Its little bravery of cardinal red.

Or "Songs for the Air":

> We may consider every cloud a lake
> Transmogrified, its character unselfed.

Few would dare to use "transmogrified" after Ransom's "Janet Waking," though I think Hecht gets away with it. These are only momentary details of style, however, an episode. Like Robert Lowell before him, he was affected more decisively by another Fugitive,

Allen Tate. He never sounds like Tate nor assumes the high oratorical mode that is part of the southerner's heritage. One might place his "Samuel Sewall" beside Tate's "Mr. Pope" to see the difference. What I have in mind is a certain "cut" in the poetic line:

> Now take him, Virgin Muse, up the deeper stream:
>   As a lost bee returning to the hive,
>   Cell after honeyed cell of sounding dream—
>
> Swimmer of noonday, lean for the perfect dive
>   To the dead Mother's face, whose subtile down
>   You had not seen take amber light alive.

These are the final tercets of Tate's "The Maimed Man," which opened the *Partisan Review* for May–June 1952, at a time when Hecht was perfecting his own style. One line—"Swimmer of noonday, lean for the perfect dive"—represents the kind of poetry, taut and rhythmically alert, that he was already approaching. There is a further consideration here. In his prose tribute to Allen Tate (*Sewanee Review*, autumn 1959), Hecht says that what he finally realized from his teacher (which Tate was for a time) was "the way a poem's total design is modulated and given its energy, not by local ingredients tastefully combined, but by the richness, toughness and density of some sustaining vision of life." And this, I think, describes the way in which we should finally approach Anthony Hecht.

In 1952 there were other presences on the scene, notably Wallace Stevens and W. H. Auden. Stevens's rhetoric is occasionally overpowering for young poets, or it used to be. Hecht seems to have been playful about this older contemporary, who is often treated rather solemnly in the Age of Bloom; so I judge from the first group of poems in *A Summoning of Stones*. In "La Condition Botanique" he speaks of

>   hopeful dreams,
> Peach-colored, practical, to decorate the bones, with schemes
>   Of life insurance, Ice-Cream-After-Death.

Then "Divisions upon a Ground," which is a parody of "Le Monocle de Mon Oncle," was reprinted in *The Hard Hours* as "Le Masseur de Ma Soeur." "The Place of Pain in the Universe," an amusing meditation in a dentist's office, surely refers to the first section of "Esthétique du Mal," where Stevens has his hero brooding at Naples in the shadow of Vesuvius:

> He tried to remember the phrases: pain
> Audible at noon, pain torturing itself,
> Pain killing pain on the very point of pain.

As for Auden, one might say that the big set-pieces of *A Summoning of Stones*, "La Condition Botanique" and "The Gardens of the Villa d'Este," could not have existed as they do without the example of Auden's virtuosity from *The Sea and the Mirror* onward. Although the interest in elaborate, even "baroque" poetry during the 1950s was entirely characteristic of the period (James Merrill was an outstanding practitioner even then), Hecht had been reading Auden since 1937 at the age of fourteen and presumably was ahead of everyone else. But he never succumbed to the Auden manner of speech, which of course has always existed on several levels. It was a matter of formal perfection, the pleasure in the finished poem. (Hecht's interesting remarks on Auden can be found in the *Hudson Review* for spring 1968.)

"The Gardens of the Villa d'Este" is a fifties poem in another obvious way. Around 1950, a holy year, the American literati moved over the Alps to Italy, which quickly became the great good place that France had been in the twenties. (Hecht was awarded a writing fellowship at the American Academy in Rome in 1951.) Poems about baroque fountains and gardens began to turn up in the literary quarterlies quite regularly. Hecht's garden is anything but *nature morte*; its delightful eroticism is immediately announced and carried through seventeen intricate stanzas. This is a serious poem, too, and toward the end the movement slows down; the poet reflects:

> For thus it was designed:
> Controlled disorder at the heart
> Of everything, the paradox, the old
> Oxymoronic itch to set the formal strictures
> Within a natural context, where the tension lectures
> Us on our mortal state, and by controlled
> Disorder, labors to keep art
> From being too refined.

It is tempting to pursue the wit of this stanza in several directions, and no doubt some readers have taken it as a *jeu d'esprit* of the New

Criticism (Brooks's paradox, Tate's tension, Warren's pure and impure poetry, and so forth) long before now. But the stanza should direct our attention to Marvell's Garden (the important literary reference), hence back to Eden itself. Richard Howard says that all the poems in *A Summoning of Stones* "are illuminated by a primal vision which asserts, beyond growth as beyond decay, beyond accident as beyond purpose, that there is a significant ordering in experience, fall from it as we must," and this theme would naturally find its fulfillment in "The Gardens of the Villa d'Este." An analogous mode of approaching the poem is by way of the water that pours over the stones and gushes from the fountains: "Clear liquid arcs of benefice and aid." This composes a counter-image to the "broken monuments" and "stoney carrion" of the earliest poems. I don't agree with some readers of *A Summoning of Stones* (for instance, the late Louise Bogan in the *New Yorker*) who saw the Italian poems, especially the "Villa d'Este," as simply a celebration of elegance, however exuberant. The "controlled disorder" is really one phase of a larger and quite important subject, as Howard says.

In *A Summoning of Stones* and again in *The Hard Hours* (1967) Hecht places the "Villa d'Este" soon after "Christmas Is Coming," a remarkable poem on several counts. It is one of the few things that he wrote in blank verse in those days (like Yeats and Tate he usually required rhymed stanzas), but certain words like *cold* and *pain* are carefully deployed half a dozen times in a poem of forty-nine lines, and the effect is almost formal. This procedure is continued by the old verse that is inserted and then repeated in fragments:

Christmas is coming. The goose is getting fat.
Please put a penny in the Old Man's hat.

The strange landscape of the poem isn't identified; it could be the setting for the Battle of the Bulge, where so many of one's contemporaries were frostbitten in December 1944:

Where is the pain? The sense is frozen up,
And fingers cannot recognize the grass,
Cannot distinguish their own character,
Being blind with cold, being stiffened by the cold;
Must find out thistles to remember pain.
Keep to the frozen ground or else be killed.
Yet crawling one encounters in the dark
The frosty carcasses of birds, their feet

> And wings all glazed. And still we crawl to learn
> Where pain was lost, how to recover pain.
> Reach for the brambles, crawl to them and reach,
> Clutching for thorns, search carefully to feel
> The point of thorns, life's crown, *the Old Man's hat.*

This almost refers back to "The Place of Pain in the Universe," with its echo of "Esthétique du Mal," and it could be considered a "tragic" version of the same theme. By this time Hecht has begun to present his subject through a kind of indirection: the old verse, a plea for charity out of the more genial world of Dickens, say, cuts across the eerie landscape to maximum effect. And the serious wit of these last lines introduces a religious perspective that is new in his poetry and that certainly anticipates a great deal.

Leaving aside a number of fine individual achievements in *A Summoning of Stones*, "La Condition Botanique" for one and "Alceste in the Wilderness" for another, I turn to *The Hard Hours*. The title suggests a crisis or at any rate a holding action in the poet's private life, but the general subject is much larger than that, and eventually personal and public destinies merge. The setting is usually urban now: Manhattan with its casual violence and its high bourgeois culture on which the civilized mind can still draw: Central Park and the Frick Collection:

> Daily the prowling sunlight whets its knife
> Along the sidewalk. We almost never meet.
> In the Rembrandt dark he lifts his amber life.
> My bar is somewhat further down the street.
> ("Third Avenue in Sunlight")

The big set-piece of the volume is "Rites and Ceremonies." Here the poet reaches beyond his own circumstances and the public atrocities of our time toward the "richness, toughness and density of some sustaining vision of life" that he mentions in the tribute to Allen Tate. The range of his subject is large—the whole sweep of western history. It is sometimes very unpleasant, and at one point he remarks: "The contemplation of horror is not edifying, / Neither does it strengthen the soul." He has permitted himself a new rhythmic and stanzaic freedom that carries him through ten pages, and the intensity of feeling often pushes against the restraint of the stanzas, as in the long passage on Buchenwald. But it is a "controlled disorder" at every stage. The third section, which begins with the caustic lines I have already quoted, is entitled "The Dream." After a preliminary passage, which touches on the martyrdoms of three saints, we move to the Corso in Rome and the homesick poet du Bellay at Carnival time; now we settle into a sequence of five-line stanzas that concludes:

> Du Bellay, poet, take no thought of them;
> And yet they too are exiles, and have said
> Through many generations, long since dead,
> "If I forget thee, O Jerusalem, . . ."
> Still, others have been scourged and buffeted
>
> And worse. Think rather, if you must,
> Of Piranesian, elegaic woes,
> Rome's grand declensions, that all-but-speaking dust.
> Or think of the young gallants and their lust.
> Or wait for the next heat, the buffaloes.

Du Bellay, the homesick spectator, is I suppose a surrogate for Hecht at this point, and in fact Hecht has already allowed him to speak in the marvelous version of "Heureux qui, comme Ulysse, a fait un bon voyage . . ." that he has placed just before "Rites and Ceremonies."

This is the most ambitious poem in *The Hard Hours*, its center, and perhaps some tentative statement of Hecht's theme is in order at this point. By far the best review of the book that I recall was Carol Johnson's in *Art International* (1968). Miss Johnson said that "if it has seemed nearly impossible for Americans to attain to tragedy without self-pitying stridence or comedy without vulgarity, we now have Mr. Hecht's poems to allay that pessimistic expectation and remind us in what proximity wit and tragedy reside—providing civilization survives them." It is the "tragic vision," then, a term we are apt to be uncomfortable with, that we have to take into account here. Many of the poems in this collection have public subjects; I suspect the ones that have had the most impact are "Behold the Lilies of the Field," which is placed near the beginning, and "More Light! More Light!" which comes near the end. They remind us that human viciousness is a recurring feature of history. (Occasionally, in reading Hecht, I have thought of D. W. Griffith's panoramic movie *Intolerance*.) In the first case the appalling execution of the Roman emperor Valerian (253–260 A.D.) erupts into a session on the modern psychiatrist's couch, and the patient identifies himself with this ancient humiliation. The public subject, that is, becomes the physical image of a private malaise. In "More Light! More Light!" the poet juxtaposes the execution of a religious martyr in sixteenth-century England ("Permitted at least his pitiful dignity") and a peculiarly brutal incident at Buchenwald. He has insisted on confronting these horrors, but in the second instance with a sardonic wit that governs the tragedy, as Carol Johnson says. "More Light! More Light!": these were Goethe's last words, and light figures prominently in the poem.

But it would be mistaken to restrict Hecht to a bleak view of experience. The tragic vision itself, or rather the romantic melancholy that it could lead to, is beautifully parodied in "The Dover Bitch: A Criticism of Life." Although Hecht has the utmost respect for Arnold (I believe that when he reads to audiences he always takes up "Dover Beach" before his own poem), he seems to suggest that melancholy is a passive state of mind that could be otherwise dealt with by the modern intelligence. One of his references for the tragic vision is *King Lear*, a play that has had a special interest for the postwar world, but more often it has been *Oedipus at Kolonos*, the great classic of reconciliation, which he is translating as a work-in-progress. His version of the chorus in praise of Kolonos has already appeared in *Millions of Strange Shadows (1977)*, and I quote the final stanzas, which I think bear out Richard Howard's thesis that in Anthony Hecht's poetry "there is a significant ordering in experience, fall from it as we must":

> O Lord Poseidon, you have doubly blessed us
> with healing skills, on these roads first bestowing
> the bit that gentles horses, the controlling
>   curb and the bridle,
>
> and the carved, feathering oar that skims and dances
> like the white nymphs of water, conferring mastery
> of ocean roads, among the spume and wind-blown
>   prancing of stallions.

An intensely personal poem, "The Vow," which stands just before du Bellay's "Heureux qui, comme Ulysse . . ." in *The Hard Hours*, makes a connection with *Oedipus at Kolonos* in another way. Hecht has twice chosen this poem as his favorite for anthologies: *Poet's Choice*, edited by Paul Engle and Joseph Langland in 1962; and *Preferences*, edited by Richard Howard in 1974. (In the latter case he paired it with *King Lear*, act 4, scene 7, when asked to pair one of his own poems with a favorite work from the past.) The subject is a dead unborn child. In the course of a short commentary in *Poet's Choice* Hecht mentions a poem on the same subject in Lowell's first book, *Land of Unlikeness*. This would be "The Boston Nativity," a harshly satirical piece from Lowell's early Catholic period, never reprinted. Hecht's poem owes nothing to Lowell except, as he explains, the courage of the "difficult" subject. Where Lowell tends to contract his poem through his abrasive tone, Hecht expands backward, as it were, through the Judaic-Greek traditions, and he boldly allows the child to speak:

> And for some nights she whimpered as she dreamed
> The dead thing spoke, saying: "Do not recall
> Pleasure at my conception. I am redeemed
> From pain and sorrow. Mourn rather for all
> Who breathlessly issue from the bone gates,
>   The gates of horn,
> For truly it is best of all the fates
>   Not to be born. . . ."

The last lines spoken by the dead child allude directly to a passage in *Oedipus at Kolonos*; as Hecht remarks, it is an "aged, bitter, Sophoclean wisdom."

In "Three Prompters from the Wings," a triptych in which Atropos, Clotho, and Lachesis take us through the stages of Oedipus's career (they represent the future, the present, and the past), Clotho submits the tragic vision to this comment:

> Nothing is purely itself
> But is linked with its antidote
> In cold self-mockery—
> A fact with which only those
> Born with a Comic sense
> Can learn to content themselves.
> While heroes die to maintain
> Some part of existence clean
> And incontaminate.

Here Hecht approaches the later Yeats, as much in his assertive trimeters as in anything else. (Yeats of course also did a version of *Oedipus at Kolonos* that is connected with *his* sense of the tragic.) Hecht's wit isn't always sardonic by any means. In the last lines of "The Vow," addressed to the unborn child, he remarks, audaciously yet tenderly: "Your younger brothers shall confirm in joy / This that I swear." The poet's first two sons are named Jason and Adam, and in fact they have already appeared in a pair of charming poems where they reenact their mythical roles in random childish gestures. (*The Hard Hours* is dedicated to the children.) But the childhood world merges, through the television set, with the fearful possibilities of the public world, and at the end of the last poem in the book ("It Out-Herods Herod. Pray You, Avoid It") the father offers this curt prayer:

> And that their sleep be sound
> I say this childermas
> Who could not, at one time,
> Have saved them from the gas.

The last decade or so has been a glorious period of creativity for Hecht. A bit to one side of his poems, but closely related to them in ways that I have already suggested, is the translation of *Seven Against Thebes* that he did in collaboration with Helen Bacon (1973). The translation with its introduction is clearly an important event in classical studies; that is, it makes accessible a dramatic masterpiece that hasn't been treated as handsomely as Aeschylus's other works. As poetry the Hecht-Bacon version is superb: see, for instance, the long choral passage in trimeters (lines 927–1109) with its pentameter interlude. (I now think that Hecht, after Yeats, is the master of the trimeter line in modern English poetry.)

The translation was undertaken at the American Academy in Rome, and modern unclassical Rome is the setting for "The Cost," the first poem in *Millions of Strange Shadows:*

> Instinct with joy, a young Italian banks
>   Smoothly around the base
> Of Trajan's column, feeling between his flanks
>   That cool, efficient beast,
> His Vespa, at one with him in a centaur's race,
>   Fresh, from a Lapith feast,
>
> And his Lapith girl behind him. Both of them lean
>   With easy nonchalance
> Over samphire-tufted cliffs which, though unseen,
>   Are known, as the body knows
> New risks and tilts, terrors and loves and wants,
>   Deeply inside its clothes.

Although the barbarians are everywhere now, the poet seems to have relaxed his severity, and indeed there is a kind of joy in physicality that runs through many of the poems in this collection: "Somebody's Life" and "Swan Dive," for instance. But youthful instinct could be "the secret gaudery of self-love," and in "The Feast of Stephen" physicality becomes sinister: Saul watches as the young thugs move in on the first Christian martyr:

> And in between their sleek, converging bodies,
> Brilliantly oiled and burnished by the sun,
> He catches a brief glimpse of bloodied hair
> And hears an unintelligible prayer.

Youth and age figure prominently in these poems, and it is part of Hecht's great talent to be able to move with ease among accumulated memories. He does this as though he were riffling through a heap of photographs, deciding what to discard, what to preserve, and actual photographs are the focal points of several poems. In "Dichtung und Wahrheit" he takes up the subject with a certain hesitation:

> The Discus Thrower's marble heave,
>   Captured in mid-career,
> That polished poise, that Parian arm
>   Sleeved only in the air,
> Vesalian musculature, white
>   As the mid-winter moon—
> This, and the clumsy snapshot of
>   An infantry platoon,
> Those grubby and indifferent men,
>   Lounging in bivouac,
> Their rifles aimless in their laps,
>   Stop history in its tracks.

This poem is on a "high" subject: the "sacred discipline" of art that might "give breath back to the past." In "Exile," dedicated to the Russian poet Joseph Brodsky in America (his Egypt), the local scene is brought to the exile's attention thus:

> Look, though, at the blank, expressionless faces
> Here in this photograph by Walker Evans.
> These are the faces that everywhere surround you;
> They have all the emptiness of gravel pits.

But this harsh first impression is gentled, and then one realizes that it would be the poet's privilege, in this instance, to give breath back to the present:

> This is Egypt, Joseph, the old school of the soul.
> You will recognize the rank smell of a stable
> And the soft patience in a donkey's eyes,
> Telling you you are welcome and at home.

"A Birthday Poem," one of Anthony Hecht's finest achievements, is in a sense about the act of perception itself. It is late June, and he peers through the "golden dazzle" at a swarm of midges, his mind open to possibilities. Perspective, the great invention (or was it discovery?) of the Renaissance, sets off ranges of space, as in a Crucifixion scene by Mantegna. The midges give way to the "blurred, unfathomed background tint" in a Holbein group portrait (a more secular age now). Then space shifts into time through "the gears of tense," and the poet comes to rest with a photograph of his wife Helen as a child:

> You are four years old here in this photograph.
>   You are turned out in style,
> In a pair of bright red sneakers, a birthday gift.
>   You are looking down at them with a smile
> Of pride and admiration, half
> Wonder and half joy, at the right and the left.
>
> The picture is black and white, mere light and shade.
>   Even the sneakers' red
> Has washed away in acids. A voice is spent,
>   Echoing down the ages in my head:
> *What is your substance, whereof are you made,*
> *That millions of strange shadows on you tend?*

And the poet allows Shakespeare (sonnet 53) to speak for him as he has previously brought du Bellay and others into the conversation, as it were. It is a moment of supreme poetic tact.

The longest poems in this collection, "Green: An Epistle" and "Apprehensions," have been much admired. "Apprehensions" especially seems to mark the direction that Hecht's poetry is taking: the long blank-verse monologue that admits a surprising amount of personal history. It is a visionary poem in which the poet stakes a good deal on sheer sincerity. This long evocation of his childhood suggests a large enveloping action: the stock market crash, which leads to other disasters, public and private; his German governess with her "special relish for inflicted pain," who somehow anticipates the "Wagnerian twilight of the *Reich*"; and so on. At the center of this unstable world, the child Anthony Hecht, living in an apartment house on Lexington Avenue in New York City, has a primal vision, what Auden (who is actually quoted) calls "The Vision of Dame Kind." It is a sultry late-summer afternoon:

> The streetcar tracks gleamed like the path of snails.
> And all of this made me superbly happy,
> But most of all a yellow Checker Cab
> Parked at the corner. Something in the light
> Was making this the yellowest thing on earth.
> It was as if Adam, having completed
> Naming the animals, had started in
> On colors, and had found his primary pigment
> Here, in a taxi cab, on Eighty-ninth street.
> It was the absolute, parental yellow.

The vision has "to be put away / With childish things" in the course of time, but it has made itself felt. The poet now looks upon the world with joy even though its tragic course never stops. A dozen shorter poems in this volume bear out the effect of the primal vision, especially "An Autumnal" and "The Lull."

Hecht is now at the height of his powers. The creative momentum that he has built has carried him into larger and possibly more dangerous enterprises. In 1978 he published a poem in *Poetry* that runs to approximately a thousand lines. This is "The Venetian Vespers," and it became the title poem of his most recent volume. In its versification and construction it grows out of "Green: An Epistle" and "Apprehensions," but it is more ambitious. It is a dramatic monologue whose main problem is to create a character, and this it manages brilliantly. "The Venetian Vespers" is Hecht's equivalent of Eliot's "Gerontion." The scale is much larger, but the structure is the same: the verse paragraphs of Eliot's poem have their counterpart in the six sections of Hecht's. Like Eliot in his time, Hecht has studied the blank verse of the Elizabethan dramatists, and the tone for "The Venetian Vespers" is appropriately set by a quotation from *Othello*, as "Gerontion" was started off by a quotation from *Measure for Measure*. Hecht's poem, however, is grander in several passages, being longer, and it frankly owes something to Ruskin: a quotation from *The Stones of Venice* provides the other epigraph. The reader with a well-stocked literary imagination will doubtless find allusions to works by Ben Jonson, Otway, Byron, Shelley, perhaps James, "Baron Corvo," Proust, and Mann. Venice has been a favorite setting for corruption, if not death, for centuries.

The literary references are only incidental to the subject, but they certainly allow Hecht to create an unusually rich poetic texture when he wants to. The narrator is a nameless, middle-aged American, the son of immigrant parents who came to Lawrence, Massachusetts, from Latvia. (We learn these facts gradually.) The child grew up in an A&P store that his father and uncle ran, but the father, caught in the ambitions of American life, went west to make his fortune; they never saw him again. His mother died when he was six. Years later he hears about the fate of his father in Toledo, Ohio: robbed and beaten and knowing hardly any English, his father was taken to the State Mental Hospital. The uncle, in a terrible, misguided access of shame, fearing a "scandal," refuses to acknowledge his brother until he dies. The day after the burial the narrator, now a young man during World War II, enlists as an aid man with an infantry company. Refusing to bear arms, he

> Was constrained to bear the wounded and the dead
> From under enemy fire, and to bear witness
> To inconceivable pain, usually shot at
> Though banded with Red Crosses and unarmed.

After two and a half years he is mustered out, "mentally unsound." Now he has come to Venice for an endless death-in-life:

> Lights. I have chosen Venice for its light,
> Its lightness, buoyancy, its calm suspension
> In time and water, its strange quietness.
> I, an expatriate American,
> Living off an annuity, confront
> The lagoon's waters in mid-morning sun.
> Palladio's church floats at its anchored peace
> Across from me, and the great church of Health,
> Voted in gratitude by the Venetians
> For heavenly deliverance from the plague,
> Voluted, levels itself on the canal.

The verse is wonderfully responsive to the shifting moods. In this passage, the reader moves from the limp rhythms of "I, an expatriate American, / Living off an annuity" (reminiscent of Gerontion's "I an old man, / A dull head among windy spaces") to the muted splendor of the lines that evoke the great church across the lagoon. If the main problem of the poem is the creation of character, the analogous problem is the creation of an action, but this is perhaps impossible. "Gerontion," an archetypal modern poem, comes full circle, but it has only the semblance of an action; and that is the case with "The Venetian Vespers," which ends thus:

> I, who have never earned my way, who am
> No better than a viral parasite,
> Or the lees of the Venetian underworld,
> Foolish and muddled in my later years,
> Who was never even at one time a wise child.

This great meditation makes the case for formal poetry as much as anything being written today. Its author has in many ways carried forward and modified a kind of tradition that I associate mainly with Tate and Auden, the leading members of the second generation of modernists (if we have Stevens, Pound, and Eliot in the first generation). He has dealt with the terrible divisiveness of the age with an extraordinary honesty and grace—what Auden called for in "The Shield of Achilles." My sense of the current scene is that his kind of poetry will matter a great deal from now on, after a period of rather shameless opportunism, and what is so reassuring is that he is writing better than ever.

Norman Williams

Poetic Devises: Anthony Hecht as a Student and Teacher of Writing

Somewhere, perhaps, in the archives of a megalopolitan midwestern university, there lies a dissertation on American writers and their mentors. It opens, one imagines, with Emerson's well-known salutation to Whitman, then devotes a lengthy discussion to Hawthorne and Melville. It might turn next to Santayana's tutelage of Eliot and Stevens at Harvard, before considering Kenyon College in the forties. Later chapters, one expects, would touch on the Black Mountain School, as well as William Carlos Williams and the Beats.

Anthony Hecht has a double place in this tradition, as both a student and teacher of writing. He apprenticed with three remarkable poets, John Crowe Ransom, Allen Tate, and W. H. Auden, each of whom contributed to his wide range of subject and tone. Hecht then went on to a notable teaching career of his own: a career with which, as a former student, I have some familiarity. In this essay, I hope to point out a few of the lessons Hecht learned from Ransom, Tate, and Auden, and to suggest some of what he conveyed in turn to his students. In the end, I think, the same qualities that distinguish Hecht's writing account for his success in the classroom: wit, erudition, technical command, and, above all, human concern.

THE APPRENTICESHIP

The story of Anthony Hecht's poetic training might begin with a piece of good fortune, if not great good fortune, in the early 1940s.

Hecht was then an undergraduate at Bard College, which at the time was a small, experimental adjunct of Columbia University. Among his teachers was a brilliant but troubled professor of literature named Lawrence Leighton. Hecht enrolled in Leighton's seminar on modern poetry, which met mornings at the professor's apartment. Professor Leighton, it turned out, was not invariably well-prepared. In fact, Leighton's five seminar students, upon entering his apartment, usually had to rouse their professor from bed, wrap him in a bathrobe, and provide him with a water glass half-full of gin. Only then, after partaking of the hair of the dog, would Professor Leighton launch into an impassioned lecture on modern poetry.

Whatever Professor Leighton's flaws, Hecht credits him with imparting a sense of urgency and purpose to the study of poetry. He also steered his students clear of the standard Louis Untermeyer anthology of contemporary poetry, instead requiring them to purchase individual volumes, including Auden's first book published in the United States *(On This Island)*, Dylan Thomas's second *(Twenty-Five Poems)*, and the three quartets besides *Burnt Norton* that did not appear in Eliot's *Collected Poems, 1908–1935*. Since none of this work had yet found its way into Untermeyer's anthology (or any other), Professor Leighton evidently did some eye-opening of his own.

World War II and the army interrupted this promising beginning in 1943. With faultless military logic, the army dispatched Hecht to Minnesota to learn German because he had studied French in college. From Minnesota, he joined the European regular infantry. Given the hazards of the job, his career might have been brief had not a discerning officer noticed that he spoke German. On the officer's recommendation, Hecht was transferred to safer work at the Counter Intelligence Corps. There he encountered a second bit of good fortune, in the person of a soldier named Robie Macauley.

Like Hecht, Macauley had notions of becoming a writer. Unlike Hecht, he had attended Kenyon College during its literary florescence in the forties. Macauley had been a classmate there of Robert Lowell and Peter Taylor, and his teachers had included John Crowe Ransom and Randall Jarrell.

All of this sounded rather luxurious, one may imagine, to an aspiring poet who spent his days interrogating captured Germans and playing cards in crowded barracks. Accordingly, after his discharge in 1946, Hecht proceeded to Kenyon, courtesy of the GI Bill, to study with Ransom and to reacquaint himself with academic life.

(Macauley, meanwhile, became a colleague of Professor Leighton's at Bard.) Perhaps no one has described Ransom's manner as well as Hecht himself:

> He had an especially beautiful and gently modulated tenor voice, with the special delicacy of his regional Southern speech, to which he brought a lilt of his own, characterized by his tendency to end his sentences on a rising inflection, as though they were more questions than statements, and conveying thereby a considerate tentativeness. This highly personal, idiosyncratic, and musical mode of speech he employed both in normal discourse and in the reading of his own poems. And we, his students, vied with each other in imitating Mr. Ransom's readings—especially of "Captain Carpenter." There was something wonderfully incongruous about the gentleness of Mr. Ransom's voice and the martial bluster of that poem.

The "musical mode of speech" Hecht mentions might be applied with some justice to the poems Hecht himself wrote while studying with Ransom. Take, for example, the "special delicacy" of the opening stanza of Hecht's early work "The Gardens of the Villa d'Este":

> This is Italian. Here
>   Is cause for the undiminished bounce
> Of sex, cause for the lark, the animal spirit
> To rise, aerated, but not beyond our reach, to spread
> Friction upon the air, causing to sing loud for the bed
>   Of jonquils, the linen bed, and established merit
> Of love, and grandly to pronounce
>   Pleasure without peer.

But there is, I think, a more specific similarity between the work of Hecht and Ransom, and it concerns the study of character. The poem Hecht mentions, "Captain Carpenter," is only the best-known example of a form that Ransom perfected: the poetic portrait or cameo. Besides "Captain Carpenter," one thinks of Ransom's poems "Miriam Tazewell," "Janet Waking," "Conrad in Twilight," and especially "Bells for John Whiteside's Daughter." Each captures, in a few deft lines, an original character and a distinctive mood. Hecht turned his hand to the same sort of endeavor in his early poem "Samuel Sewall."

Before turning to that poem, it may be well to consider briefly the method of "Captain Carpenter." The poem relates the tale of an indefatigable and chivalrous soldier who is deprived, one by one, of his appendages—a story likely to remind movie-goers of the Black Knight in Monty Python's *In Search of the Holy Grail*. Ransom's poem is memorable not only for its gruesome plot, however, but also for its mock-heroic tone. Note, for example, the awkward syntax, archaic diction, and comic rhyme in this stanza, which nevertheless strikes an elegiac note in its final line:

> But God's deep curses follow after those
> That shore him of his goodly nose and ears
> His legs and strong arms at the two elbows
> And eyes that had not watered seventy years.

Hecht takes a similar, though more whimsical tack, in his portrait of Samuel Sewall. Rev. Sewall, a minister, politician, and chronicler of colonial Massachusetts, described in one of his famous diaries a "rebuke," suffered at the hands of one Madam Winthrop, for refusing to wear a powdered wig in public. Hecht takes that passage as the occasion for his poem

> Samuel Sewall, in a world of wigs,
> Flouted opinion in his personal hair;
> For foppery he gave not any figs,
> But in his right and honor took the air.

The historical narrative, diction, and quatrain stanza form here all recall "Captain Carpenter," though Hecht's inclination toward the tetrameter lightens the tone. The antiquated style is even more striking in a later stanza of Hecht's poem, which also demonstrates his genius for rhyme

> But yet she bade him suffer a peruke
> "That One be not distinguished from the All";
> Delivered of herself this stern rebuke
> Framed in the resonant language of St. Paul.

The poem concludes with Sewall's rejection of Madam Winthrop's advice on the matter of wigs. Instead, he visits the Widow Gibbs the next Sunday, a "pious lady of charm and notable bust," and proposes marriage within the week. Though Hecht's conclusion lacks the bitterness of "Captain Carpenter," those familiar with Sewall's life may detect a note of irony. For all his derring-do in the matter of powdered wigs, Rev. Sewall earlier presided and delivered death sentences at the Salem witch trials—an act for which he alone of all the judges did public penance. Yet in Hecht's poem, his judicial excesses do not perturb the scrupulous Madam Winthrop, nor does his apology command her respect. Only wigs count in the opinions of proper Boston, as chivalry alone matters to medieval England.

Hecht has confined most of his subsequent "poetic cameos" to the double dactyl, a light verse form he invented with John Hollander.[1] But his interest in character also has continued in his serious work. In "The Grapes," a poem from his most recent book, Hecht has written a moving study of a European chambermaid. And in "The Venetian Vespers," an extended dramatic monologue about an American expatriate and the title poem of that book, he has delved more deeply into character than any poet now writing.

After a year of study at Kenyon College with Ransom, Hecht returned to New York in 1947. There he enrolled in tutorials with Allen Tate through New York University, or, as Hecht has put it, "I connived, with his consent, to get something out of the G.I. Bill of Rights and his patience and generosity at the same time."[2] Tate had invited Hecht to New York after meeting him at a summer English program at Kenyon in 1946. Hecht has aptly described the weekly tutorials and Tate's teaching method in general:

> The gentleness in conversation always prevailed. After a while, during that first year of our acquaintance, I began to feel that he was almost too kind. He never seemed quite tough enough on the poems I brought him. In a fairly primitive and simple-minded way, I had expected him to "pick out the bad things" with some superior, antiseptic critical forceps, and to advise on the best way of dressing the wounds and restoring the tissue. It was never anything like this, of course. To begin with, I must have presented him with an endless number of stinkers, for I had something new for him, sometimes several things, every week. But as our conversations proceeded I came to see that he was telling me about the way a poem's total design is modulated and given its energy, not by local ingredients tastefully combined, but by the richness, toughness and density of some sustaining vision of life—sustaining, at least, throughout the world of the poem, and perhaps with some resonance to it after the poem is done.

Hecht here suggests the connection between writing and life on which Tate insists, a moral quality that also distinguishes Hecht's own work. It is precisely that urgency which draws us to Tate's poems, despite their dense, difficult, and sometimes obscure style. Consider, for example, these lines from "Ode to the Confederate Dead":

> Autumn is desolation in the plot
> Of a thousand acres where these memories grow
> From the inexhaustible bodies that are not
> Dead, but feed the grass row after rich row.
> Think of the autumns that have come and gone!—
> Ambitious November with the humors of the year,
> With a particular zeal for every slab,
> Staining the uncomfortable angels that rot
> On the slabs, a wing chipped here, an arm there:
> The brute curiosity of an angel's stare
> Turns you, like them, to stone.

Hecht has achieved this same kind of moral force in several of his own war poems, including "Japan" and "It Out-Herods Herod. Pray You, Avoid It." Where Tate, as a southerner, is haunted by the Civil War, Hecht, as a soldier and a Jew, is compelled by World War II. Hecht's poem "Japan" chronicles his changing view of Japan and the Japanese as he passes from childhood to maturity. As the poem progresses, the images grow darker and more taut. The poem begins with a youthful and innocent vision of Japan:

> . . . the academy of stunts
>   Where acrobats are taught
>   The famous secrets of the trade
>   To cycle in the big parade
> While spinning plates upon their parasols.

With the war, however, he comes to see a more diabolical side:

> Now when we reached them it was with a sense
> Sharpened for treachery compounding in their brains
> Like mating weasels; our Intelligence
>   Said: The Black Dragon reigns
>   Secretly under yellow skin,
>   Deeper than dyes of atabrine.

And later in the poem, describing a parasite that attacks Japanese rice workers, Hecht writes with brutal directness:

> For, planting rice in water, they would raise
> > Schistosomiasis
> > Japonica, that enters through
> > The pores into the avenue
> And orbit of the blood, where it may foil
> The heart and kill, or settle in the brain.
> > This fruit of their nightsoil
> Thrives in the skull, where it is called insane.

A second war poem of Hecht's, "It Out-Herods Herod. Pray You, Avoid It," is perhaps even more striking. It concerns Germany rather than Japan and works on a very emotional and personal level. As the poem opens, the poet's children are watching a television western, "As, with a Sunday punch, / The Good casts out the Bad." That is not the way the poet sees things, though; once his children have said goodnight,

> All frequencies are loud
> With signals of despair;
> In flash and morse they crowd
> The rondure of the air.
>
> For the wicked have grown strong,
> Their numbers mock at death,
> Their cow brings forth its young,
> Their bull engendereth.

The poem develops into a meditation on the poet's helplessness as a father and as a Jew in the face of a criminal government:

> Yet by quite other laws
> My children make their case;
> Half God, half Santa Claus,
> But with my voice and face,
>
> A hero comes to save
> The poorman, beggarman, thief,
> And make the world behave
> And put an end to grief.
>
> And that their sleep be sound
> I say this childermas

Who could not, at one time,
Have saved them from the gas.

Although Tate may have encouraged Hecht's serious side, Hecht never lost his light touch. I note in this regard a rather quirky subject that has attracted both Tate and Hecht: the fate of literary characters once their story concludes. Tate takes up the question in his widely anthologized poem "Last Days of Alice," a mournful meditation on the aging Alice of Lewis Carroll:

Alice grown lazy, mammoth but not fat,
Declines upon her lost and twilight age;
Above in the dozing leaves the grinning cat
Quivers forever with his abstract rage.

Tate's poem concerns the relationship between the older Alice and her double in the looking-glass, as well as the infinite regress and narcissism that suggests. All of this is described in rather dispiriting terms:

Alone to the weight of impassivity,
Incest of spirit, theorem of desire,
Without will as chalky cliffs by the sea,
Empty as the bodiless flesh of fire.

Bearing in mind that allusion to "Dover Beach" in the third line, we may proceed for relief directly to Hecht's poem "The Dover Bitch." The subject is another heroine has-been, namely Matthew Arnold's old girlfriend. If Tate's Alice was an indolent noodler, though, Hecht's character is a resolute middlebrow who distrusts poetic maunderings:

. . . She told me later on
That after a while she got to looking out
At the lights across the channel, and really felt sad,
Thinking of all the wine and enormous beds
And blandishments in French and the perfumes.
And then she got really angry. To have been brought
All the way down from London, and then be addressed
As a sort of mournful cosmic last resort
Is really tough on a girl, and she was pretty.
Anyway, she watched him pace the room
And finger his watch-chain and seem to sweat a bit,
And then she said one or two unprintable things.

As may be seen, Hecht's tone here contrasts markedly with Tate's. While Tate finds the older Alice symbolic of all he deplores in modern life, Hecht adopts a colloquial and accommodating posture, not untouched by a certain aromatic wit. "I still see her once in a while," the poem concludes,

> And she always treats me right. We have a drink
> And I give her a good time, and perhaps it's a year
> Before I see her again, but there she is,
> Running to fat, but dependable as they come.
> And sometimes I bring her a bottle of *Nuit d'Amour.*

The third of Hecht's mentors, W. H. Auden, was his teacher only in the broadest sense. In 1950, after teaching Tate's course at New York University for a year (Tate had moved to the University of Minnesota) and earning a master's in English at Columbia, Hecht returned to Europe to share a cold-water flat in Amsterdam with an army friend. That friend was scheduled to marry a Dutch woman in the spring of 1950, but, when plans went awry, the two bachelors motored to the Italian island of Ischia. Their trip was prompted strictly by economics: a newspaper advertisement promised half a palazzo for eight dollars per month, including the services of a full-time maid.

Ischia in the 1950s was something of a backwater, in contrast to the jet-set spa it has become. It included a small community of English and American expatriates who met each evening at an outdoor cafe. Or, as Hecht has put it, "If one had nothing to do, one could toddle down, have a drink and chat." Auden was a regular member of the group—some of whom he recalled in his poem "About the House"—and according to Hecht contributed much conversation on art, writing, and current events. On learning that the young Hecht was also a poet, Auden asked to see his work and later invited him over to discuss it—a discussion Hecht has described as invaluable. For his part, Auden must have been impressed with Hecht's ability, since he enlisted his aid in reviewing manuscripts for the Yale Series of Younger Poets. (That year's winner was John Ashbery.)

One need look no further than Auden's poem inspired by Ischia, "In Praise of Limestone," to see his effect on the younger Hecht. Auden's work is a free-ranging meditation, composed in loosely metered lines of alternating length, on fickleness and fanaticism, north and south, virtue and sin, and art and exhibitionism, with the limestone of Ischia serving as a central conceit. Auden's opening lines give an indication of the poem's design:

> If it form the one landscape that we, the inconstant ones,
>   Are consistently homesick for, this is chiefly
> Because it dissolves in water. Mark these rounded slopes
>   With their surface fragrance of thyme and, beneath,
> A secret system of caves and conduits; hear the springs
>   That spurt out everywhere with a chuckle,
> Each filling a private pool for its fish and carving
>   Its own little ravine whose cliffs entertain
> The butterfly and the lizard; examine this region
>   Of short distances and definite places:
> What could be more like Mother or a fitter background
>   For her son, the flirtatious male who lounges
> Against a rock in the sunlight, never doubting
>   That for all his faults he is loved; whose works are but
> Extensions of his power to charm? From weathered outcrop
>   To hill-top temple, from appearing waters to
> Conspicuous fountains, from a wild to a formal vineyard,
>   Are ingenious but short steps that a child's wish
> To receive more attention than his brothers, whether
>   By pleasing or teasing, can easily take.

This same discursive method is followed in Hecht's poem "La Condition Botanique"—a poem which, perhaps more than any other, established his early reputation as a master of prosody. Though based on the Brooklyn Botanical Gardens, Hecht's work takes as its point of departure that very same island of Ischia:

> Romans, rheumatic, gouty, came
> To bathe in Ischian springs where water steamed,
> Puffed and enlarged their bold imperial thoughts, and which
> Later Madame Curie declared to be so rich
>   In radioactive content as she deemed
>   Should win them everlasting fame.

Hecht has adopted a far more intricate form than Auden, shaping his stanzas like lozenges, their lines ranging from four to six beats, with each line rhymed to its metrical mate. But, as in Auden's poem, the subject matter ranges widely, touching on Finns, Turks, French verb wheels, bachelor oysters, and the Grand Army of the

Republic before it is all over. I close this section by quoting two of the stanzas that roam farthest afield (and which are favorites of mine), both dealing with the dreaded specimen *Dionasa muscipula*, or

> The Mexican flytrap, that can knit
>   Its quilled jaws pitilessly, and would hurt
> A fly with pleasure, leading Riley's life in bed
> Of peat moss and of chemicals, and is thoughtfully fed
>   Flies for the entrée, flies for the dessert,
>   Fruit flies for fruit, and all of it
>
>   Administered as by a wife—
> Lilith our lady, patroness of plants,
> Who sings, *Lullay myn lykyng, myn owyn dere derlyng,*
> Madrigals nightly to the spiny stalk in sterling
>   Whole notes of admiration and romance—
>   This, then, is what is called The Life.

In these poems, the young Hecht seems in many respects the equal of his masters. In "Samuel Sewall" he sketches character and circumstance with the same deft touch as Ransom. "Japan" and "It Out-Herods Herod. Pray You, Avoid It" show the same gravity and concern found in Tate's poems about war. And in "La Condition Botanique" Hecht discourses as freely and as widely as Auden.

The lessons Hecht took from Ransom, Tate, and Auden surfaced not only in his work but in his classroom. Hecht's lively humor, his wide range of knowledge, and his prosodical skills were all much appreciated, but behind them lay something even more fundamental: a conviction that ethics and aesthetics cannot be unbound.

THE TEACHING

Anthony Hecht began teaching shortly after his first book, *A Summoning of Stones*, was published in 1954, and he has continued ever since. I first met him in 1975 at the Bread Loaf Writer's Conference in Vermont, a sort of two-week summer mini-series based on Thomas Mann's *The Magic Mountain*. The setting is a former mountain resort with a fin-de-siècle ambience and an abundance of consumptives, neurotics, and Jesuits, or at least an abundance of jesuitical debate. The campus itself was left to Middlebury College in 1915 by a lumber baron who, as his life's work, composed two volumes of philosophical dialogue between a teenage girl and a pine tree. This seems completely fitting, as do the signs on the highway that bisects the campus, warning motorists of possible flightiness ("CAUTION: STUDENTS") and expressing a blunt opinion of the local poet ("FROST HEAVES").

When I attended Bread Loaf, Hecht was teaching there for his third (and last) consecutive summer. The Bread Loaf "experience," one should note, has two distinct facets—a formal curriculum consisting of lectures, workshops, and individual tutorials by established writers; and an informal array of meetings and minglings with fellow students, most of whom share avid, idealistic, and often arrogant attitudes about writing.

Like many of the younger students there, I arrived at Bread Loaf with certain dogmatic opinions of my own, none very original. I held, first of all, that poetry must be founded on a succession of "deep images." Meter and rhyme, I believed, bore the same relationship to modern poetry as the tutu bears to modern dance: that is, useful only for parody. Finally, I thought, the poets against whom all others must be measured were Sylvia Plath, James Wright, and John Berryman.

I was, then, a little disappointed to find that the Bread Loaf staff that year included no father-haters, rural surrealists, or suicides. I also was mildly put out to find myself assigned to Anthony Hecht as a teacher, rather than, say, Marvin Bell, who at least came from the Midwest and wrote free verse. On the morning of the second day, I purchased Hecht's book *The Hard Hours* and took myself to the shade of a maple to study its contents. Dipping in at random, I found an elegant tribute to some Italian gardens, a speculation on centaurs, and even a poem with a French title, "Le Masseur De Ma Soeur" (but missed, of course, the reference to Wallace Stevens and even the pun). I was ready to dismiss the whole thing as further evidence of the decay of the academy when I reached the first poem in the book, "A Hill." Following a description (in lines that did not rhyme!) of the bustle of Rome, the poem takes a strange and decided turn:

> the noises suddenly stopped,
> And it got darker; pushcarts and people dissolved
> And even the great Farnese Palace itself
> Was gone, for all its marble; in its place

Was a hill, mole-colored and bare. It was very cold,
Close to freezing, with a promise of snow.
The trees were like old ironwork gathered for scrap
Outside a factory wall. There was no wind,
And the only sound for a while was the little click
Of ice as it broke in the mud under my feet.
I saw a piece of ribbon snagged on a hedge,
But no other sign of life. And then I heard
What seemed the crack of a rifle. A hunter, I guessed;
At least I was not alone. But just after that
Came the soft and papery crash
Of a great branch somewhere unseen falling to earth.

And that was all, except for the cold and silence
That promised to last forever, like the hill.
. . . .
I was scared by the plain bitterness of what I had seen.
All this happened about ten years ago,
And it hasn't troubled me since, but at last, today,
I remembered that hill; it lies just to the left
Of the road north of Poughkeepsie; and as a boy
I stood before it for hours in wintertime.

What was this if not the very "deep image" I sought? In fact, the poem asserts that this image holds more meaning for the poet than all of the accumulated culture of Europe, including the "great Farnese Palace itself." It began to seem that Hecht might possess some virtue after all and that his workshop could be worth attending. (I might add that this poem still surfaces in my mind at odd moments, while grocery shopping, for instance, or filling out tax forms.)

I was struck, in those Bread Loaf workshops, by Hecht's knowledge of the technical aspects of verse and by his kindness toward those of us not similarly skilled. It was not unusual for him to remark, as a sort of casual prologue, that a particular student poem might be read in tetrameter, with a rhyme between lines two and four and an off-rhyme between six and eight, which was, however, not carried through. He might then mention that the third line could be interpreted as three amphibrachs, recalling Poe's *Ulalume*: "The skies they were ashen and sober."

Those of us following the uncapitalized and jagged lines on the mimeographed sheet would blink in amazement, since what we were looking at had all the earmarks of free verse, with nothing even approaching a rhyme. I remember thinking that there might be more to this poetry business than I had thought, and perhaps I should consider law school after all. But before I could become too morose, some well-meaning soul at the rear of the room generally would speak up: "I agree with everything you just said, of course, and also wanted to say I really like the part where he compares the sunset to a sinking ship."

Hecht never so much as grimaced at comments like these. He might respond that, while that particular metaphor did not seem completely apt to him, the author had managed two or three other sequences where sound and sense harmonized perfectly. He would go on to suggest, in a spirit of possibility rather than criticism, other directions for the poem that did not even include shipwrecked sunsets. Unlike many student conversations at Bread Loaf, the tone in Hecht's class was never authoritarian, and the terms were never absolute. Humor and kindness prevailed. And in this way, the author, if he or she were shrewd, understood that revision was in order, while the class contributor was left feeling pleased with his critical acumen.

After those two weeks at Bread Loaf, I did not see Hecht again for two years, when he taught at Yale University in the spring of 1977. There, with a tweed jacket and burled pipe instead of summer shirts and sandals, he looked very much the Ivy League don. But any appearance of stuffiness was soon dispelled by his jovial laugh and his distinct fondness for wordplay. I was in my second year of law school (I went) and was quick to take advantage of its policy encouraging enrollment in outside courses—though economics and government, rather than poetry, were probably what the dean had in mind. Still, I signed up for Hecht's creative writing course on Tuesday and Thursday mornings, directly following contracts and corporate law. It convened high in one of Yale's gothic towers, in a concrete chamber lit only by small, leaded windows and an iron chandelier and furnished only with a chalkboard and three long tables, arranged in a cul-de-sac.

Despite these feudal surroundings, I remember the course as a distinct breath of fresh air after the quibbles and Latinisms of law. Hecht's learning was such that he could provide a short and witty history, with illustrations, on virtually any topic raised by a student's poem, including, for example, German art, the life and times of Emily Dickinson, or the music of Cole Porter. I recall in particular a late autumn day when, weary from an hour-and-a-half of puzzling out the treatment of junior and senior lienholders under the

Uniform Commercial Code, I arrived in a state of near collapse. A line in an otherwise forgettable student poem that day referred to the lion as king of the beasts, and this humdrum observation occasioned a detailed discourse by Hecht on animal hierarchies, minerals, angelic orders, monarchies, planets, and butterflies, in which Aristotle, Dante, Linnaeus, Copernicus, Shakespeare, and Milton all figured to a greater or lesser extent. I left the class revived and—what is closest to the heart of a teacher—resolved to further reading. The difference, I think, between the earlier lecture on secured creditors and the impromptu discourse on hierarchy was Hecht's insistence on a human context. For him, a ranking of animals or aristocrats might be curious or amusing, but the remarkable fact was the social need to devise it at all. For the bar exam, in contrast, one needed to know exactly what does become of a good faith purchaser for value of goods subject to a prior security interest, while the evolution and peculiarity of that result (not to mention the peculiarity of the question itself) did not matter one whit. This distinction also may go some way toward explaining the difference between poetry and law, or even good and bad teachers.

Hecht returned to the University of Rochester for the fall semester, but he generously offered to correspond. Because his letters convey his conversational style and teaching method firsthand, I take the liberty of quoting a short section of one here, in which he argues against an allusion to Breughel in a poem that I sent:

> If I may venture a small suggestion, I think you might do well to cut out the reference to Breughel, which seems almost obligatory. You have so well succeeded in creating one of his winter landscapes in words, with his very colors and even his skaters, that a reader instantly delights in discovering his painting within your words; and I think it is better to let the reader discover the relationship on his own, rather than supply it for him. I think you could let "in our latitude" carry the burden of what is implied by the painter's name: that paintings of miraculous events and the events themselves are set in a more tropical and benign climate. Of course, this is not a matter to be pressed too hard. There were northern saints and northern miracles; it is merely a convenient fiction to ignore them. Even Breughel himself painted nativity scenes, one of which we saw this summer in the Correr Museum in Venice.

This passage conveys the generosity and concern one always finds in Hecht's teaching. One can imagine a less tactful correspondent writing, "Cut the Breughel. It hits you over the head like a frying pan, and anyway it's wrong." The message might come across, but one would miss the charm. That would not be Hecht's style.

Hecht's poetry, as I hope I have suggested, shows the mark of his remarkable apprenticeship with John Crowe Ransom, Allen Tate, and W. H. Auden. While one can trace similarities in subject matter and style, Hecht also learned something more from his teachers, and he conveyed something more in his classroom. Though technique was always part of the discussion, and though it is an essential and outstanding part of his poetry, the point on which Hecht always insisted was the connection between expression and experience. As Hecht learned from Tate, a poem "is given its energy, not by local ingredients tastefully combined, but by the richness, toughness and density of some sustaining vision of life." For an author known for his erudition and technique, Hecht's final lesson may seem surprising. I think it's something like this: that the quality of one's writing, like the quality of one's life, depends directly on the depth of one's human concern.

NOTES

1. Here is one example by Hecht himself:

    Higgledy piggledy
    Rodya Raskolnikov
    Belted two dames with a
    Broad-bladed axe:

    "I am the victim of
    Misericordia,
    Beaten," said he, "by re
    Ligion and sax."

    From *Jiggery Pokery: A Compendium of Double Dactyls*, ed. Anthony Hecht and John Hollander (Atheneum, 1984).
2. "A Few Green Leaves," p. 1.

Daniel Hoffman

Our Common Lot

Anthony Hecht began writing in the years after World War II, when the New Criticism defined the expectations of readers of poetry, when Donne, the metaphysicals, and Hopkins were at the apogee of their influence and the preeminent modernist poets were Eliot, Yeats, Stevens, and Auden, formalists all. Within a decade all this had changed, changed utterly, as Pound and then Williams, then Olson and his Black Mountain epigones burst upon the decorous scene, blasting sensibility with free forms, American feet, projective verse, breath lines, and, with the advent of the Beats, visionary poems, drug trips, and political as well as aesthetic revolt against the perceived status quo. Most of the poets of Hecht's generation show the effect of these disruptive influences, moving from early formalism to later free verse of one kind or another. But not Hecht. He has been true to his first self, having discovered his poetic persona in the act of creating an individual voice through modulation of received traditions. His poems form a continuum in which pleasures of eye, of ear, of mind enrich the texts, as irony, wordplay, music, and intelligence gird his lines.

Indeed, Hecht has deliberately stood apart from his free-versing contemporaries, of whom he has written,

> They speak in tongues, no doubt;
> High glossolalia, runic gibberish . . .
>   Some come in schools, like fish.
> These make their litany of dark complaints;
>   Those laugh and rejoice
> At liberation from the bonds of gender,
>   Race, morals and mind,
> As well as meter, rhyme and the human voice.

The strictest metrist of them all, Hecht would seem superficially to have continued unchanged the Eliot-Ransom line in which he began, for even in his most recent work he continues his characteristic use of intricate metrical organization and crossed rhymes that make his stanzas look like seventeenth-century poems. Yet Anthony Hecht is not, and never was, merely a conventional versifier. He combines a metaphysical style with a keen play of language and an attitude to experience that makes his work unmistakably his own. The ironies in his superbly crafted poems are not merely verbal, for Hecht is a modern man who actually believes in God and whose view of American life is not, like those of the Whitman-inspired, optimistic. In the midst of inescapable discrepancies between what we expect of life and what experience gives us, Hecht is open to sensuous pleasures; the very texture of his versing is a play of sound, a search for aural consonances that doubly delight the mind and the ear. But at the core of his poetry there is a Hebraic stoicism in the presence of immitigable fate. This quality is suggested by the title of his second book, *The Hard Hours* (1967).

From the beginning Hecht's work has been implicated in history: he is not one to confront experience *ab ovo*. In his earliest book, *A Summoning of Stones* (1954), he declared his commitment to the life of society, ergo taking history as his province, rather than being an artist who dwells in the isolation of the self. This is implied in "Alceste in the Wilderness": Hecht's poem places Molière's misanthrope in the solitude he had claimed, at the end of the play, was preferable to society's corruption, but that solitude proves at once savage and ravaged by death and desiccation. "Versailles shall see the tempered exile home, / Peruked and stately for the final act." Yet in another referential poem Hecht declares his own freedom from a slavish conformity, poetic as well as social: "Samuel Sewall, in a world of wigs, / Flouted opinion in his personal hair"—the metrical variation of that last half-line flouting regular iambics.

In another respect *A Summoning of Stones* resembles the early work of Hecht's friend Louis Simpson; as did Simpson in *The Arrivistes* and *A Dream of Governors*, Hecht writes of an American's discovery of Europe, for instance, in "The Gardens of the Villa d'Este," which begins, "This is Italian." But Hecht's poem is an exploration of the aesthetic bequest of Europe, not of the terror or pity history had exacted in such places during the recent war; that darker theme will emerge in *The Hard Hours*. Here, in a stanza characteristically baroque in rhythmic and metrical pattern, Hecht uses the occasion of beholding a formal garden to define, analogically, the intentions of his own formal art:

> For thus it was designed:
> Controlled disorder at the heart
> Of everything, the paradox, the old
> Oxymoronic itch to set the formal strictures
> Within a natural context, where the tension lectures
> Us on our mortal state, and by controlled
> Disorder, labors to keep art
> From being too refined.

In *The Hard Hours*, much control of much disorder. The poems embody anarchic emotions yet allow their expression with a shaping consciousness, as of grief in "The Vow," or madness in "Birdwatchers of America" and "Third Avenue in Sunlight." At times Hecht's dramatic lyrics armored in biblical allusions remind one of the diction and vehemence of Lowell ("These eyes, which many have praised as gay, / Are the stale jellies of lust in which Adam sinned"). But in poems that dramatize the hard hours of his generation's history, Hecht speaks with a tragic irony that is his own unmistakable voice. "More Light! More Light!" plays out against the implications of Goethe's dying cry two episodes from history: the burning at the stake of an accused heretic in the Middle Ages, and this:

> We move now to outside a German wood.
> Three men are there commanded to dig a hole
> In which the two Jews are ordered to lie down
> And be buried alive by the third, who is a Pole.
>
> Not light from the shrine at Weimar beyond the hill
> Nor light from heaven appeared. But he did refuse.
> A Lüger settled back deeply in its glove.
> He was ordered to change places with the Jews.

In the absence of the light of either Goethe's humanism or the Word, the Pole's refusal may suggest that he, like their Nazi captor, is too scornful of Jews to kill them himself. As for them, "Much casual death had drained their souls away," and they obey the order to bury the Pole. But then the Nazi makes them dig him out and get back in. The gravity of Hecht's quatrains molds this fable of "casual death" as unassuageable, without transcendence.

World War II made young Americans unwitting participants in the inexorable action, whether chaos or design, of history. Some, like Jarrell and Simpson, recorded their pity and fear at imminent death; some, like Dickey, brooded years later on the destruction and killing that had been their duty. For the American who is a Jew, the war had a meaning even more fraught with terror, pity, and guilt. It was supposed that Germany, next to the United States, had the most assimilated Jewish community in the world, yet those Jews were the victims of genocide. So horrifying are the facts of the Nazis' extermination policy, managed as a murder industry with death camps organized like factories, that one might think the bare recital would make trivial any imaginative elaboration. The effect of the Nazi era on the consciousness of Jewish American poets was to cast a threatening shadow over the presumed security of life itself. Hecht, thinking of his own children, says that he "could not, at one time, / Have saved them from the gas," as though his forebears had never left Germany for America. Just as soldiers spared in combat feel irrationally guilty when they think of their luckless buddies, many American Jews felt guilt at having been spared the fate of their brethren in Belsen. For instance, Irving Feldman, in the title poem of *The Pripet Marshes* (1965), imagined his Jewish friends, Americans all, whom he would "seize as they are and transport . . . in my mind to the *shtetlach* and ghettos," where "in a moment the Germans will come." All Jews are potential victims; in "The Six Million" Feldman writes a *kaddish* for those who were killed. Stephen Berg, too, cannot escape the menace, the suffering, the guilt of this unforgivable tragedy. In *The Daughters* he writes a poem based on the report "that the French poet, Robert Desnos, broke out of a line of naked prisoners on their way to the gas chambers at Buchenwald and went from prisoner to prisoner reading palms, predicting good fortune and happiness." The victim of history's insanity offers in this surrealistic gesture the transcendent consolation of the release from suffering in death, for "The lovely season is near."

In "Rites and Ceremonies" Hecht, who as a soldier twenty years earlier had seen the death camps, the survivors, and the dead, writes a ten-page meditation not only on the ovens of Buchenwald, where they "are perished as though they had never been," but on the historical roots of persecution. The present agony, evoked in the first section ("The Room"), is set against earlier examples: in part 2 ("The Fire Sermon"), the burning alive of Jews in the Middle Ages who, during the plague, confessed after torture to poisoning the wells; and in part 3 ("The Dream"), a redaction of du Bellay's account of a pre-Lenten Festival of Misrule in which Jews were scourged as scapegoats. These sufferings, contemporary and historical, lead in the final section, "Words for the Day of Atonement," to a moving, austere prayer for forgiveness of "the whole Congregation of the Children of Israel, and the stranger dwelling in their midst. For all the people have inadvertently sinned." This long poem, by its structure as well as its language, makes possible the transcendence of its painful subject. In its length of design, in its deployment of varied forms and rhythms suggesting *Four Quartets,* as well as in the title of the second part and in liturgical phrases taken from "Ash Wednesday," Hecht's "Rites and Ceremonies" repeatedly evokes Eliot. This homage to the preeminent religious poet of our time is intentionally double-edged. Hecht is the most accomplished poet younger than Wilbur to perpetuate in his own practice the aesthetic Eliot's influence had dominated. But like Karl Shapiro, he doubtless felt dismay that this principal maker of modernism, despite his public professions of Christian piety, had never made any attempt to suppress his early poems with their crude caricatures of "Bleistein with a Cigar" and "Rachel *née* Rabinowitz," nor had he ever repented of his exclusion of Jews in *The Idea of a Christian Society* (1940) and *Notes Toward the Definition of Culture* (1949), as though Buchenwald had no relevance to the conditions of his own salvation. Unlike Shapiro, who rejected Eliot's aesthetic, Hecht remains true to the innate formalism of his own poetic character, writing a major poem which rivals the work of the predecessor to which it avowedly refers. Its further effect is by inference to implicate in the enormity of genocide—the great sin of history—those social attitudes expressed and made to appear respectable by Eliot, who spoke from the pulpit, from university chair, from the columns of eminent journals: attitudes in which the deeper, more violent prejudices of the masses are always grounded; hence they are as blameable as the cruder rantings of Pound, whose vulgar anti-Semitism was a strand of his insanity. "For all the people have inadvertently sinned."

In other poems in *The Hard Hours* Hecht writes of personal themes such as were the burdens of confessional poems by many contemporaries. But Hecht characteristically makes of private tensions statements of the human condition rather than revelations of his own anxieties. "Three Prompters from the Wings" is at once reminiscent of Auden's tone and trimeter movement, and, in its structure, of Ransom's "Spiel of the Three Mountebanks," as the three Fates tell by turns the tale of Oedipus, seen by the Future, the Present, and the Past. "Behold the Lilies of the Field" is indeed a confessional poem—the speaker is on a couch, telling his story to his therapist; but in this dramatic monologue the confessor is a character in the poem, by no means necessarily the poet himself. Phone calls from the patient's mother merge into a dream of the humiliation of a conquered king who is stripped, exhibited naked and in chains, and finally flayed alive and stuffed by his enemies. The father figure subjected to these punitive fantasies proves to be the emperor Valerian, the dream transposed from the tenth chapter of Gibbon's *Decline and Fall.* For Hecht, private fantasies recapitulate history, and history is personal suffering writ large.

Millions of Strange Shadows (1977), only the third book by this scrupulous poet, is committed to the formalism of his earlier work, with its elegant and slightly elevated diction and sinuous syntax in rhymed stanzas or blank verse. But some new poems are more directly personal than hitherto, in particular "Apprehensions." This long autobiographical monologue recounts boyhood memories of a brother's illness, his father's ruined investments in the Crash and subsequent attempted suicide (as the Depression caused depression), and the presence throughout of Fräulein, the "Teutonic governess" whose "special relish for inflicted pain," savored in tabloid accounts of horrible murders and dismembering, will a few years later be inflicted by her race upon the world. In the midst of such apprehensions the speaker has an epiphanic moment when, before a storm, the visible world of city streets and apartment house walls becomes numinous (as in "A Hill," the opening poem of *The Hard Hours*). But this transcendence is only momentary, "to be put away / With childish things" in a world where "sex was somehow wedded to disaster, / Pleasure and pain were necessary twins." He meets his Fräulein "By secret assignations in my dreams . . . As the ghettos of Europe emptied." She merges into the Nazi woman *kommandant* who had parchment lampshades made from the skins of her victims in Belsen.

How different in tone is the self-ironical wryness of "The Ghost in the Martini," in which the middle-aged poet, asked by a voluptuous admirer of twenty-three what he was like at her age, hears the inner voice of the awkward, genuine self he has outgrown. This poem, sophisticated and lubricious at the same time that it uncovers—and covers—inner wounds, gives unstintingly of those pleasures of cadence, plays of words and thought, that are Hecht's thumbprints. In this and in many other poems (among them "Sestina d'Inverno," "A Birthday Poem," "Coming Home," and "The Feast of Stephen"), some comedic, some ironical, some deeper in tone, Hecht's style, "by controlled disorder," gives artistic coherence to a world in which, as he tells his son Adam, "there will be / Many hard hours, / As an old poem says . . . / I cannot ease them for you; / They are our common lot."

Joseph Brodsky

Anthony Hecht and the Art of Poetry

Anthony Hecht is, without question, the best poet writing in English today. If I am not willing to lavish superlatives on him, it is neither because of the considerations of good taste, nor because of a foreigner's natural prudence with epithets; it's simply because on the heights this poet inhabits there is no hierarchy.

Technically speaking, there are two elements at work in our perception of the world: auditory, based on the word; and visual, based on the image. While the first activates and releases the mind, the second deals exclusively with the eye and confines the mind to the object's finite nature. When it comes to literature, the emphasis on the auditory provides for highly spiritual, or tragic, or purely didactic works, while the emphasis on the visual gives us epics and pastorals. In short, this is the Bible versus Homer. So *lyric* poetry, which is but the fusion of these two elements, both echoes and proliferates the development of our civilization. Apart from anything else, lyric poetry is a sharply focused version of it. If only because a poem occupies such a small place on the paper, each word, each comma, as well as every object mentioned in it, carries an astonishing burden of its previous usages—the burden that hurts a lesser poet into vagueness, a better one into precision.

Anthony Hecht's ability for visualization is absolutely extraordinary. It's not that his eye possesses both microscopic and telescopic capacity nor that his ear is infallible. In the case of this poet, we encounter, among other things, a unique development of the species: the total *identity* of the eye and the ear. While this poet sees, he speaks, and the word makes his eye linger on an object. The simultaneousness of this process animates the object and promotes it from the status of reality into a category, indeed into a state of mind. Or, to put it bluntly, into a vision, where the reality of this world, after all, belongs.

Which is to say that his poetry, and poetry in general, is neither an art nor a branch of art but something more crucial. If what distinguishes us from other species is speech, then poetry, which is the supreme version of language, is nothing less than our anthropological goal. Conversely, whoever regards poetry as an art or a form of entertainment commits an anthropological crime, first of all against himself.

If, nonetheless, Anthony Hecht's poetry is tragic, and to me it is, it is necessarily so, and not only because it comes from this world but because it echoes the world beyond this one. The writer of Hecht's precision can't feel comfortable in both worlds and his eye is bound to find flaws either in angels, if only because angels are inferior to humans since they are not created in God's own image, or in a creed-sponsored notion of infinity. For, to a writer, every creed or doctrine that normally signifies the point of spiritual arrival is but a point of departure for his metaphysical journey.

Every poetic career starts as a personal quest for sainthood, for self-betterment. Sooner or later, as a rule rather soon, a man realizes that his pen accomplishes more than his soul. This discovery often leads to an unbearable schism within the individual and is, in part, responsible for the demonic reputation that poetry enjoys in certain witless quarters. Still, this is just as well, for the seraphim's loss is nearly always the mortal's gain. Besides, the split is never complete, neither goal is abandoned, and in the voice of a good poet we always hear the quarrel of the spheres with the pavement: the first is responsible for the pitch, for the diction; the latter, for the content.

Given the level of today's locution, both in poetry and in the fresco, the nobility, the dignity as well as the humility of Hecht's diction are such that it may seem that his speech is directed not to humans but to the dwellers of the extreme abode. And there is something to it, for to imagine the author of *The Hard Hours* and *The Venetian Vespers* engaged in conversation in a drawing room is as hard as it is to visualize Einstein teaching math in a high shool. Still, it's not angels nor the deity that are Hecht's addressees, it's something beyond, and I think that he simply talks back to the language, of whose beauty, wisdom, sensuality, inevitability of form, irony, and everlasting nature this poet is the clearest mirror.

Part II: Texts

Edward Hirsch

Comedy and Hardship

I first discovered *The Hard Hours* as a freshman in college when I wandered into the poetry section of the campus bookstore and somewhat haphazardly picked it off the shelf along with a few other books whose titles attracted me. I have forgotten the other books, but I was immediately arrested by the voice in *The Hard Hours*—its low, plaintive, apocalyptic urgency, its wry irony and unmistakable anguish. I took the book home and didn't so much read as devour it. The poems seemed haunted, puzzling, necessary. They fused the personal and the political in radical ways; they cried out in the wilderness to be heard. Sometimes they were playful, knowing, cynical; other times they summoned up the most horrific human experiences with a cool, dispassionate fury. Informed by what one of the poems defined as a necessary "Comic sense," they also testified to the darkest aspect of our natures. One listened to the naked suffering in such poems as "More Light! More Light!," "Rites and Ceremonies," and "Behold the Lilies of the Field," and was never quite the same afterward.

The Hard Hours is a book of modern crisis lyrics. The crisis generally comes from inside the self—the individual at the mercy of his own psychic traumas and wounds—but just as often that crisis (so severe as to amount to a kind of psychotic breakdown) is generated by a personal impotence in the face of overwhelming external circumstances and forces. American poets have often written as Emersonian individualists, as if the self were an imperial entity that can create and determine not only its own destiny but also history itself, yet in *The Hard Hours* (and this is one of the central reasons that hours *are* so hard) the integrity of that self begins to disintegrate as it is invaded from the outside by forces much larger and stronger than it. Power is real; the individual is neither independent nor immune from the cruelty or authority of others. The self, the house of being, is physically and emotionally vulnerable, and experience is crippling. The Adamic poet has eaten the bitter fruit and fallen not only into Time, but also into the political realm of History.

During a period when the Deep Imagist poets were inventing a kind of pastoral sublime that would mostly predominate in American poetry for a decade or so, Anthony Hecht was exploring his own urban, anti-transcendental mode in poems of great colloquial wit and majestic formal intensity. Hecht's poems of the sixties are urbane, decorous, stately; their characteristic diction combines an informal contemporary speech with a high, somewhat Jacobean language. But despite a New Critical sense of manner and decorum, Hecht's work is empowered by an almost religious fervor. At times one feels as if he is reading the work of an Old Testament prophet who has been transferred to a contemporary American setting. That prophet has gone to school on the witty ironies and traditional forms of W. H. Auden, John Crowe Ransom, and Allen Tate. At the same time he writes as a father dispossessed of his children, a lover irremediably separated from his beloved, a Jew in a post-holocaust world. The poems have a raw passionate intensity, a vital historical sensibility, and a furious vision of evil. But that vision is also accompanied by a crucial sense of human comedy. Indeed, that comic sense may be the most misunderstood feature of what is surely one of the fiercest books in contemporary poetry.

One of the striking features of *The Hard Hours* is the way the poems continually deflate a certain type of rhetoric, searching out and exposing the false and phony, puncturing the heroic gesture. It is as if the poet had decided that he could only speak truly—indeed could only be believed—after he had first cleared away the sentimentalities and undermined the poetic tendency to inflate both language and experience. The satirical revision of "Dover Beach" remains the most notorious example:

> So there stood Matthew Arnold and this girl
> With the cliffs of England crumbling away behind them,
> And he said to her, "Try to be true to me,
> And I'll do the same for you, for things are bad
> All over, etc., etc."

"The Dover Bitch," subtitled "A Criticism of Life," ultimately questions the relationship of poetic language to reality. The serious idea behind the broad deflating humor is that people have to be treated as they really are, not as opportunities for the grandiose self to declaim rhetorically. That's why the woman whom the speaker claims to know intimately—a distant cousin to the ordinary woman in Auden's poem "Who's Who"—gets so angry:

> To have been brought
> All the way down from London, and then be addressed
> As a sort of mournful cosmic last resort
> Is really tough on a girl, and she was pretty.

The poem playfully fixes the woman addressed by Arnold's poem as a living flesh-and-blood person, flawed but nice, a generous woman of easy virtue "Running to fat, but dependable as they come." In the process it critiques a melodramatic language as well as a sentimental Victorian ideal. Finally, it addresses and adjusts the gap between the romantic and the actual.

A similar satirical impulse animates "The Thoughtful Roisterer Declines the Gambit," Hecht's version of a sonnet by Charles Vion de Dalibray. The thoughtful roisterer is the quintessential streetwise character more concerned with his own safety than with acts of heroism. His cunning commonsensical approach—he'd rather be an anonymous and cowardly civilian who is still alive than a celebrated and courageous soldier who is dead—challenges the longstanding European ideal of selfless and noble service to the state. He not only pokes fun at that ideal, but he also mocks the very idea of dying "For comparative strangers, like Richelieu or the King."

> So far as I'm concerned, you can drop the act
> About the Immortal Fame and Illustrious End.
> I shall die unsung, but with all of me intact,
> Toasting His Noble Majesty and His Grace.
> And if I die by the mouth, believe me, friend,
> It won't be the cannon's mouth, in any case.

Read in the context of the nasty violence and grim suffering that pervades the entire book, the thoughtful roisterer is a more emblematic figure than he may initially appear. He is sly, cynical, antiheroic; he recognizes that he may not live, but he certainly isn't going to volunteer to die for an apparently meaningless ideal. He at least wants to survive intact. And throughout *The Hard Hours*, the question of survival is very much at issue.

There are two recurring dangers or threats to the survival of the figures who move through the landscape of Hecht's second book: madness and history. One emerges from inside the self, the other impinges on it from the outside, but both have to be dealt with and overcome, even if possible outmaneuvered. Often they are intertwined as—to paraphrase a statement by Wallace Stevens—a violence from inside the mind tries to counter the violence from outside it. These inner and outer forces are introduced in the second and third poems of the book, one a "personal" lyric, the other a "historical" one. The first poem in the book, "A Hill," recounts an epiphanic experience in Italy, a vision of "plain bitterness" that ruptures time and turns into an elemental boyhood memory of an almost aboriginal loneliness. After this, "Third Avenue in Sunlight" and "Tarantula, or, The Dance of Death" introduce the two emblematic faces of the horrific. How to deal with them constitutes one of the central psychological tactics in the book.

The rhyming quatrains of "Third Avenue in Sunlight" condense the story of a college friend of the speaker's who suffers what amounts to a total nervous breakdown that he only barely manages to survive. The attack of so-called "savages" stands in the poem as a metaphor for the wild, nearly naked, and unleashed forces of the psyche:

> But still those savages,
> War-painted, a flap of leather at the loins,
> File silently against him. Hostages
> Are never taken. One summer, in Des Moines,
>
> They entered his hotel room, tomahawks
> Flashing like barracuda. He tried to pray.
> Three years of treatment. Occasionally he talks
> About how he almost didn't get away.

The narrator who moves along Third Avenue in sunlight ("Nature's error") inhabits a parallel physical as well as psychological space. He also drinks in the daytime, avoiding the predatory sunlight. Sympathetic to his old friend, he nonetheless seldom sees him anymore, keeps his distance, refuses to fall into either his own or his friend's fateful web of madness:

> Daily the prowling sunlight whets its knife
> Along the sidewalk. We almost never meet.

In the Rembrandt dark he lifts his amber life.
My bar is somewhat further down the street.

In psychological terms, the speaker in "Third Avenue in Sunlight" is a more serious and contemporary version of the thoughtful roisterer trying to keep intact. One thinks of him in relation to those in *The Hard Hours* who, in a sense, don't manage to get out of the hotel room when the furies attack: the tormented speaker in "Behold the Lilies of the Field" who recalls the sight of his emperor slowly being flayed alive and converted into a hideous life-sized doll, or the despairing woman in "And Can Ye Sing Baluloo When the Bairn Greets?" who never escapes the yawning abyss of sexuality, or the speaker in "The Man Who Married Magdalene" who knows he will one day wake up in Bellevue "and make psalms unto the Lord." What Baudelaire called "the wind of the wing of madness" ("Birdwatchers of America") is continually passing over the main characters in *The Hard Hours*.

Death is the victor—physically as well as psychologically—in "Tarantula, or, The Dance of Death." Indeed, death itself, incarnated in the flat voice of Tarantula, is the speaker in the poem, a narrator who comes of age during the medieval plague that virtually levels Europe: "That was the time I came into my own./ Half Europe died." It is as if the plague were speaking in cool tones, in carefully measured, modified sapphics about the series of orgiastic trancelike deaths in which victim after victim goes "out of his head." Nothing can save them from a particularly gruesome and horrific death. Like an adolescent king who has finally reached full maturity, the plague reigns supreme in this protracted moment, coming into its own. (One wonders if there is a primal and repressed sexual guilt associated with that "coming into my own": in the next poem, "The End of the Weekend," a couple's sexy retreat is shattered by a black presence beating its wings "in wrath" in the attic. When the speaker climbs the stairs he discovers "Some small gray fur . . . pulsing in its grip." Thus sex is associated with a predatory animal death.) Nothing can stop the contagious plague from spreading during "a black winter." There are no heroes in this poem, and few survivors. Exemption is accidental. Death itself is the principal witness.

In the ethical cosmology of *The Hard Hours*, there is little room for heroism. The feverish dancing and quasi-ecstatic deaths in "Tarantula" are ironic and awful but, in a way, far more horrific are the holocaust deaths of "More Light! More Light!" and "Rites and Ceremonies." That's because in these poems the barbarism has a human face. Heroism is misguided and even innocent. The hero tries to maintain an impossible purity of action, but in actuality there is no purity nor saving grace for anyone. Think of the parable of the Pole and the two Jews in "More Light! More Light!" It serves as the book's most bracing example—and it *is* an example—of the way that "casual death" drains away the soul and barbarism dehumanizes its victims. Those victims are not even permitted a "pitiful dignity." The language of the poem is steady and neutral, even documentary, the outrage distanced, the riveting story told without much commentary:

> We move now to outside a German wood.
> Three men are there commanded to dig a hole
> In which the two Jews are ordered to lie down
> And be buried alive by the third, who is a Pole.
>
> Not light from the shrine at Weimar beyond the hill
> Nor light from heaven appeared. But he did refuse.
> A Lüger settled back deeply in its glove.
> He was ordered to change places with the Jews.
>
> Much casual death had drained away their souls.
> The thick dirt mounted toward the quivering chin.
> When only the head was exposed the order came
> To dig him out again and to get back in.
>
> No light, no light in the blue Polish eye.
> When he finished a riding boot packed down the earth.
> The Lüger hovered lightly in its glove.
> He was shot in the belly and in three hours bled to death.
>
> No prayer or incense rose up in those hours
> Which grew to be years, and every day came mute
> Ghosts from the ovens, sifting through crisp air
> And settled upon his eyes in a black soot.

In this bleak twentieth-century exemplum, heroism is unrewarded and suffering is neither redemptive nor transcendental. It doesn't signify. The Pole acts humanely (and without any sign higher than his own conscience) and yet he suffers a death as slow and brutal as that of his victims, the Jews who have already lost their souls and now lose their lives, too. The dehumanization is complete—even the guard is metonymically identified only as his "Lüger." There are no mourners or saviors in this poem. There is only the relentless stripping certainty of the death camps. And the eventual passing of time. The Goethean ideal of light has been replaced by the banal darkness of evil. Humanism, like the Age of Reason, is dead. Civilization—represented by the shrine at Weimar—is effectively over.

There *is* a survivor in "Rites and Ceremonies." His is the ethic of the solitary witness. He has "come home" from the camps, but twenty years later he still can't forget a large room filled with human hair, nor a trainload of some five hundred people who are about to be "made into soap," nor the constant screaming of little children going to their deaths. He stands as a twentieth-century Job cataloging a series of unspeakable horrors and crying out in his anguish to "Father, adonoi, author of all things." At night when he sets out to pray he feels himself being sucked back into the ovens with the millions who "have come to this pass." Prayer is for him a reenactment of suffering. He is a tainted survivor (tainted only because he has survived) whose afflicted testimony to an invisible God is one of the only memorials for the victims. He is akin to the patient in "Behold the Lilies of the Field" who is "made to watch" the worst atrocity imaginable, who can't turn away from the torture and whose only redemption (sanity) is in the excruciating attempt to find an adequate language for suffering. In their struggle to acquire a language equal to the cruelest extremities of experience, both of these narrators are stand-ins for the poet who is, after all, trying to write a civic poetry after Auschwitz and Buchenwald.

The second, third, and fourth sections of "Rites and Ceremonies" enlarge and universalize the catalog of slaughters, beyond the twentieth century. Each of these holocausts is horrific, unbearable, metaphysically equal. They are all unjust. The cowards and heroes are burned together; the weak and the faithful are destroyed just like the strong and the faithless. At times the voice in the poem reaches a pitch of grief nearly impossible to listen to—indeed, it is archaically addressed to God the Father. There is an intermittent and inconsolable religious anguish in *The Hard Hours* that is perhaps unequaled since Hopkins's late "terrible" sonnets.

> Father, among these many souls
> Is there not one
> Whom thou shalt pluck for love out of the coals?
> Look, look, they have begun
> To douse the rags.

> O that thou shouldst give dust a tongue
> To crie to thee,
> And then not heare it crying! Who is strong
> When the flame eats his knee?
> O hear my prayer,
> And let my cry come unto thee.

Alternating with this pleading outcry to the Deity, there is another voice in "Rites and Ceremonies" that is more social and daily, more matter-of-fact. This understated voice not only gives a flat listing of the horrors ("In Marseilles, one hundred and fifty Friars Minor. / In the region of Provence, three hundred and fifty-eight / Of the Friars Preachers died in Lent") but also presents a series of dark conclusions. One finds a powerful and negative anti-heroic moral in each of the final three sections: that the slaughter of innocents is "not a judgment" (2, "The Fire Sermon"); that "The contemplation of horror is not edifying, / Neither does it strengthen the soul" (3, "The Dream"); and that "Merely to survive is not an index of excellence, / Nor, given the way things go, / Even of low cunning" (4, "Words for the Day of Atonement"). These are the conclusions of experience stripped of its last illusions.

It is against the backdrop of recurring historical cruelty, of scapegoating and victimization, of compromises and conditions, fevers and losses, that one understands what Hecht means by a "Comic sense." Here is the defining passage from the Yeatsian second section of "Three Prompters from the Wings":

> Some sentimental fool
> Invented the Tragic Muse.
> She doesn't exist at all.
> For human life is composed
> In reasonably equal parts
> Of triumph and chagrin,
> And the parts are so hotly fused
> As to seem a single thing.
> This is true as well
> Of wisdom and ignorance
> And of happiness and pain:
> But is linked with its antidote
> In cold self-mockery—
> A fact with which only those
> Born with a Comic sense

> Can learn to content themselves.
> While heroes die to maintain
> Some part of existence clean
> And incontaminate.
>   ("Clotho: or, The Present")

To live as an adult is to live in a compromised, tainted, and impure world. It is to know triumph mixed with chagrin, happiness balanced by pain. The hero who needs to maintain purity can't in fact live in the world as it is. He wants a simpler and cleaner place. The survivor, on the other hand, learns to accept the cold self-mocking compromises of reality. As opposed to the sentimentalization of the Tragic Muse, he must learn to content himself with a more complex and impure Comic Muse.

It is with this kind of self-knowledge that the Jewish father recognizes at the end of the book that at one time he could not have spared his children from the German ovens ("It Out-Herods Herod. Pray You, Avoid It"). While his sons live in an allegorical world of televised fairy tales and westerns where "The Good casts out the Bad," he understands a harsher and more complicated reality, not only the presence but also the sustaining power and often the victory of evil. Thus the book ends with a tender prayer for their safety:

> And that their sleep be sound
> I say this childermas
> Who could not, at one time,
> Have saved them from the gas.

This is the voice of lonely acknowledgment and recognition. And this recognition is one of the central insights of Hecht's lyrical poetry of mature adulthood.

The Hard Hours is a masterpiece of comedy and hardship, of madness descended and sanity triumphant, of evil encountered in the various guises of history, and of suffering witnessed and remembered. No one who reads it ever forgets its fierce clarities. American poetry is forever richer because of its dark knowledge and wisdom.

Peter Sacks

Anthony Hecht's "Rites and Ceremonies": Reading *The Hard Hours*

[Dante's] art is, in the original Greek sense, an imitation or rehearsal of nature, an anticipation of fate.
  —George Santayana, *Three Philosophical Poets*

They seem to fulfil a destiny which not only satisfies the inexorable and arbitrary patterns of the music, but might be a perfect counterpart of the happiest of fates. Or perhaps not altogether the happiest. . . .
  —Hecht, "On the Methods and Ambitions of Poetry"

Anthony Hecht's poetry has deservedly been admired for its mastery of form, a mastery rarely found in American poetry of the last three decades. Yet even among those who do write formal poetry Hecht stands with the yet more distinguished few whose work goes beyond virtuosity or formal elegance to meditate upon the very conditions that give rise to its formality—conditions or rather *imperatives* that may challenge and perhaps in extreme cases almost subvert the poet's finest accomplishments. Hecht's work therefore offers us something rare: the opportunity to study some of the deeper implications and functions of contemporary formal poetry; the chance to clarify what achievements we may look for in such poetry, achievements by which to discriminate against less responsible examples of formal verse; and the possibility of experiencing how some of the most powerful poems of our time test themselves against the pressures of their own compulsions, and against the furthest limits of their calling.

In Hecht's case, the imperatives to formality are various, and the following essay will explore several of them. But we may note at the outset that they will range from the private to the communal or transpersonal, since few serious commitments to formality (particularly within lyric verse) lie outside the intersection of these domains. Indeed, at their most rigorous such commitments will often force us to question our very assumptions of privacy or autonomy, and we shall see how Hecht's themes have always advanced that questioning. Unlike the all too many writers who currently "strive to render / The cross-word world in perfectly declined / Pronouns beginning with ME," Hecht attends to the bonds of aesthetic form in such a way as to represent his larger sense of the bonds that determine not only the mysterious forces of nature or history, but also the contours of any responsible human self.[1] Such bonds and contours may be those of aspiration, for as Hecht has written the poem is "Governed by laws that stand for other laws, / Both of which aim, through kindred disciplines, / At the soul's knowledge and habiliment." Or they may be those of darker necessity, embodying what is painfully ineluctable. Recalling the two epigraphs above, we may say that Hecht's poems formally represent the designing forces of fate itself. In fact, few contemporary poets have so thoroughly explored how each of us may be directed by the "Three Prompters from the Wings."

It is this larger sense of the relation between formality and fate that sets Hecht's work apart from the trivial and gratuitous stylizations that mar so much contemporary formal verse. And it is this concern, with its ceremoniously enacted responsiveness to the frequently hidden mesh of personal and impersonal compulsions, that gives so many of Hecht's poems the property of *ritual*. Not by chance did he entitle one of his most ambitious and passionate sequences "Rites and Ceremonies."

By regarding many of Hecht's poems as "rites and ceremonies" I want not only to stress their formal properties but also to ask what these properties represent and what kind of acts they perform. In doing so, I will concentrate (for chronological reasons) on *The Hard Hours* (1967), though with a schematic mention of the earlier *A Summoning of Stones* (1954), and a brief glance ahead to *Millions of Strange Shadows* (1977) and *The Venetian Vespers* (1979). Like his individual poems, Hecht's entire career thus far has great formal coherence, and my reading of the one book should suggest an approach to his work at large. While giving needed specificity to such terms as "fate" or "ritual," "compulsions" or "imperatives," I will follow the self-revisions and developments of these and other related topics throughout Hecht's work. Along the way I'm hoping to account not only for the particular satisfactions that Hecht's poems provide, but also for their occasional ability to disturb both their author and their readers almost to the point of numbed silence. Alongside poems in celebration of nature, human artifice, love, or erotic desire, we shall encounter poems as shattering and bleak as any of our time, works that will also compel us to qualify my opening remark about Hecht's mastery, by realizing the degree to which such mastery may involve something as disconcerting as "being mastered."

The fifteen poems chosen from *A Summoning of Stones* to be reprinted with *The Hard Hours* have great consistency of style and subject. Even a much briefer consideration than they require and reward can take the reader well into a discussion of Hecht's later work. For example, the very first poem, "Double Sonnet," draws attention both to a young poet's willingness to engage the traditional forms at an almost hypertrophically demanding level and to his understanding of the kind of thematic arguments generically associated with the sonnet form—matters of love and rule, of mastery and unmanning speechlessness, of the precarious humanization of "numbers" by "sheer extravagance," and most important, of the terrifying oscillation between "a grace won by the way from all / Striving in what is difficult," and "the unbidden terror and bone hand / Of gracelessness." This oscillation, or rather *fall*, intensifying those from ease to unease, or from mastery to unmanning, confirms the more than merely aesthetic dimensions of "grace" and hence of Hecht's formal style itself. And while the emphasis and meaning of grace will deepen throughout Hecht's work, we will also notice just how characteristic is the structural and stylistic embodiment of the very fallenness on which these poems meditate. Not only is a fall part of the paradigmatic movement of many of Hecht's poems, but fallenness and its opposing grace are both paradoxically reflected by these poems' highly wrought submissions to entire networks of formal bonds. As suggested above, these bonds become an image of fate or destiny; and "destiny" (as Hecht concludes in a sestina whose aesthetic laws themselves enforce his point) is "neither to our mind nor of our making."[2]

Admittedly, this kind of formal subjection, particularly to mediating codes and conventions, marks almost every seriously ambitious poet's entry into poetic tradition. But as I am suggesting, Hecht's early work deepens these rites of initiation by enacting them within the context of the human Fall. For just as the young poet's achievement of formal mastery depends on a renunciation of lawless instinctual expression, and on a submission to the exaggeratedly formal displacements and shapings of poetic language, so mankind is doomed not only to the various "bonds of gender, / Races, morals and mind"—not to mention those of mortality—but also to the world of law and artifice. Indeed, if there are to be any imagings of Edenic innocence and timelessness, these can occur now only through labor and ingenious art. "Disinherited heirs, / Old Adams," we peer through plate glass windows of a greenhouse to envision our original garden; "most perishably flawed," we depend on the "searching discipline" of art to keep the "eye still clear, as though in spite of Hell."[3]

What gives these early poems much of their subtlety as well as their syntactic complexities and sinewy uses of paradox is therefore the poet's recognition that his unusually heightened, at times almost baroque formality is a consequence and sign of a fall from natural grace, while also being an inescapably difficult means to the very conception or imitation of such grace. But these poems have tensile power as well as subtlety, and there are several reasons for this. The first is the doubling whereby the poet's confrontation with the bonds of aesthetic form embodies his explicit regard for the laws that also bind our loves ("As Plato Said," "Imitation"), our wars ("A Deep Breath at Dawn," "A Roman Holiday"), or our desires, whether for the regained vision of youth or for an image of immortality itself ("The Gardens of the Villa d'Este," "A Poem for Julia"). Beyond this, several kinds of forceful energy are actually aroused by these double bonds. Admittedly, such laws as those of desire or aggression are not merely forms but rather *forces*.

> Yet I am mastered by uncommon force
> And made to think of you, although it blends
> Not with my humor . . .
> . . . .
> But it is a compelling kind of law
> Puts your design before me.
>   ("As Plato Said")

>   Then shall the sullen god
> Perform his mindless fury in our blood.
>   ("A Deep Breath at Dawn")

But even where formal rules are precisely those of artificial codes, the poet's energies are invigorated and braced by them, as by a challenging obstacle that provides the very opportunity and standard by which to prove his powers. With their highly mediated deployments of formal diction, syntax, meter, and rhyme these early poems move with the assurance and energy of perfectly rigged ships, buoyed and partly driven by the thrill of prowess thus demonstrated. That such prowess is bought only by discipline, and that such empowerment exists only in tension with a kind of submission, is one of the paradoxes that will recur with many (and usually darker) modulations throughout Hecht's work.

These poems are further enlivened by their energetic resistance to what might otherwise become arid formalism or its concomitants in mere determinism or in puritanical bids for perfection. In "Discourse Concerning Temptation," one of the several explicit references to the Fall, "man's brief and natural estate" is situated uneasily between the poles not only of Paradise and Hell but also of "formula" on the one hand and menacingly profuse nature on the other. The "gentleman of severest taste / Who won from wickedness by consummate strife / A sensibility suitable to his chaste / Formula" is consequently haunted and undone by the world his formulas exclude. And "The Gardens of the Villa d'Este" moves through a brilliant description of the formal gardens and sculptured fountains to reveal how the artificially plotted site works an effect that is "binding," yes, but whose bonds work provocatively "upon the gland." The poet's own devices, resembling the gardens with all the seductively "deft control / And artifice of an Hephaestus' net," are themselves designed to work as "more than formulas." For craft is nothing without the energy of a necessitating purpose, form is nothing without the counter-thrust of passion, and the poem's underlying ritual, like that which once observed the month of May (compare Herrick's "Corrina's Going A-Maying") would be frivolous without its deliberate processional of desire. These verbal gardens and their contrived elicitings of natural impulse have a *path* that would lead, precisely by its formal inevitability, to bed and to the renewals of May.

"More than formulas," then, for several reasons—amongst which should be added the poet's sense that the world itself, like each of his vigorous yet topiary stanzas in "The Gardens," is a paradoxical interplay of order and its unruly opposite:

> For thus it was designed:
> Controlled disorder at the heart
> Of everything, the paradox, the old
> Oxymoronic itch to set the formal strictures
> Within a natural context, where the tension lectures
> Us on our mortal state, and by controlled
> Disorder, labors to keep art
> From being too refined.[4]

This formally burgeoning celebration of "controlled disorder" brings to mind Hecht's statement: "The poem wishes to pay its homage to the natural world, from which it derives and strives to imitate. And there is in nature a superfluity, an excess of texture."[5] An additional reason for several of the poems' densely woven ceremonial fabrics may thus be their imitation of superfluous texture, as well as their formal payment of homage—an act that maintains the traces and forms of ritual offering.

The urge to pay homage compels much of Hecht's later work. But that urge becomes grimly complicated by realities that are far harder to celebrate. In fact if we look at "Christmas is Coming" (an early harbinger of "Rites and Ceremonies") or ahead to most of *The Hard Hours* we find harrowing reprises of structures and themes already discussed. The laws determining experience and art become more sinister compulsions; paying homage comes to require the bearing of painful witness; the fall from grace involves not merely a descent into time, mortality, and artifice, but rather an entrapment in situations of psychic and political anguish. Where before we had lost unmediated innocence and ease, now we come more closely to know evil and suffering. And now the resistance to concord or graceful order will derive not so much from the irrepressible "excess" of nature or desire, as from the disruptive forces of cruelty and pain—forces whose binding insistences give them a deeply troubling formality of their own.

As might be expected, Hecht's rites and ceremonies change accordingly. The initiations of a poet into the traditional codes of art are now mirrored by harsher scenes of origin, and by more frightening rituals of subjection. Celebration turns toward acts of witness and expiation; ceremonies of seduction or renewal give way to those of affliction or attempted catharsis. So, too, the pursuit of grace proves more urgent, even desperate, as the meaning of grace itself moves from that of assured rightness or beautiful deportment to that of merciful deliverance or redemption. I will return later to these ideas, particularly those of catharsis and grace. But for the moment I should turn from further abstract cataloguing to the poems themselves.

Our point of entry to *The Hard Hours* is its title and related epigraph. "Hard" now applies not to the almost timeless lapidary emblems of a summoned order, but to the painful rigors of temporality and of "the times" themselves. Title and epigraph force us back through more than six centuries to an earlier expression of suffering, a suffering which itself occurs by looking back through time to all that has been lost forever: "Al that joye is went away, / That wele is comen to weylaway, / To manye harde stoundes." The early English poem has a Latin title ("Ubi Sunt Qui Ante Nos Fuerunt") so that it, too, reads like a translation of yet prior pains. We shall see how many poems in Hecht's book of hours work precisely by returning to past sufferings that themselves look back to or translate yet earlier originals. Both within and between themselves, these poems provide successive mirrorings and echoings of pain. These may be distributed across space ("But miles and miles away / suffers another man"), though more essentially they reverberate through time (as in "Rites and Ceremonies" or "More Light! More Light!"). In the words of du Bellay, one of Hecht's favored poets (whose use of *durer* points to the blend of pain and duration in *The Hard Hours*): "rien ne dure au monde que le tourment."[6] Inescapably, such persistences point to a suffering whose recalcitrance seems to be both psychologically and historically fated.

With this in mind we approach "A Hill," the extraordinary *paysage démoralisé* that stands at the beginning of the collection, rather as "un colle" stood at the beginning of Dante's journey. The poem itself is *about* an involuntary return to a fearful kind of beginning, a scene of "plain bitterness" that has inscribed itself on the mind with something close to infernal insistence. What is interesting here is that this early scene disrupts not only the subsequent conscious mind but also the very network of coded phenomena—

friendship, urban architecture, markets of exchange, the accumulations of conventional currencies and representations—that we have come to associate with the bonds and matrices of the cultured self. Against this network, and at the very moment when the civilized scene appears to hold out "gestures of exultation" or intimations of "godliness" (for this poem, too, enacts a kind of fall), an even more compelling imperative forces itself upon the mind. The bonds of artifice or social life are thus disrupted by a yet more severe bondage to a scene of desolation encrypted so deeply in the psyche that its first surfacing is not even recognized as an actual recollection. If we have come to notice the dispossession associated with obedience to the forms of culture and society, "A Hill" portrays a far more frightening and antithetical dispossession—a seizure by the returning perception of a scene of such menacing blankness that it threatens to rip apart those very fabrics of consciousness, society, or art that might have been designed in part to cover its adversarial reality.

Yet the scene is eventually recognized, and it is given both its moment in the time of childhood and its geographical place. The mind also comes to repossess a portion of its own experience, however devastating. Furthermore, there is an undeniable empowerment in the very ability to sweep away the entire realm of Roman piazza and marble palace and to confront us so immediately with their drastic replacement. At the beginning of his book, the poet thus signals one of his powers as being that of making such radical substitutions or regressions, suggesting perhaps that his art will return to the unadorned grounds preceding those of art. Henceforth, no marble palaces will be allowed to exist without the eclipsing awareness of an unaccommodatingly bare hill. No social or aesthetic forms will be free from personal recognitions of desolation.

Reinaugurating an earlier threshold experience, the poem thus acts as a threshold itself: enter this book, recognize this bare hill, pass over the mental boundaries such a crossing implies. At the same time, the poem performs an act of apparent self-grounding (however abysmal), both in returning to a childhood scene and in establishing the hill as a landmark figure for the radically subversive and self-isolating powers of the poet's mind. That such an act should be involuntarily suffered as much as it is performed, and that the recognition of one's own powers of displacement should be bound up in obedience to a psychological imperative—this is of course the kind of paradox that Hecht is inviting us to explore.

Although the ritualistic elements of "A Hill" should already be clear, it may be worth pausing to emphasize their presence, however compressed and internalized. The most obvious, particularly for an opening poem, would be an initiatory rite of passage in which an individual is withdrawn from society, placed in an isolating (and often darkened) scene of instruction, and then "restored / To the sunlight and [his] friends." A society would thereby control a dangerously liminal phase of the individual's transition, while also allowing the initiate to learn certain truths that may otherwise be occulted by social life. Since this poem includes no ushering or supervision within the rite, no real sense of a reinvigorated relationship between individual and society, and only a ravaging scene of dubious and solitary instruction, we see at once that its ritual elements may be anti-types as much as types, although their presence certainly gives a formal gravity and a more than personal depth to the described experience.

Similarly, although there is again a terrifying elision of all that might otherwise graduate the procession, we might see elements of a ritual revisitation, by which an individual leaves his given surroundings in order to revisit a prior scene of crucial importance. Why this particular site holds such force is left implicit in the poem—indeed the unassimilated and uninterpretable barrenness contributes most of the hill's power. This tremendous power of negation even tends to eclipse our speculations on the psychological properties of landscape, or on the tomblike quality of an isolated hill in whose presence this revisitation might distantly resemble the practice of returning to a burial site in order to erect or unveil a memorial. We are not certain of anyone or anything having been buried here, however metaphorically. Perhaps the hill marks the kind of obscured, unconscious loss that lies at the core of melancholy.

By the same negative token, if anything is being preserved or recognized it is the mind's ability to be confronted by plain bitterness, or by the abrupt force of its own displacements—what, after all, assures us that the remembered boyhood self might not have been prey to yet another dissolving trance of involuntary memory while originally staring at the hill? In addition to figuring what we called the poet's radically subversive "powers" of replacement and self-isolation, the hill might thus mark something like an abyss, a capacity for infinite regression within a self that is discontinuously constructed (and possibly undone) by memory. We recall the textual echoes and translations from the "hard hours" back to the "harde stoundes" of an "Ubi Sunt."

One further ritual trace, related to those already mentioned, is the ceremonial "descent" to a scene of revelation, in which the initiate or adept would be confronted with various emblems, or would be induced to experience a moment of possession. Of course Hecht's scenario of possession offers no sacred tokens, no identification with some inspiring god or demon. And the ceremony is as much one of dispossession as of increased power. But his revealed scene does take on the visionary aspect of an eternal presence ("that promised to last forever"), however negative. And the "papery crash / Of a great branch somewhere unseen falling to earth" does have the impact of an absolute, admonitory sign, referring not just to a fall but to a sudden amputative disjoining of branch from tree—perhaps figuring that of the self from some larger matrix, or of part of the self from a more entire identity. Curiously, the gradual return from the revelatory scene to the sunlit market in the piazza is marked by the latter's own fragmentation ("Then prices came through, and fingers"), as if that fabric, like that of the self, can neither be perfectly restored nor regarded as anything but a fragile assemblage of discrete elements, a texture capable of being unraveled to such loose threads as "a piece of ribbon snagged on a hedge."

The poem is thus deeply subversive on several fronts; and the power of its subversions is surely increased by the way it seems to have enacted various overlapping rites, almost all of them in a negative or dispossessing mode, despite the empowerments we already noticed. In this vein, the negated allusion to Dante ("It was nothing at all like Dante's") both summons a visionary model and disavows it, thereby pointing to the fact that Hecht's infernal vision is not assimilable to some graduated architecture of a spiritual world any more than to the Farnese Palace. Even to call it "infernal" assigns it the kind of interpreted location that it resists. The blank unassimilability of the memory is its point—along with the utter lack of contexts that might have drawn the recollection into a schema of justice, hope, or guided instruction.

Similarly, any effort to compare the poem with, say, a Wordsworthian "spot of time" must chart its severe difference from even the grimmest of Wordsworth's memorial returns. The blank verse narrative is the same, even the structure whereby the recollecting imagination usurps "ordinary" consciousness. But Hecht offers no obvious recuperative admiration for a growing poetic power and no suggestion of how that power might positively engage the larger designs of nature and society. "A Hill" joins vision with an intransigently bleak anti-vision, certainly not like "the visions of saints, /

And perhaps not a vision at all."⁷ Reading it is our price of admission to *The Hard Hours*, and almost all the following poems occupy the region dominated by its primordial scene. As late as *The Venetian Vespers*, Hecht will be attending to such "first precocious hints of hell, / Those intuitions of living desolation / That last a lifetime." Whether or not any poem can offer a redeeming context for such "plain bitterness" or create a texture capable of withstanding the threat of such primordial barrenness—these are questions we take with us as we read on. Few poets have formally inducted the reader with such an uncompromising challenge; for in many respects such questions menace not only the possibility of art, but also the very lives we seek to construct above the bare grounds of desolation.

The speaker of "A Hill" had no choice but to recollect or rather repeat an experience of devastation. "Third Avenue in Sunlight" portrays a more deranging version of this kind of compulsion. Here a character called John, "unfettered but unfreed," is psychologically bound to restagings of primitive conflicts such as those associated with the ritual game of Cowboys and Indians, a game that shapes or reflects the paranoia from which he cannot escape: "But still those savages, / War-painted, a flap of leather at the loins, / File silently against him." Just as no marble palace was proof against returning fear of bleakness in "A Hill," so the game of scouting for savages occurs "behind the museum in Central Park"; and John's later drinking will occur in "the Rembrandt dark." For no offerings of culture, nor in this case religion ("He tried to pray"), nor even psychiatry ("Three years of treatment") can stave off the returning madness ("Daily the prowling sunlight whets its knife / Along the sidewalk").

If we look for some kind of framing sanity or assurance from the narrator, his closing statement ("My bar is somewhat further down the street") offers only a chilling suggestion that he, too, may be prey to distresses of his own that drive him out of the sunlight into the shady bars. (In fact we may wonder just whose perception regarded the sunlight as a prowling killer, since that moment of description floats freely between John and the narrator.) Indeed, perhaps the story of John, and his encapsulated confession, is a delegated and displaced confession by the speaker of the poem. And if John's act of confiding "to a stranger" was no talking cure, there's little to suggest that the oblique confession of this poem provides substantial relief. Instead of a cure for madness or distress, we are given only a dark hint of its possible displacement and replication "further down the street." As in "A Hill," the possible frames of civility and discourse are threatened by the dark negations that remain encysted at their core. And while the tightly rhymed quatrains seem to leash and even mock the madness with a kind of droll, black humor of formality, they nevertheless embody a feeling of entrapment; and they, too, come to seem mocked by what no form can rationalize or contain.

The immediately succeeding poems, "Tarantula, or, The Dance of Death" and "The End of the Weekend," carry the argument into yet harder terrain. The first performs a ritual dance or chant of possession in which the Plague "comes into his own" precisely by dispossessing his victims. Once again the poem focuses not merely on the grip of madness ("the mind rots") but on the way in which the entire resources and forms of a civilization, from attempted hygiene to religion, are mocked by the imperatives of this disease—the trance, the bondage of the will, the "powerless[ness] against contagion." From the beautifully mannered submission to bonds in *A Summoning of Stones*, we have come to the ghastly rictus of the dying, convulsed "like souls in sin."

Like the several versions of predators that haunt the following poems, the tarantula has a grip nothing can break. And that hold has or is a formal, ritual property, associated both with dance and with the very form of the poem. The quatrains are carefully bound to their *abab* rhymes, but with a dramatic shortening of each final line, which is cut down from five stresses to a mere two. So we are locked into a system of repeated abbreviations. Almost like puppets on the poem's strings, we are led along only to be pulled up short. The stanzaic form thus mimes the harsh reductions of each death, leaving us with a shrunken residue resembling the "blind head of bone" that "Grinned its abuse" at the more ample trappings of the flesh. The poem's final residue ("That was the black winter when I came / Into my own") also echoes the opening line ("During the plague I came into my own"), thereby closing the circular trap of possession while also confirming the approximately balladic dance form by its refrain. As if this weren't enough, the refrain's placement subtly reminds us of a yet more compulsively repetitious dance form—that of the villanelle. For without their short fourth lines, these stanzas would be tercets, and if we look at the first two tercets we notice how closely they promise a villanelle. The rhymes are almost in place, and the sixth line echoes the first while also prefiguring the poem's end.

The fact that such significant formal mastery should be placed at the disposal of the Tarantula may leave us wondering whether the strongest compulsions of formality may not themselves be deadly! Could it be that the very impulses toward such formal control, and the effects that such control enforces, are not merely subversive or over-mastering, but somehow lethal? Or does our performance of death's dance in the form of a poem allow us safely to act out and to bind our own instinctual fall toward mortality? Do the satisfactions of form then temporarily appease our longing for the grave? Or might we prefer to say that death is horribly alien, and that rituals like the danse macabre of this very poem try homeopathically to mimic and perhaps exorcise his power? In either case, the poem's function would be the same. But whether death compels us from within or from without, surely our notion of a saving, apotropaic performance is already mocked from inside the poem itself: "Runes were recited daily, charms were applied. / That was the time I came into my own. / Half Europe died."

One cannot help noticing that "The End of the Weekend" concludes with yet another victim held "pulsing in [the] grip" of a predator. In this case the raptor's grip becomes an emblem of the punitive dispossession by which the narrator's sexual adventure is interrupted. Perhaps the interruption occurs as sexual desire is forced to witness a mocking image of its own predations. Or perhaps desire is bound and rebuked by a totemic authority, with its "wings of wrath" and "golden eyes"—an authority hard to disentangle either from symbols of paternal sway, or from the tyranny of death itself. (In "Three Prompters from the Wings" Oedipus himself feels the grip of an internalized owl sink "Into the soft and bloody / Center of his mind.") Furthermore, to seal the fixity of this grip, the poem remains clutched in the eternal present of the traumatic scene. Once again we have returned to childhood, but now it is as if the restorative way back to a later present has been cut off.

It is clear from these opening poems that Hecht may himself be bound by the need to represent what it might be like to live (or die) in the grip of forces beyond our rational control. Even the uncharacteristically informal verse of "Message from the City" describes circumstances that limit our best selves ("Love and constraint, / conditions, conditions"). And once again, the speaker returns to a childhood memory—this time of watching another fated fall, if only of raindrops going to meet "their dooms." So, too, the beautiful nativity poem "Jason" weds its ritual celebrations to a deep sense of "the story as foretold," whereby an individual child (yet another "little boy alone") is bound to the more than personal destiny encoded by his name. Whatever that destiny may be, the child is no more free than he is nameless, for to be named at all is to be governed in part by the preceding codes of a society, its language, its legends, even its dreams. As will be true in related poems such as "Adam" and "The Vow," the poet's task and accomplishment is to counter the bonds of external constraint and even loss by those of love.

With "Behold the Lilies of the Field," Hecht elaborates far more severe variants of his opening themes. Since the poem is about competing compulsions and demands, we notice that the title is itself a command, repeating the line from Jesus' parable—itself meant to adjudicate between adversarial claims. The command will be echoed within the poem by the auditor, who seeks to calm and control the primary speaker's confession ("take it easy. Look at the flowers."; and yet more imperatively at the end, "You must rest now. You must. Lean back. / Look at the flowers"). Whether the auditor is a friend, a doctor, or a psychoanalyst, let us put his directives alongside those of Christ, and let us call these the imperatives of religion or of psychoanalysis, or of whatever discourse may be designed to absorb or ease the speaker's anguish.

For much of the poem, the auditor will actually try to curb the speaker's account ("That's enough for now. Lie back. Try to relax") while the speaker rebels against these imperatives by submitting to greater compulsions of his own. Clearly, we are in familiar territory, recognizing the grip of an imperative that intransigently resists outside forms of control or integration while forcing the speaker back to a scene that was itself marked by the formal compulsion to witness.

Before we enter that scene, however, we wonder what induces the speaker's recollection. On being told to look at the flowers, he thinks of the narcissi or jonquils (a significantly close distinction) that he had once given his mother. The offering had not been adequately appreciated, and the son's wounded desire for that appreciation turns somewhat vengefully (and perhaps no less narcissistically) to a related but more severe disappointment—his witnessing of his mother's dishonesty on the telephone and his subsequent conceding to her degradation:

> "Your mother's a whore,"
> Someone said . . .
> Meaning she had lost all sense of honor,
> And I think this is true.

At this crux, the speaker moves by way of attempted negation ("But that's not what I wanted to say") to a moment of loss and confusion ("What was it I wanted to say?"), then back to an involuntary reaffirmation of his mother's dishonesty ("it was so amazingly true"). This in turn brings on the final disorientation and dispossession ("Where was I?") from which he will not emerge, for he now moves as if beyond his opening confession, and beyond his initial identity, to a larger scenario of dishonoring, one that plunges him back into the ancient world. Where before he had witnessed his mother's deceit, here he will watch the horrible degradation and death of his leader, a Roman emperor, with whom "passed away the honor of Rome." Our interpretation of this dreamed or fantasized witnessing of an historical event (the torture and execution of Emperor Valerian by the Persian king Sapor) may therefore view it as a colossal restaging of the mother's fall. If Valerian functions as a paternal figure, we may say that he merely disguises the true object of abasement; or since his fall costs the honor of Rome (mother Rome?), perhaps he is a blamed ruler-scapegoat who must now bear not only that abasement but also the son's vengeful anger, however disguised in the form of an involuntary witnessing. Of course, since the ancient scene is historically "prior" to that of the mother's dishonesty and occurs within a deeper level of the confession, we may prefer to say that the paternal degradation has priority. But whatever our interpretation, and however unreal the content of the fantasy or "recollected" projection (curiously enough, the historian Gibbon himself narrates yet doubts the supposed torture of Valerian), we cannot doubt the speaker's compulsion to restage his role as witness, a compulsion replicated within the scene by his being "tied to a post and made to watch." He repeats variants of this enforcement at least five times: "It was always the same and we always were made to watch." "And we were not allowed to close our eyes / Or to look away."

He is thus forced to observe as Valerian is flogged, stepped on, and eventually flayed. The emperor's skin is stuffed to make "A hideous life-sized doll," a totemic effigy used to instruct young girls about the male anatomy. At this point the narration comes very close to primordial fantasy, a staging of the Oedipal scenario by which sons *and* fathers are degraded yet elevated to symbolic effigies. Now, too, the speaker is ransomed home by his mother—as if his relation to her can be renegotiated after the ritual martyrdom and symbolization of the father and after the son's own abasement as the surviving commodity of an exchange.

Of course there is no cure or resolution here. There is no evidence that the speaker is "restored to himself" from his projected identity as a Roman witness. We are faced with yet another possible loss of self, another dispossession like those in the preceding poems and more particularly like that by which John had been entrapped in restaged fantasies of wars against "savages." As in "A Hill" or "Tarantula," there is the repeated confrontation with the very antithesis of civilization. And once again, the primary thrust of the poem's discourse is against containment or moderation. As marble palace gave way to bare hill, or John gave way to imaginary tomahawks, or Rome gave way to barbarians—so the language of rational cure or spiritual advice gives way to the compulsive narration of anguish and abjection.

What makes this so troubling now is that the material of this narration is so closely tied to that of history itself. Whatever the speaker's private motives, we may ask how we ourselves can witness history without falling prey to a version of his trauma. What kind of discourse can absorb what we are forced to see? What cultural form can contain our compulsive restagings of those moments when "we were not allowed to close our eyes / Or to look away"?

We come to these questions because "Behold the Lilies" has revealed something more than the poems discussed thus far. Admittedly, "Third Avenue" suggested a possible displacement of confession. But now we actually observe a speaker moving from a confession of domestic dishonoring to a vastly displaced version of that dishonoring within history. If the poet in "Third Avenue" could speak through John, and if the speaker in "Behold the Lilies" can narrate through a fantasized historical version of himself, to what degree may we suppose that his predicament and obsessions are displaced versions of the poet's own?

I do not ask this in a narrowly biographical sense (later poems like "Green: an Epistle," "Apprehensions," or "The Venetian Vespers" may be more appropriate for such inquiry), but as a way of pointing to the more general relation between the poet and the speaker as forced witnesses. Apart from the importance of its historical context—this poet writes as a survivor of war, and during a decade of assassinations and of national degradation in yet further wars (particularly when the media were perfecting their ability to bring distant atrocities home to the domestic viewer)—the question cannot be slighted because other poems in *The Hard Hours* will replay scenes of enforced witnessing. And they, too, will meditate on the possible complicities of our "passive" entrapment within history, as well as on the costs borne by a survivor who, like all poets, can only re-present cruelty, never prevent it. In each case, as the intensely psychological character of "Behold the Lilies" drives home, the most affecting representations of political or historical suffering are those with the most intimate connections to our private selves. Indeed, such representations force us to reconsider the very distinction between what is private and what is historical.

"Behold the Lilies" leaves the speaker lost between the divergent demands—look at the flowers, look at scenes of anguish. In addition to representing the language of religion, or medicine, or normalizing culture, "look at the flowers" could also (as the old figure suggests) mean "look at poetry." Particularly if thus seen as a displaced version of the poet, the speaker is caught between a culturally determined aesthetic language that cannot save and a personal and historical imperative that insists on being represented, however disruptively or incurably. It is this predicament that motivates so much of *The Hard Hours* and that "Rites and Ceremonies" will most desperately repeat.

En route to that restaging we pass an odd and disturbing poem about exorcism. The poem "Pig" alludes to Christ's exorcism of a possessed man whose devils were cast into a herd of Gadarene swine. But the poem chooses to remain focused sympathetically on the victimized swine, as if to outweigh the benefits of salvation with the cost of damnation—not just any damnation but that of the very victim used to purchase a cure. The poem is fascinated by the possibility of exorcistic release but cannot break free from the irreducible residue of a suffering that is ultimately only displaced, not undone. In fact, far from casting out, the haunting repetition within the final lines ("O Swine that takest away our sins / That takest away") allows us to weigh precisely the sensation of having something repeat itself or linger without period in the mind (this is the only poem in the book to end without a full stop). Even the word "save" cannot be freed from its having been used to exclude and damn the victim: "Save one full of offense / Into which the thousand fiends of a human soul / Were cast and driven hence."

This kind of subversiveness lies behind many of the subsequent poems, whether in the playful demolition of Matthew Arnold's sentiments in "The Dover Bitch" or in the comprehensive meditation on Fate in "Three Prompters from the the Wings." While this latter portrayal of a totally overmastered "master of himself" pursues several of Hecht's themes at once, it centers perhaps most disturbingly on the possibly self-reflective problem of Oedipus's quest for purification. If we have already noticed Hecht's deep concern with the dilemmas of attempted confession, exorcism, or deliverance from dark compulsions, we may be especially troubled by this ironic portrait of the unknowingly self-destructive compulsion of Oedipus's own desire to "maintain / Some part of existence clean / And incontaminate." And if Oedipus's final catharsis and vision require nothing short of his own annihilation, we may wonder to what degree the poet or reader can use Oedipus cathartically without suffering a similar fate. For how would our quest for catharsis, if thoroughly successful, dispossess or blind us any less than was the case for Oedipus? Is there something inherently ruinous in the quest itself? And even if one wished to use Oedipus to exorcise one's very desire for such a purifying quest—would that be any less blind or misguided?

The poem reinforces a deep skepticism regarding these questions, for it simultaneously undermines our every claim for self-knowledge or self-possession. Even the Fates are suspect, for although their voices seem to come autonomously from outside that of the lyric poet, and although they seem to be the "authoresses" here, we know that they are mouthing lines which they themselves have been given. Is it that man projects a Fate that dispossesses him, even while Fate itself is dispossessed by virtue of being a mere projection or "instrument"? No stable ground halts the infinite regress of doubt, as we move back to the following truths: that "Blind men will choose as master / To lead them the most blind"; that "What the intelligence / Works out in pure delight / The body must learn in pain"; and that only through literal self-blinding does Oedipus reach his final apprehensions.

Even more thoroughly than "Third Avenue," or "Behold the Lilies," or "Tarantula," or "Pig," "Three Prompters" thus forces us to surrender any illusions about the possibility of purging whatever most distressingly compels us, or at least of doing so without great pain and destruction. And it is at this dark hour, before that of "Rites and Ceremonies," that we might refer to one of Hecht's most revealing statements regarding the relation between poetry and ritual form, a relation that centers precisely on the question of catharsis. Discussing literary presentations of "order and design among the disparities of the universe," he includes instances when our perceptions of such order "remain mootly an intuition, as when, in tragedy, some outrage against the natural order (whatever that may be) having been committed, that order erupts in violence, carnage, and holocaust, and by this means extirpates the poison, to cleanse and rectify itself. This is as true of *Hamlet* and *Lear* as of *Oedipus Rex;* and the lyric poem, far more modestly no doubt, also predicates a great order, though not perhaps through action, as in a tragedy, or through assertion, as in didactic work, but through its metaphors."[8]

At this point, Hecht adds to metaphor the elements of poetic form, but we should dwell for a moment on the revealing juxtaposition of lyric poem and cathartic tragedy. Clearly there could have been other ways of pointing to the lyric's ability to suggest images of "a great order." Why then conjoin the lyric poem to classical tragedy unless one's vision of the poem somehow draws it into the same affective field as those examples of violent eruption and extirpation? Obviously, Hecht qualifies the comparison, and he does not speak of the poem's eruptions; but he will end this very essay with an explicit claim for the cathartic powers of the poem, and he will do so only after returning to the very theme of violence and terror:

> In any case [the constructs of the poet] undertake to reconcile for a moment what is natively inharmonious, dissonant, wayward and incommensurate, and they do not always instantly provide us with repose. Often enough their configurations are based precisely on tension, and on tension at a terrible and perilous pitch. They invite within the world of their discourse our sweetest triumphs and deepest desolations, and exhibit to us freshly and frighteningly all the terrible violence which may be implied in the formula of the bomb, but which that formula could never try to duplicate. But a poem could; for poems already have. And at last, in allowing us to contemplate, even within a single poem, such diversity of experience, both the good and the bad, brought into tenuous balance through all the manifold of devices of art, the spirit is set at ease by a kind of katharsis, in which we are brought to acknowledge that this is the way things are, and by which is recovered for us at the end the inexhaustible plenitude of the world.[9]

This is a tremendous burden for the poet, one which brings the characteristic elements of ritual and grave responsiveness to so much of Hecht's work. But surely the burden is made far heavier by the skepticism with which so many actual poems in *The Hard Hours* complicate our belief in the practical accessibility of catharsis. Even if one keeps in mind the above shift of emphasis between catharsis as eruptive extirpation on the one hand and contemplative reception of diverse abundance on the other, the poems themselves press extremely hard against the possibility of passing from configurations based precisely on "tension at a terrible and perilous pitch" to any final "setting at ease." It is this hard and oppositional pressure, similar to that of the bare hill against the marble palace, or of speaker against auditor in "Behold the Lilies," or of victim, witness, and even predator against any systems of defense or reconciliation, that drives so many of Hecht's poems to the very limits of form and efficacy.

This brings us to "Rites and Ceremonies," a poem that was itself more than twelve years in the making. Once again, we face a recapitulation of many preceding themes and techniques (even more than its surrounding poems, "Rites and Ceremonies" is of course *about* recapitulations), and more extensively now, the lyric voice is drawn outward and backward to the dark impersonations in which "The famous ancient questions gather." The manner in which the voices of others (ranging from David the Psalmist to Shakespeare and George Herbert) impose themselves upon or within the voice of the poet, represents at a formal level not only the relation between "tradition and the individual talent" but also the pressure of history upon the self.[10] At the same time, since so much of this poem will struggle with the question of poetry's efficacy or integrity in the face of history, the inclusion of other voices gives a disturbingly totalizing dimension to the question. More than being measured against its own occasions, preceding poetry is now weighed against more recent and more extensive examples of "plain bitterness" or historical anguish. While familiar to Hecht's readers, the tense structure of this oppositional weighing is therefore deeper and more comprehensive than those we have already observed. Like Adorno (though of course more positively, since this is after all a poem), Hecht now implicitly questions the adequacy of poetry in the wake of the Holocaust. But more far-reachingly than Adorno, Hecht implicates even previous poetry within the scope of the inquiry.

Appropriately enough, the poem's totalizing gesture opens part 1, "The Room," not only with the ancient voice of the Psalms but also with praise for the author of creation—praise that will be complicated by troubling allusions, even interruptions, and that will turn against itself in the form of a question about salvation.

> Father, adonoi, author of all things,
> > of the three states,
> > the soft light on the barn at dawn,
> > > a wind that sings
> > in the bracken, fire in iron grates,
> > > the ram's horn,
> > Furnisher, hinger of heaven, who bound
> > > the lovely Pleaides,
> > entered the perfect treasuries of the snow,
> > > established the round
> > course of the world, birth, death and disease
> > > and caused to grow
> > veins, brain, bones in me, to breathe and sing
> > > fashioned me air,
> > Lord, who, governing cloud and waterspout,
> > > o my King,
> > held me alive till this my forty-third year—
> > > *in whom we doubt—*
> > Who was that child of whom they tell
> > > in lauds and threnes?
> > whose holy name all shall pronounce
> > > Emmanuel,
> > which being interpreted means,
> > > "*Gott mit uns*"?

The language melds a contemporary voice to that of the Psalms and Book of Job, thereby already summoning a context of praise and complaint that shadows any simpler celebrations. And the verse form itself oscillates off balance, ill at ease and vulnerable within the otherwise tight weave of rhyme and ceremonially extended syntax. The web of creation includes the speaker himself, whose autonomy is thus heavily qualified at the very outset. And just when the self is introduced (referred to in the context of survival—"held me alive till this my forty-third year"), doubt interrupts the poem as if from another voice or from within another region of the psyche. This interruptive voice and the force of its subversions deepen throughout the poem, at times becoming the dominant strain. But already how radically (and emphatically!) it undermines the entire opening paean, for it casts doubt not only on the author of creation, but also on the very auditor to whom this poem is being addressed. The doubt is thus deeply self-reflexive, jeopardizing the very bases and rationales of the poem. And the conjoinedly dubious identity of God and addressee remains one of the principal features and questions of the entire poem.

After this admission the poem further questions the existence of a possible savior, doing so in such a way as to contaminate the child's holy name, Emmanuel, by translating it into the language of the most recent and extensive oppressors in the poem. The translation of course also horribly ironizes the borrowed languages of Isaiah (7:14) and Matthew (1:23), wrenching them into the antithetical and disempowering context of Nazism, a context the speaker now enters directly with personal recollections of World War II.

The shift is reinforced formally by the turn away from incantatory psalmlike diction to that of immediate, conversational reportage and from the antiphonally woven verse form of the opening lines to the choppy, though still rhymed octaves that follow:

> I saw it on their belts. A young one, dead,
> Left there on purpose to get us used to the sight
> When we first moved in. Helmet spilled off, head
> Blond and boyish and bloody. I was scared that night.
> And the sign was there,
> The sign of the child, the grave, worship, and loss,
> Gunpowder heavy as pollen in winter air,
> An Iron Cross.

Within the macabre initiation ritual the figure of the child recurs, now associated with a young dead German soldier and the Iron Cross. Between the words "Gott mit uns" and the Iron Cross, it is now impossible for us to name or image these arch-symbols of salvation without seeing them joined to adversarial meanings—just as pollen is now linked in mind with gunpowder. Such enforced tensions characterize much of what follows, as the speaker now falls prey to the kind of compulsive repetition that had marked traumatic scenes in the earlier poems. Despite having returned home from war, and despite the passage of twenty years, he is locked within the eternal present of the concentration camps. At the very moment of attempted prayer, he is compelled to remain within that endless captivity: "At night, Father, in the dark, when I pray, / I am there, I am there." As in "Behold the Lilies," the psychological imperative and the historical horror to which it is bound resist the curative contexts of religion or other discourses of absorption. And the specific annulment of religious consolation is sharpened by the accusation of passivity in the face of the Holocaust "Which a great church has voted to 'deplore.'" From the irony of "Gott mit uns" the poem has now moved to overt criticism, each time making it more difficult for us to find comfort within the very language that might otherwise have responded to our needs. Even our attitude to the Judaic prayer of a doomed victim in the gas chamber is now hopelessly complicated by overwhelming doubts about the prayer's efficacy. So, too, pity and terror are surely here, but any flow of catharsis is arrested by the opposed image of entrapment and suffocation

> As the rubber-edged door closes on chance and choice.
> He is saying a prayer for all whom this room shall kill.
> *"I cried unto the Lord God with my voice,*
> *And He has heard me out His holy hill."*

The lines of the Psalm are thus brought into desperate tension with the very lines to which they are formally bound. Faced with this unbearable impasse, which ends the poem's first section, we can only read on, knowing that we shall have to return to the questions it has raised—questions about the existence of God and salvation and about the efficacy of any possible language of redemption or redress. If such language fails literally to save "those whom this room shall kill," what other function may it perform? Are the rituals of prayer or even memorial futile on every level? With these questions we also ask whether or not the speaker himself is to be "restored" from the endlessly traumatic presence within which he has remained entrapped.

Like the third section of *The Waste Land*, the second part of the poem is entitled "The Fire Sermon," and its speaker, too, will meditate on the possibilities of being "plucked" out of the fire. Hecht's subject is more overtly historical than Tiresias's "foresuffering" of degradation. For the poem moves back from the Holocaust to an earlier scenario of persecution, in which Jews were burned as scapegoats for the plague. The predominant blank verse, occasionally lengthened or cropped, is suited to the narrative account, although the form will change abruptly to a far more stylized ritual mode when we arrive at the inevitable "ceremony" of execution and the emerging prayer. Pointedly ironizing the language of tourism and architectural history, the poet directs us away from Strasbourg Cathedral to the envisioned scaffold (a harsher and now moralized version of the movement from Farnese to bare hill) on which the victims are to be burned. The critique of a culpably unconcerned aestheticism (admiring the minster facade, while ignoring—and perhaps in order to ignore—what the church committed) is now joined by an attack on clergy, town council, and an academy that would later honor Goethe. For all these came "To watch the ceremony," thereby implicating their represented codes and values in such a way as to render them not only unhelpful but malevolent. Once again we are left wondering where to turn, and what language to use, as the victims are assembled, "Children and all, and tied together with rope."

As the fires are lit, the narrative account is replaced by prayer. And the particular poetic form of the prayer, as well as some of its actual lines, takes us directly back to the work of one of Hecht's masters, and one of the most affecting poets of prayer, George Herbert. Appropriately enough, Herbert's poem is called "Denial." The first of its six stanzas follows:

> When my devotions could not pierce
>   Thy silent ears;
> Then was my heart broken, as was my verse:
>   My breast was full of fears
>   And disorder.

Again and again, the final unrhymed lines keep the stanzas broken and exposed, until persisting beyond the crisis of its inaudibility, the prayer finally heals its spirit and rhyme by an optative vision of divine repair ("That so thy favors granting my request, / They and my mind may chime, / And mend my rhyme").

Hecht's version will have no such ultimate mending, and will close by almost repeating its entire opening stanza with a recursively entrapping emphasis on the absence of hearing. These are the final four stanzas:

> Father, among these many souls
>   Is there not one
> Whom thou shalt pluck for love out of the coals?
>   Look, look, they have begun
>   To douse the rags.
>
> O that thou shouldst give dust a tongue
>   To crie to thee
> And then not heare it crying! Who is so strong
>   When the flame eats his knee?
>   O hear my prayer,

>   And let my prayer come unto thee.
>   Hide not thy face.
> Let there some child among us worthy be
>   Here to receive thy grace
>   And sheltering.
>
>   It is barren hereabout
>   And the wind is cold,
> And the crack of fire, melting of prayer and shout
>   Is blown past the sheepfold
>   Out of hearing.

I take this to be an extremity in Hecht's art. At its most masterful, at the point where it perfectly mimes the virtuosity of Herbert himself and draws upon trains of allusion stretching back through Eliot and Saint Augustine to the prophet Amos, the prayer casts itself against the limits of its calling and remains unheard. Or, if heard, remains unable to call down the interventions of mercy or grace. By repeating the form of Herbert's poem without its reparation, and by quoting the entire sentence:

> O that thou shouldst give dust a tongue
>   To crie to thee,
> And then not heare it crying!

Hecht breaks open the wounds of the earlier poem, revives its greatest pain, then leaves it unredressed. In fact an unappeased refrain, "Out of hearing," now prolongs Herbert's line "But no hearing." It is as if this insistent and unassimilably "broken verse" were the timeless voice of poetry itself lamenting the limits of its efficacy.

From here, the poem opens a third section, "The Dream," which narrates yet another ceremony of torment. It does so despite recognizing that "The contemplation of horror is not edifying, / Neither does it strengthen the soul." We are thus still within the grip of Hecht's compulsion to witness—despite the possible futility of that act—returning now to Renaissance Rome to stand beside the exiled du Bellay as he watches the rites of Carnival. Seeming to urge distraction ("take no thought of them"), the poet cannot help but direct du Bellay's attention to the abused victims of the Church. Characteristically he sees how they themselves replicate generations of pain and exile, thereby keeping alive the painful verses of Psalm 137, "If I forget thee, O Jerusalem, . . ." Despite another bitter and final pointing toward distraction ("wait for the next heat, the buffaloes") it is the Psalm's covenant of remembrance that takes us to the fourth and last section of the poem.

"Words for the Day of Atonement" questions the very merits of survival, and alludes skeptically to the prophecies of a "saving remnant." Thus cutting against the fundamental last hope of Judaic prophecy, the poem accuses all whose present lives "in this wilderness of comfort" are unworthy of the sufferings of those who died. In keeping with its occasion, the poem lays bare our guilt, and it questions,

> Where is there one
> Mad, poor and betrayed enough to find
> Forgiveness for us, saying,
> "None does offend,
> None, I say,
> None"?

Formally paring themselves down to the negation of "one" by the repeated "none," the lines are also rhymed to create an effect of necessity and durability—a durability extending at least since the ravings of King Lear on the heath. The allusion complicates Hecht's question by deriving its saving edict of forgiveness from the deranged and powerless fantasy of a dethroned (and of course fictionalized) king. If this is where forgiveness must arise—if at all—how bear the madness, poverty, betrayal, tragic waste, and fictionality of its source? No wonder Hecht frames his question with the prior query of whether or not to ask it: "Shall we ask, / Where is there one . . ."?

The questions call for an answer, "Listen, listen," but are met by the same fate as the prayer in "The Fire Sermon" ("But the voices are blown away"). This time, however, the poem struggles forward ("And yet, this light, / The work of thy fingers. . . ."), and prays yet again for compassionate forgiveness. This new prayer, with its obsessive yet almost soothingly hypnotic repetitions, throws itself against the entire fabric of doubt that has been woven throughout the poem. And the desperate outpouring of its invocation brings in its wake a calm recognition of its own compulsions. Since so much of this entire poem's argument and development has been conducted at the level of form alone, we may expect some formal expression of this transition; and indeed the ten straight lines of outpoured prayer are followed by four modified repetitions of the Herbert stanza, complete with mended rhymes. As if this submission to the formal design of a poet of submission were not enough, the language of purification and humiliation ("washed," "humbled") includes several allusions to Job (the treasuries of snow, the fathering rain) and hence to a contrite surrender to powers beyond those even of our doubts. And it is only consequent to the penitential submission implied both by these allusions to Job and by the return to the mended stanzas of God's "domestic servant" that the poem finally introduces an incomprehensible and irresistible promise:

> Who shall profess to understand
> The diligence and purpose of the rose?
>   Yet deep as to some gland,
> A promised odor, even among these snows,
>   Steals in like contraband.

The promise rises like a physiological imperative (compare the glandular bonds in "The Gardens of the Villa d'Este" or in the later "Goliardic Song"). As the word "contraband" indicates, we are locked tightly within Hecht's characteristic war of compulsions. If Eliot had spoken of being redeemed from fire by fire, Hecht might speak of being redeemed from bondage by yet other bonds. Against the laws of inner guilt and outer oppression, there now rises the illegitimate yet saving law of a different kind of submission, that of atonement and of the humble acceptance of a promise that surpasses rational doubt. If "The Fire Sermon" had brought Hecht to a limit of poetic efficacy, this later description of a diligent purpose beyond understanding nevertheless brings him to an equally extreme imperative: to counterweigh his own skepticism and guilt by a vital responsiveness to the possibility of forgiveness. The declaration follows immediately: "Forgiven be the whole Congregation of the Children of Israel, and the stranger dwelling in their midst. For all the people have inadvertently sinned."

It is this responsive and creative willingness to balance the image of universal forgiveness against that of universal sin, that allows the conclusions of the poem. The guilt of the witness and survivor has now received its fullest acknowledgment and possible forgiveness, and a restored community has shared its dispensation with the stranger (perhaps a figure for the poet) in its midst. As it must, this restoration of community now undergirds the poem's final rite, which once again is one of prayer.

>   Father, I also pray
> For those among us whom we know not, those
>   Dearest to thy grace,
> The saved and saving remnant, the promised third,
>   Who in a later day
> When we again are compassed about with foes,
> Shall be for us a nail in thy holy place
> There to abide according to thy word.
>
>   Neither shall the flame
> Kindle upon them, nor the fire burn
>   A hair of them, for they
> Shall be thy care when it shall come to pass,
>   And calling on thy name,
> In the hot kilns and ovens, they shall turn
> To thee as it is prophesied, and say,
> *"He shall come down like rain upon mown grass."*

Returning to the opening address of the entire poem, the prayer also formally amplifies its opening version. As before, the line lengths oscillate, but their flow is now channeled into two stanzas, each of which closes a single period with three solid lines of full and equal length. This provides a sense of amplitude and security; and the rhyme scheme itself has been augmented from an *abcabc* form to the more extendedly inclusive (we may almost say long-suffering) *abcdabcd* design.

As deeply as he had voiced his skepticism, and as clearly as he still depicts the continuing forms of oppression, the poet now honors the sheer will to posit grace, survival, and salvation. Although the powerful language of Ezra, Isaiah, Daniel, and the Psalms is brought once again into terrible tension with the "hot kilns and ovens," and although the final line (from Psalm 72) might be practically as futile as those spoken in the gas chambers of "The Room," we are now invited to rethink what "futility" might mean. There is no sudden access of belief, and no miraculous escape from future pain. In the wake of the Holocaust we are not asked to believe in any actual rescue from the ovens. The bleak assurance here is that in the very midst of inevitable and recurrent torment, the human spirit will be present at its most courageous and vigorous—surviving in and through its very ability to hold fast to the image of God's merciful descent. Poetic language at its highest gives form to this indomitable expression, in which the needs and the will of the spirit converge so powerfully as to render almost irrelevant the question of whether or not God "actually" exists. And it is this power of giving life and form to spirit, despite its inability to summon more than the image of divine intervention, that vindicates the existence of such poetry in the face of whatever historical circumstances may entrap or oppose it. It is therefore for those who can say these words that the poet finally prays. In the tremendous conflict of opposing bonds that informs so much of Hecht's work, and among so many resistant forces and insistences, this final "contraband" imperative refuses to be silenced. It is as strong as Hecht's compulsions to bear witness, and as recalcitrant as its negative versions in traumatic recollections, oppressive barbarisms, or self-lacerating guilt. Perhaps we should say that the poet's homage to a resistant spiritual strength is here exactly equal to his despair.

Of course it would be unrealistic to expect this balanced pitch of tension to be maintained indefinitely. And the poems that conclude the book do include several representations of unmitigated despair. Several of these, like "Birdwatchers of America," continue the explicit attack against the optimistic symbols of religion or art—and by implication, against the very languages and codes these represent. Even the normal language of everyday life is opposed and threatened by these poems about "things of which we seldom talk." In "Birdwatchers," Hecht uses his paradigmatic structure, a substitutive fall, to replace the opening stanza's benign image of peace (the dove of Picasso or Catholicism) by a grotesquely ironic version both of that image (now the "outrageous bird" of prey) and of the peace it represents (the corpse on which it crouched "seemed in ultimate peace / Except that he had no eyes"). And in case we were inexperienced enough to think that this ghastly anti-epiphany might be somehow arbitrary or avoidable, it is entrenched within the psyche of a fixated woman, "whom we hear at night"—yet another in the book's series of witnesses who remain traumatized by what they have seen.

In fact the contrast between the repeated anguish of looking, and the "ultimate peace" of blindness, surely reflects back on the poet's painful calling. So many of these poems have represented images of sightlessness—as if for all their gruesomeness these had exercised more than simply macabre fascination for the poet. We may think of Oedipus in "Three Prompters," the corpse in "Birdwatchers," the blindfolded figure in "The Origin of Centaurs," the effigy of Valerian with "blanks of mother-of-pearl under the eyelids" (as opposed to the speaker who was not allowed to close his eyes), the "Blind head of bone" in "Tarantula," the blind men of "Sloth," or finally the soot-covered eyes of the dead Pole in "More Light! More Light!" Whether these symbolize the exaggerated punishment of those who have seen too much, or the castrative submission to overmastering fates, or the ambivalently desired release from seeing (and writing), their hold on the poet is almost predatory.

The last three poems of the book create an extraordinary finale. "More Light! More Light!" enacts the multiplication of historical agony that we have seen elsewhere; and it does so within a repetitive structure of commands whose totalitarian rigor becomes yet another image of fate itself.[11] The strict quatrains with their ballad rhyme-scheme reinforce this by their allusion to narratives of unavoidable fatality. And once again, the poem has a ritual quality, for it describes savage ceremonies of execution and entombment, the last of which even involves a grotesque kind of game. As the German officer orders the Pole to bury the two Jews alive, then reverses the order after the Pole's refusal only to reverse it yet again and finally to kill all three, he is degrading their very desire for survival. And the poem itself plays against our desire that at least someone survive the transaction. We become horribly implicated in this poem, beyond merely wondering "what would *we* have done?" For if we are somehow made to witness the events, we also survive them—in the company of the only other survivor, the Nazi killer. It is this manner in which Hecht has trapped himself and his readers within the uncanny association of narrator-observer, survivor, and killer that most thoroughly seals the darkness of the poem and enforces the most despairing vision of the relation between poetry and the bearing of historical witness.

This time, there is no question of prayer. In the earlier execution, centuries ago, the spectators prayed for the victim's soul, their prayers more than ironized as the dying man "howled for the Kindly Light." In the later scene "No prayers or incense rose up" as the Pole lay bleeding to death. In a literal sense within the poem there were no witnesses (least of all, God!); or if *we* have been somehow "present," the unavailability of any offered forms of response leaves us arrested in a frozen silence so mute as to render us almost absent. Perhaps this is the ghostly position most of us occupy in relation to the historical events around us. If we resist association with the killer, perhaps in our muteness we should recognize our similarity to the only final attendants on the corpse: "every day came mute /

Ghosts from the ovens, sifting through crisp air, / And settled upon his eyes in a black soot."

"And Can Ye Sing Baluloo When the Bairn Greets?" maintains the pessimistic mood with another horrified fixation whose bonds no religion or contemplation can break ("There is no cure for me in the world of men"). And the title's question, regarding a singer's ability to comfort a child, points toward the last poem in the book, "It Out-Herods Herod. Pray You, Avoid It." This perfectly situated closing rite is in the form of a balladic lullaby, and the singer points to the ritualistic nature of his song by calling it a childermas, a mass sung to memorialize the innocent victims of Herod. With this poem, Hecht returns to the painfully balanced conclusion of "Rites and Ceremonies," although there is a hard-edged terseness now, as of a lullaby sung through clenched teeth. In fact the title not only mentions the arch-villain of the childermas, but quotes Hamlet's speech against overacting, thereby warning about the possible relation between tearing a passion to tatters on the one hand and a murderous hypocrisy on the other. Accordingly succinct, the poem juxtaposes a father's sense of reality against his children's simple "laws" by which "The Good casts out the Bad." The themes of exorcism, and of opposing codes, are familiar, as is the poet's susceptibility to what cannot be contained ("The giant and witch are set / To bust out of the clink"). Also familiar is the question of what the poet's role should be. Now even more darkly than in "Rites and Ceremonies," he shows there will be no salvation, that he is unable to save even his own children. And yet he sings despite this knowledge, in order that his children's sleep be sound.

No cathartic casting out, no redemption, no belief—only the recognition that his song can soothe and that it must be sung. Whether it can truly soothe anyone who does not still believe, as the children do, that a hero will come to "make the world behave / And put an end to grief"—this is a question almost too painful to ask. Not merely because one can only answer in the negative (the closing rhyme binds "childermas" itself to "gas"), but also because it associates the unbelieving singer with those actors whose inevitable pretense puts them in constant danger of out-Heroding Herod.

"Pray you, avoid it." Despite the fact that the only prayer held out by the title is a kind of anti-prayer against the theatrical "make-believe" that is necessary for an unbeliever's childermas, the poet is once more up against the unavoidable. If we ask what necessity the ballad form suggests this time, it is perhaps this last necessity of the poet's burden—to perform his final rite despite the knowledge that he cannot save, and that Good cannot cast out the Bad. We might say that this is Hecht's fate as a poet. That he refuses to "avoid" his task and chooses to sing rather than to yield to a mute despair—this is his strength (or perhaps in the context of fate we should say character). And that the grave courage of his song should include such a deep attention to its own necessities of form and to the rightness of its sound (which is also of course the granted "soundness" of his children's sleep)—this is his art.

Hecht's succeeding books deserve studies of their own, and I shall close by merely offering a few condensed suggestions of how this particular discussion might be extended. Clearly, Hecht's poetry maintains its formal properties throughout the intricacies of *Millions of Strange Shadows* and the masterful blank verse achievements of *The Venetian Vespers*. So, too, these poems are still attentive to the issues outlined above. Their ritual properties persist (though these are now occasionally further below the surface), as do their fascinations with such matters as our fallenness, our acts of witness, or the attempts to construe our "shadowy fate's unfathomable design."

To generalize, *Millions of Strange Shadows* seems to recoil somewhat from the lacerating extremities of *The Hard Hours*, as if the poet longed now for a quality of repose, a dream of stillness or abeyance from the hours themselves—particularly now that time is increasingly viewed as the medium of sheer degeneration. With their "arrested flights" and "fixtures," the poems often seek to "Stop history in its tracks" in order to measure (and as if to inhibit) our unstoppable decline. On the one hand, the book has an autumnal, Virgilian cast, and many of the poems do offer iconic images of arrested motion or achieved poise that then act as standards against which (or even upon which) to measure the erosions of time and history. On the other hand, this "frieze" aspect occasionally seems to mirror the stunned or nearly immobilized response of a poet who is weary of witnessing to no avail or who yearns for his own version of the diver's retrospective dream in "Swan Dive"—that he may "achieve the chiselled stone / Of catatonia."

Of course not all the poems are about such stasis, though many do refer to the stillness of statuary, or photographs, or intervals of sheer waiting as in "Peripeteia" or "The Lull." In "Peripeteia" the poet dreams (among other things) of a release from arrested spectatorship and fictionality—although the releasing touch that should disrupt the fictive medium (of *The Tempest*) is of course itself the figment of a dream. And while "The Lull" allows its scene to "Harden to an etched / And iron immobility," a "trance of stillness" in which all things "manifest / The deep, unvexed composure of the blessed," it is never unaware of the storm to come. So that while these pauses are often associated with epiphanic definitions of reality, we are seldom freed from the sense of another, perhaps more pressing and certainly more destabilizing reality that is being held at bay. If there seems to be a cost in several of these poems' iconic stillnesses, however vigorously perceived, or in the poet's virtual satisfactions of an "unwavering taste" for the cool eventuality of death, it is perhaps in the way their statuary poise wards off the specifically dynamic intensity that had driven *The Hard Hours*. Admittedly, such warding off is never irresponsible nor blind, for as "The Cost" makes clear, the poet is never unaware of torment; it is rather that immediately following *The Hard Hours* Hecht's need for a poetry of recuperation (here one that does justice to the meditative freedom and suppleness of the mind) requires a certain muting of sorrow, an ability to explore with refreshing verve such things as "the spin / And dazzled rinse of air" that surrounds a young Roman couple whose very balance and grace astride their tilting motorcycle depends on their not "tak[ing] thought / Of all that ancient pain" carved upon Trajan's column. However, since *Millions of Strange Shadows* begins by meditating on this couple's "slender purchase," and ends with "The Lull," in which "Rapt in a trance of stillness . . . *for the moment* the whole world is real" (my emphasis), it is impossible to avoid wondering how long the pause can be sustained.

In order to move beyond "the lull," or to return to the intensities of *The Hard Hours*, Hecht has therefore once again had to shatter his own defenses against torment and loss. An almost impossibly harsh demand might have required him to pursue a more vulnerably narrative art, perhaps of a biographically self-examining nature, whether mediated through other speakers or more directly addressed. And yet with his distinctive courage, this is precisely the demand Hecht follows, beginning in part with poems like "Green: An Epistle" or "Apprehensions" and then moving to their consummation in "The Venetian Vespers." As one might expect, the form for these poems is blank verse, allowing the long reaches of verse paragraphs in which narrative and reflection extend themselves unbrokenly through all the nuancings of voice at its most intimate. If many of the poems in *Millions of Strange Shadows* had possessed the stillness that precedes the storm or thaw (even "Apprehensions" had the speaker "called away" from the window just as it began to rain), poems like "The Short End" or "The Venetian Vespers" move into fierce immolations or into the drenching rains of acknowledged personal losses and their possible assuagements.

While continuing to analyze the various bonds and compulsions that constrain yet drive these extraordinarily adventurous poems, our extended discussion would chart their new openness to the discourse of popular culture (the way, for example, the speaker in "The Grapes" recognizes her destiny by an image in *Time* magazine, or the woman in "The Short End" achieves her ultimately consuming fantasy within an advertisement in the *New Yorker*). For these are among Hecht's most recent registrations of our bondage to the network of laws or codes around us, his way of continuing to show where the most personal and the most impersonal of laws intersect. Before, it may have been the grip of the plague, or the oppressions of Nazism—now it may be the insidious way in which our self-definitions are determined by the fictions of mass culture.

I cannot here detail Hecht's recent rites and ceremonies of initiation, of revenge, of self-destruction, or most extensively of mourning. But in "The Venetian Vespers" we would have the amplest opportunity to explore how fully the speaker returns to the very origins of selfhood, and how he accommodates this most personal of narratives within the encompassing ceremony of an "evening worship." With moving recapitulations of the deaths of both parents, the speaker also enacts the deep renunciations required for mourning, the acceptances of mediating artifice, the ceremonious and humbling descent of a curbed spirit into the "lees of the Venetian underworld," the achieved receptivity to accessions of rainfall and of light. For here, too, in its most extended form, Hecht has restaged his extraordinary yet characteristic counterpoint of bonds—between the compulsively nightmarish reality of suffering and the "obsessional daydream / Of our redemption."

NOTES

1. "A Lot of Night Music," *Millions of Strange Shadows*, 20.
2. "Sestina d'Inverno," *Millions of Strange Shadows*, 31.
3. "La Condition Botanique" and "A Poem for Julia."

4. As in Herrick's "Delight in Disorder," though here with far more virtuosity, the poet affirms the equivalent of a "wild civility." Elsewhere, Hecht has written of "The urgent lawless measure of love" (*Millions of Strange Shadows*, 80).

5. "On the Methods and Ambitions of Poetry," 492. Hecht has of course given additional reasons for his choice of formal verse—the necessity for pausing and thus potentially discovering something unexpected during the process of composition, or (quoting Richard Wilbur) the use of a medium in which "the difficulty of the form is a substitution for the difficulty of direct apprehension and expression of the object." I am trying to suggest what other motives may accompany these reasons.

6. Or compare Hecht's own "Morning will taste of bitterness again. / The heart turns to a stone, but it endures" ("Clair de Lune").

7. We may think of Elizabeth Bishop's "In the Waiting Room" or many of Beckett's works for other distinctly "postmodern" examples of how traditional topoi of revelation or inspiration are now more often associated with dispossession and desolation than with empowerment.

8. "On the Methods and Ambitions of Poetry," 498.

9. Ibid., 505.

10. One further determinant for the presence of other voices is surely the poem's intensely elegiac nature. From "Lycidas" to "The Quaker Graveyard in Nantucket," elegies have almost always been marked by such inclusions. In fact, a longer reading of "Rites and Ceremonies" or even more particularly of "The Venetian Vespers" should take account of their deep relationship to the elegy as a genre.

11. The title of course alludes to the supposedly last words of Goethe, and the poem does mention Weimar, on whose outskirts lay the camp of Buchenwald. Less known perhaps is the fact that the center of Buchenwald was marked by a colossal oak tree called the "Goethe oak." Earlier in the poem, the line "*Die Vögelein schweigen im Walde*," quoted from Goethe's "Wandrers Nachtlied II," offers an ironic reminder of that poem's close: "Warte nur, balde / Ruhest du auch."

Alicia Ostriker

Millions of Strange Shadows: Anthony Hecht as Gentile and Jew

A teacher of literature to the undogmatic and semiliterate young confronts twice a year the question of how, on the first day of class, to begin suggesting that, given a choice between art and truth, they should demand both. The task is never easy and is not made easier at a time when no corps of belligerent students besieges the ivory chamber. The professor may lecture on until June, explaining enthymemes and stanza patterns, glossing allusions, and in general indicating that poetry is a superior entertainment. The students, to whom neither art nor truth is a matter of urgent concern, will write it all down and never know why.

Several possibly overlapping reasons exist for traditional formal excellence in poetry, or, to put it another way, several messages may be transmitted by it. The most obvious from a sociological point of view would be that the mastery of poetic skills, or the ability to appreciate them, flatteringly distinguishes us from the loutish multitudes. Other reasons for the production and consumption of high poetry might include nostalgia for a classical past believed to be happier or nobler than the present; our poignant need for the consolations of art after the depredations of life; our intuition that aesthetic gestures are somehow analogous to moral gestures. Traditional forms of verse in particular tend to endorse by implication ideas of order in private and public life. All this, insofar as the devices exist prior to the matter of the poem, has little to do with "form as an extension of content," save that formal elegance, coherence, precision, and subtlety tend to be signals of social privilege and political conservatism.

Yet at the same time there is what Euripides called love of loveliness, and there is what Yeats called "the fascination with what's difficult." The heart goes out, bewitched by art as if by magic. Finally, there is the Platonic or Pythagorean faith that the order to which a poem aspires is an imitation or embodiment of some Real Order which ordinary material reality obscures. As Anthony Hecht suggests in a poem called "Peripeteia," a disciplined poem may be

> Governed by laws which stand for other laws,
> Both of which aim, through kindred disciplines,
> At the soul's knowledge and habiliment.

Because Hecht is among the handful of living American poets who understand and practice the discipline of formal excellence, his work permits itself to be regarded by the critic as essentially emotionless, haut bourgeois, the sort of topiary work that amuses but does not stir us. Possibly this makes sense with some of Hecht's earliest poems—a title like "Le Masseur de ma Soeur" is awfully arch, and perhaps he has on occasion employed artifice purely as a defense against feeling. One can scarcely avoid noting of Hecht at all times that his stanza patterns are ingenious and graceful and his blank verse supple, his learning classical and his milieu cosmopolitan, his language opulent and his wit charming. Or one notes his sense of "loss," his tone of subdued yet ironic despair—these are, after all, correct modern stances—neglecting to observe the cause.

I need therefore to say that Hecht for me has been primarily not a littérateur but a pedagogue and moralist of the specific sort defined by Keats in "The Fall of Hyperion." "None can ascend this height," Keats is told, "But those to whom the miseries of the world / Are misery, and will not let them rest." For such a poet, technical accomplishment has a consistently moral edge. At one end of his range is the temptation toward mere stylishness, decorum, "civilization" in the trivial and idle sense. Hecht's gifts make this possible just as Keats's gifts made possible a pure lassitudinous sensuousness; either alternative suggests refuge from the pained awareness of an awakened intelligence "That but to think is to be full of sorrow / And leaden-eyed despairs." At the other end is the temptation to ungoverned rage. Hecht hints at this temptation in the title—"It Out-Herods Herod. Pray You, Avoid It"—of the poem which, far from ranting, meditates in tidy trimeter quatrains on his children's innocent expectation that good will defeat evil, and on himself,

"Who could not at one time / Have saved them from the gas." Poetic control may signify a self-control without which one would simply explode with grief and fear. There is also I think a third temptation in Hecht, of which more anon, to a despair that would simply surrender to silence.

And there is another complication. Hecht belongs only in part to that civilized tradition represented in our century chiefly by T. S. Eliot and thereafter by John Crowe Ransom, Allen Tate, and Robert Lowell. He is only half assimilated to what Matthew Arnold called Hellenism. His other half is emphatically a Jew. His is the high culture of those post-enlightenment German Jews whose glorious error was to believe in the ideals of German/European culture more than their hosts did. Among his relatively recent poetic ancestors we may think of that classic Jew, that tormented wit, that romantic skeptic, that exalted and profane lyricist Heinrich Heine. Among his ancient fathers is the author of *Lamentations*; as Babylon to Jeremiah, so Buchenwald to Hecht. At its most energetic and disturbing, then, Hecht's art registers a Hellenic delight in beauty and order undermined by the Hebraic conviction that the beauty and order of high culture have been founded on suffering and cruelty.

The two most anthologized pieces of *The Hard Hours* (1967) are "The Vow" and "More Light! More Light!" "The Vow" teaches that human beings of good will yearn, through love, to propagate in joy, against odds—Hecht's wife has miscarried, but "Even as gold is tried, gentile and Jew." To the ghost of the dead child, the poet swears blessing for the mother and future children. His stanza is lyrical, his language eloquently echoes both the Bible and Sophocles. The double worlds of reference are a means of giving depth to private grief and desire, or rather, of sounding the depth that is already there; and they are a means of vowing commitment to the reconciliation of gentile and Jew, which has proved "too bold a mixture" for the child's survival.

"More Light! More Light!" teaches that human beings of good will can be first brutally degraded then brutally destroyed by the millions, notwithstanding the heavenly light of a Christ or the secular light of a Goethe. The atrocity of a Christian burned at the stake by other Christians is paralleled by the atrocity of a German ordering a Pole to bury two Jews alive: there is nothing new under the sun. Here the poet uses an efficient pentameter quatrain narrative, and the persona of an enlightened tour guide ("We move now to outside a German wood . . .") who appreciates the ironic significance of "the shrine at Weimar" and is simply letting us know. The first of these is a private poem, the second a public, and Hecht writes more of the latter.

Eros, in the Manichean world of *The Hard Hours*, stands against the implacable cruelty of nature and man and usually loses. In the loose blank verse vision poem "A Hill," the hallucinated scene is barren and wintry, a landscape of "plain bitterness." "Tarantula, or, The Dance of Death," speaks maliciously in the voice of the plague. The poems of pogrom and holocaust remind us not by preaching nor beating the breast but by telling a few vivid stories: that human brutality is abominable, unutterable, and worse; that we witness and are helpless to mend; that "The contemplation of horror is not edifying, / Neither does it strengthen the soul." On the contrary. The contemplation of horror weakens the soul, according to Hecht, yet we have no moral choice. The voice of "Behold the Lilies of the Field," which I believe is the most remarkable poem in the volume and which may not be well known only because it is almost unbearably anguishing to read, is that of a modern neurotic petulantly obsessed with his mother. Gradually we learn of his experiences as a Roman legionnaire, captured by barbarians and "made to watch" (the phrase is a refrain) the systematic daily flogging and final execution, by slow flaying, of the emperor Valerian. "In the end I was ransomed. Mother paid for me," he says. If this voice were not nameless, we could well compare it with Prufrock's, for the reedy tones of the surrendered will, less ironic than Prufrock's, and sadder, and older. At the same time, there is a depth of bitterness in Hecht to which Eliot never descends. The "Fire Sermon" section of his "Rites and Ceremonies" juxtaposes an account of the mass burnings of Jews throughout Europe during a medieval plague with an appreciation (again the tour guide appears) of medieval architecture. Not the decline of an Age of Faith but its height is the source of torment. Neither the Christian God nor the Jewish "Father, adonoi . . . *in whom we doubt*" is exonerated.

Millions of Strange Shadows is a book less excruciatingly painful than *The Hard Hours*, though still filled with *paysages moralisés*. In a sense it is a book about the poet's struggle to transcend despair without resorting to self-delusion. The assumption throughout is that to think is to be full of sorrow, and a major theme is the idea of "the cost," or the trade-off between happiness and knowledge. In the poem of that title, a young Italian couple speeding around Trajan's column on a Vespa represents beauty and vitality retained at the price of ignorance. Knowledge in this poem, as typically in Hecht, is historical. To think is to remember, for example, that "Trajan, of his imperial peers / Accounted 'the most just,'" left hosts of "the nameless young" dead in the fifteen-year Dacian wars with which he purchased no more than seven years of Roman peace. The elliptical speaker of "Green: An Epistle," examining intertwined illusions of pastoral innocence and manly (possibly patriarchal) virtue, bitterly observes that the evolution of vegetable life has been an obscene "everlasting war" and the evolution of virtue a matter of the growth, burial, and hardening—as vegetation to coal to diamonds—of unacknowledged "resentment, malice, hatred . . . vindictiveness." This poem has an almost Baudelairean muscularity.

Two other ancestral poets provide the volume with impressively bleak pieces. Hecht's free translation of Voltaire's "Poem Upon the Lisbon Disaster" makes available the view that all is not for the best in a world of arbitrary earthquakes, even if a God may be said to preside. This is, if one likes, an early Absurdist manifesto, rendered in tones of jolly rationality; or it is an item in the long litany of challenges that Jews—believing and unbelieving—have mounted against their God. In "A Voice at a Séance," Hecht ventriloquizes what sounds unmistakably like the familiar drone of Old Possum at his most disembodied—a sort of *Beyond the Four Quartets*—telling us that there is little to expect on the other side of the grave either:

> It is all different from what you suppose,
> And the darkness is not darkness exactly,
> But patience, silence, withdrawal, the sad knowledge
> That it was almost impossible not to hurt anyone
> Whether by action or inaction. . . .
> . . . .
> What you learn has nothing whatever to do with joy,
> Nor with sadness, either. You are mostly silent.
> You come to a gentle indifference about being thought
> Either a fool or someone with valuable secrets.
> It may be that the ultimate wisdom
> Lies in saying nothing.
> I think I may already have said too much.

This is so good that it almost seems parody, but I suspect that it is something subtler and more crucial than parody for the poet, perhaps a way of discovering the degree to which he too endorses the silence of a final apathy. If the echoes behind echoes fade back from the composite ghost of *Little Gidding* to the dusty voices that spoke in Hades to Ulysses, so much more grave the experiment. My own conviction is that this position does not represent "ultimate wisdom" in the least, and my impression is that Hecht too rejects it. This voice is, rather, a voice of temptation for the poet: its seductive argument for despair and silence is one that must often afflict the exquisitely and morally conscious mind. Yet it goes against Hecht's own deeper grain, which in this volume seems to want to move through indictment to a qualified affirmation of men's and nature's possibilities.

Hecht dwells recurrently on weather conditions in *Millions of Strange Shadows*, each evoking a climate of mind and each beautifully realized in terms of pure descriptive persuasiveness, the pedagogue's syrup. Heat signifies mindlessness. It is a hot summer night in "Black Boy in the Dark," a poem about America as sweetly melancholy as an Edward Hopper painting, and as mysteriously perfect in its phrasing. The art of echo gives Hecht his multireverberant response to Kennedy's assassination: "We were there, / We suffered, we were Whitman." Heat again, bodily and sensual, is the climate of the locker room and the climate in which a group of splendid-bodied athletes murders Stephen, the first Christian martyr, under the direction of Saul.

Cold and a bare landscape associated with childhood seem to be an objective correlative for undeluded perception in Hecht. Such was the grim landscape of "A Hill." In "Peripeteia," however, its valence alters, becomes less frightening. The umber and stubbly landscape is remembered during the poet's precious moments of solitude in a theater as the lights dim, and it is seen as the possible precondition in his life of an artist's discipline, the goal of which is the soul's self-realization. In "After the Rain," "The air is a smear of ashes / With a cool taste of coins," and there is a "plain, uniform light" that Hecht likes. A similar light, appearing before rather than after a storm and intensified to the point of revelation, appears in "Apprehensions," a blank verse poem that owes something of both matter and manner to Auden, something more to Wordsworth, a bit to Frost, and most to the poet's own moral-aesthetic loyalty toward an experience of primal illumination. "Apprehensions" is probably the finest poem in the volume; it is certainly the most intimate, and stylistically the barest; more important, it offers a rare view of the world as benign.

Again, the poet is a child. He watches from his window over Lexington Avenue in New York:

> A storm was coming up by dark gradations.
> But what was curious about this was
> That as the sky seemed to be taking on
> An ashy blankness, behind which there lay
> Tonalities of lilac and dusty rose
> Tarnishing now to something more than dusk,
> Crepuscular and funerary greys,
> The streets became more luminous, the world
> Glinted and shone with an uncanny freshness.
> The brickwork of the house across the street
> (A grim, run-down Victorian chateau)
> Became distinct and legible; the air,
> Full of excited imminence, stood still.
> The streetcar tracks gleamed like the path of snails.
> And all of this made me superbly happy,
> But most of all a yellow Checker Cab
> Parked at the corner. Something in the light
> Was making this the yellowest thing on earth.
> It was as if Adam, having completed
> Naming the animals, had started in
> On colors, and had found his primary pigment
> Here, in a taxi cab, on Eighty-ninth street.
> It was the absolute, parental yellow.
> Trash littered the gutter, the chipped paint
> Of the lamppost still was chipped, but everything
> Seemed meant to be as it was, seemed so designed,
> As if the world had just then been created,
> Not as a garden, but a rather soiled,
> Loud urban intersection, by God's will.

What precedes and follows this epiphany in the poem is unalleviated bad news: disorder and sorrow within the family, a sadistic German governess, sensational murders in the *Journal-American*, and Hecht's ubiquitous World War II, in which "The ovens blazed away like Pittsburgh steel mills, / Chain-smoking through the night, and no one spoke." The juxtaposition of the hideous bad joke of "Chain-smoking" with the silence of God and man during the Holocaust is vintage Hecht. Yet the vision of primal light is real, even if it cannot save. Stylistically, the comparative lack of finesse Hecht permits himself in the verse that describes it—he is writing here slightly more clumsily, more naively than usual, and one notes how his habitual Latinisms drop away as the description of "the yellowest thing" advances—seems a way of affirming its reality. This is the case despite the speaker's later assertion that the vision had to be "put away / With childish things, as, in the end, the world / As well as holy text insist upon." For the holy text is of course Saint Paul's, whereas the vision is to all appearances straight out of *Genesis*, while evoking in effect that "More Light!" for which Goethe called. It is both sacred (but pre-Christian) and secular. It is also, interestingly, both male and female, for the speaker has introduced his experience as belonging to the type "that W. H. Auden / Designates as 'The Vision of Dame Kind.'" Father God and mother Nature seem equally responsible for what the innocent eye is enabled, through a brief window, to see.

Millions of Strange Shadows includes several love poems, more personal and warm than earlier work, and a rollicking "Goliardic Song" celebrating Venus Pandemos—a figure who, though the poet does not mention it, is a probable ancestress of the medieval Dame Kind. It includes a sex-and-self-loathing poem better and funnier than "The Dover Bitch" (which itself was good and funny) called "The Ghost in the Martini," with which Heine himself might be pleased. Of the several poems about art, the most complex is one called "Gladness of the Best." The title is from George Herbert, to whom the poem turns out to be an homage. The poet contemplates a Book of Hours, and in its illuminated motif of vines and flowers "whose thick clamberings entwine / Heaven and earth and the viewer's raddling eye," he finds the visible counterpart of what in music is "fugal consort, branched polyphony." But this intertwining, a "dense, embroidered art / Of interleaved and deftly braided song," is in turn

> the trope
> Or figure of that holy amity
> Which is our only hope,
> Enjoined upon us from two mountain heights.

The "holy amity" to which we are enjoined and in which we may hope to join—this pun is a serious one—is itself double. We hope both for human amity and for the existence of a loving God. The two heights are of course Sinai and the place of the Sermon on the Mount. It is fitting that a coalescence of "gentile and Jew" in Hecht should appear under the rubric of art and that it should remind us that truth and beauty need not necessarily be twain.

The final poem in the volume, called "The Lull," does a reprise of

Hecht's meteorological renderings. The scene is a July backyard, sunny and mild, until the light changes:

> A casual, leafy sprawl
> Of floated lights, of waverings, these are
> Swags of mimosan gentleness, and all
> The quiet, bourgeois riches of Bonnard.
> Or were, until just now the air
> Came to a sudden hush, and everywhere
> Things harden to an etched
> And iron immobility, as day
> Fades from a scurry of color to cross-hatched,
> Sullen industrial tones of snapshot grey.
> Instinctively the mind withdraws
> To airports, depots . . .

But this, we remember, is the light of reality for Hecht. In it things are perceived as quiddities and seem the product of "design." Caught in "a brief / Mood of serenity," the accidental pebbles, stones, and trees of the poet's environs become able to "manifest / The deep, unvexed composure of the blessed." One thinks immediately of Wordsworth's "Tintern Abbey," and "that serene and blessed mood / In which the affections gently lead us on." For Hecht here as elsewhere, it is "the trustful eye, / Content to notice merely what is there," which leads us and in which we must trust. The poet has already told us that a storm is coming. But it does not arrive during the course of the poem, as it does in "Apprehensions." This time Hecht does not take away what has been given nor claim that it is childish. The apprehension of evil has lapsed, and "for the moment the whole world is real." We need to stress the concept of wholeness as well as that of reality here. A poem like this teaches that we can, in lucky moments, perceive beyond or behind a world of division and pain another world—Platonic, perhaps—which is whole. It is to retrieve such moments that an artist develops his craft.

Linda Orr

Pastiche and Pain: After Anthony Hecht's Translation of Voltaire

> *And why should they take thought*
> *Of all that ancient pain?*
> —Hecht, "The Cost"

"Poem upon the Lisbon Disaster" is a philosophical poem against philosophy, for there can be no reasoning about horror, not even any semblance of knowledge. Yet that keeps no one, especially Voltaire and Hecht, from thinking, from trying to understand what he knows he can't. Hecht's translation, virtually penultimate in his second book, precedes "The Lull" that wants to have the last word, even as its very title sadly implies the degree to which, in the words of an earlier poem, respite is "founded on disaster." At the very least, disaster and happiness are ineluctably intertwined, if only through their complicity with form and language.

The Voltaire/Hecht poem is structured by arguments, both facetious and serious, that explain and at the same time refute explanation of why an earthquake rocked Lisbon in 1755; and in the process this long poem from *Millions of Strange Shadows* emphasizes what is "Voltairean" in all of Hecht's books, for it articulates, to cite the translation itself, a particular stance in Anthony Hecht's ongoing investigation into "the root of evil." The translation, flexible and correct, manages to sound squarely like a Hecht poem, even as it keeps and creates markers to remind us that the poem was written in 1756 by Voltaire, that feisty beak-nosed Frenchman in a wig.

Beyond the virtuoso performance of Hecht's diction, "Poem upon the Lisbon Disaster" evokes the issue of translation itself both for Hecht and in general, but equally important, of the adequacy of words (in any tongue) before catastrophe. We are meant to wonder, since horror is untranslatable, whether it can matter how often it is re-translated, or how formally it is fixed in verse. Is there such a thing as quakeproof language?

The central position of translation in much of Hecht's work brings to the fore the inevitable problematic of language, which translation represents in perhaps its most essential form. I think the fundamental status of translation in Hecht's entire canon makes a theoretical statement, whether he capitalizes on it or not. Translation embodies the dialectic or conflict of Hecht's poetry. The presence of translations in each book forces a sense of history on the reader, harking back to eighteenth- or sixteenth-century France or to ancient Greece and Rome. And the "foreign" poems sound a note of difference that is the minimal condition of any critique, cultural or historical. But the translations also lend themselves to an intertextual theory of literature that (superficially) appears to bar the "real" and strong personal or political emotion and to close literature in on itself. Whereas in *The Hard Hours* the original authors of the translations are indicated in the table of contents, they (Voltaire, Sophocles, Ronsard, Horace) drop out of the table of contents in the two later books. This isn't dishonesty (the names appear at the end of each poem) but a sign of how integral the translated texts are to Hecht's own poetry.

Such a theoretical status of translation tends to break down both the idea of a text's originality and the subjectivity of the author. Translations even take on an intricate gamut of distances from that blurred original since sometimes Hecht marks "after" Baudelaire or "from" Ronsard or "freely from" Horace, and his Brodsky poems are "versions." It's as if words, forms, and poems themselves circulated through ages and languages, renewed or at least redisposed. This both shows a sense of generosity if not community and erects the figure of literature (and history) as a kind of palimpsest if not a huge (serious and respectful) game of telephone or gossip.

The Lisbon poem's subtitle, "Or, An Inquiry into the Adage 'All Is for the Best,'" alerts the reader that this poem is a kind of philosophical treatise. The subtitle quotes its literary model and ideological opponent, Pope's "Essay on Man." In contemporary terms, one could say that Voltaire proposes a close analysis of that one aphoristic sentence, "All is for the best," and yet the poem actually begins in exclamation: "Woeful mankind, born to a woeful earth!" That is, irony initiates the argument, which promises reason but can only utter unreasoning exclamations of rage, pain, and despair.

On the other hand, though those indecorous bursts of rhetorical emotion seem momentarily to address "woeful mankind," a quick shift reminds us that mankind has no voice, cannot participate in the argument. The poem seems in fact addressed to a "you," savant at times or proud sophist, philosophical "optimist" in a school with Pope, Bolingbroke, Leibniz. The "I" himself only now and then ventures his humble opinion. (Mankind is always "they.") Yet "you" drops out midway, when the knotty questions end up in God, Who alone makes human reason possible but Whom nothing can comprehend. The "I," via the quoted "I" of a subtle caliph, addresses Him at the end in an ambiguous humility, whose actual impudence Hecht's translation appears to stress.

Like point of view, logical structure is fluid, and more: it keeps giving way, as the poem loops back on itself. Questions and reasoning break down into rage and into the simple statement, both philosophical and lyrical, of pain and suffering that brings the poem to periodic halts. The questions pour back in, persistent, restless, and the almost uncontrollable process starts again. The arguments never "build"—just as the child in "The Venetian Vespers" can never seem to "build" a vocabulary.

Actually it isn't even the case that the questions and analyses exist on their own before dissolving into rage and pain. The narrator puts the arguments into his opponents' mouths so that they're covered in sarcasm a priori. That is, the anger and bitterness are barely transformed into this mock-dialogue. "Seeing these stacks of victims, will you state, / 'Vengeance is God's; they have deserved their fate'?" Maybe the narrator is quoting his opponents verbatim, but his effective strategies of argument also emphasize what is implicit, the obscene presumptions supposed to justify catastrophe: 1) That the victims got what they had coming. 2) That we petty mortals can't see It but there's a Master Plan in which all of this makes perfect sense for the Greater Good of the cosmos. 3) That those bastards were getting uppity anyhow, complaining and demanding a better life. (In eighteenth-century terms: they thought they could escape their natural, God-given inferiority by believing that radical hocus-pocus about Man's Perfectibility.) 4) That God must be testing us for the rewards of eternity. (Dismissed is the old Manichean argument that God doesn't have control over matter, which spawns evil.) And "All is for the best" is simply the shorthand that marshals every one of the premises above.

More than the earthquake, it is the poet's own anger that makes the poem's ground rumble: the anger at the sophists, the Ph.D.'s who theorize people's indifference to one another, their blindness to one another's sorrow, and legitimize it. As long as trauma doesn't strike them and their families, the haughty "tranquil minds" can show such easy objectivity, since the objectivity is based, in fact, more on the high ground than on any faculties of reason.

Moreover, the sophists are in league with the profit-makers. Here is another bit of delicate consolation doled out by the "optimists":

> "Drop dead with peace of mind;
> Your homes were smashed for the good of humankind;
> . . . .
> The North shall profit by your vast demise,
> And by astute investment realize
> Your momentary loss and fatal pain
> Conduced, through general laws, to ultimate gain. . . ."

Voltaire plays on the economic metaphor that Hecht so frequently meditates upon and modernizes. The word *bien* in the French line *Tous vos maux sont un bien dans les lois générales* means first "good" ("All evils are a good in the general laws"), but, coming after the preceding line, its second meaning as (worldly) goods, property, is lightly activated. Hecht takes that second meaning and runs, extending one line into three, in an instance of inflation that happens rarely (three times all told) in the poem.

These lines, specific perhaps to a concrete historical situation (was France profiting from the end of the Portuguese Empire?), are archetypical enough to suggest specific instances of exploitation over and over in history.[1] In the Voltaire/Hecht poem, the narrator tries for a while to counter the optimists' fundamentally greedy or self-serving arguments, but it's a waste of time, is itself "unprofitable"—except that it produces the poem. Babies died, not just criminals and decadents. By what cost-benefit scheme may this be justified? Similarly, by what account is Lisbon any more wicked than Paris? In this particular instance, Hecht fashions a gem out of Voltaire's already nice, condensed line ("Lisbon is swallowed up, and they're dancing in Paris"): "Lisbon is gone, yet Paris drinks champagne." Hecht gets more resonance when "pain" rhymes in the couplet with "champagne," and he lays a subtle stress on *consumption* into the bargain.

But the poets, whatever their tropes, can counter sophistical arguments just so long—"you claim," "you say"—before turning to an imperative that is also a direct attack.

> Do not presume to soothe such misery
> with the fixed laws of calm necessity,
> With The Great Chain of Being, hymned by Pope.

The poet will have no more of a Deistic bookkeeper God. Indeed, he inveighs against all that's fixed, calm, in conformity with alleged law and necessity; that "chain" of cosmic hierarchy has been used to whip others for too long (one thinks of the governess and the little boy in Hecht's "Apprehensions," contained in the same volume as the Lisbon poem). As the final line of the passage just quoted may imply, Voltaire knew English enough to appreciate the pun on Pope. Considering the institution of the Catholic Church as the largest imperial power of the day, he can even attribute a blasphemy to its own hierarchical cosmology: the "chain," he reminds us, "depends from God, Who is unchained."

We may wonder exactly what Hecht had in mind when he translated this poem of "ancient pain." It seems of course inevitable that a book published in 1977 might be heavy with the legacy of Vietnam. As the arguments of "Poem upon the Lisbon Disaster" fray into scenes of massive human destruction and cries of pain, it's hard not to think of that Indo-Chinese experience. The description of torn, piled bodies under the rubble of their houses brings back pictures of devastated villages. Voltaire—because of the French language itself?—remains fairly abstract:

> Come running, look at these frightful ruins,
> This debris, these rags, these unfortunate ashes.

Hecht's verse is perhaps more Yeatsian, especially in its signature end rhyme:

> Approach and view this carnage, broken stone,
> Rags, rubble, chips of shattered wood and bone.

But both he and Voltaire zero in on "Women and children pinioned under beams . . . piled under severed limbs" (Hecht). Perhaps a kind of Leibnizian serenity, to stretch an analogy, could obtain in a nation whose broadcast media had translated and *fixed* horror for the tranquil American living- or diningroom. Vietnam and Cambodia (El Salvador and Nicaragua) were and are as far away from us as eighteenth-century Lisbon. Or as Lisbon was from eighteenth-century Paris. Impatience, even stridence, are understandable from those who would—as Hecht unremittingly has chosen to do—"look squarely at the real," without recourse to self-serving moral platitude.[2]

The arguments, which are supposed to structure "Poem upon the Lisbon Disaster" and which by the authors' rhetorical arrangement are always already steeped in sarcasm if not bitter rage, burn out in periodic pauses. Brainteasers interrupted by one or another picture of gratuitous horror, by an outrageous philosophical discussion carried on against a background noise of moaning, give way to some of the best statement poetry I know. If Voltaire has a sentimental, rhetorical excess that is matched in some ways by Hecht's baroque preciosity, each writer's elaborate style is used to set up a contrasting simplicity, an austerity in the face of pain.

The "philosophical" poem in this instance must modulate into a litany on pain and a metaphysical lyric of unknowing. Its first sustained passage is a "translation," so to speak, of the river that flows beside the dying, which the interlocutor cannot hear; and it ends thus: "It is not pride that speaks, it is felt pain." We perceive here the rhythm of the poem and its language, which persistently churn up the "inquiry," the quest for wisdom, only to come again precisely upon pain. Which makes no sense. Finally, the poem "builds" to the central issue of reason as *scandal*, an impossible syllogism, from which can issue only lyricism and disguised anger.

> From Flawless Love ills can have no descent;
> Nor from elsewhere, since God's omnipotent;
> Yet they exist.

Hecht arrests the line, by the brutal caesura after two iambics, just as Voltaire splits his normally regular alexandrine in two. But then Hecht, as he often does, guards against too literal a translation of Voltaire's exclamations, in the interest, likely, of maintaining seriousness. While Voltaire goes off into that eighteenth-century melodrama which can irritate or make us laugh ("O sad truths! / O astounding mixture of contrarieties!"), Hecht comments with a sentence: "Such paradox has checked / And baffled the weak human intellect."

Hecht's poetry of not-knowing apparently requires a preparatory space; thus, his rich, virtuoso couplets seem to hunger for resolution, while resolution itself states that no resolution is possible. The arguments don't, therefore, grow in logic; rather, the statements grow in intensity:

> Whatever ground one takes is insecure:
> There's nothing we may not fear, or know for sure.

These lines reverberate because of the pun on "ground," which brings together physical and metaphysical universes, earthquake and argument. Here is another example nearer the end of the poem:

> It is of loss and grief our lives are made.
> The past is but a memory of despair,
> The present ghastly if it points nowhere,
> If the grave enfolds our spirit with our dust.

The Ecclesiastean tone is softened (or is it made more horrible?) by the verb "enfolds," which is Hecht's own touch. Some poets have come close to a strict non-narrative diction of stark simplicity (Cavafy, Justice, Kees); others have worked that simplicity off metaphor of varying lavishness (Stevens, Merrill, Strand); but Hecht has his own unique sense of rhetoric and historical language that highlights the more direct lines.

The Voltaire/Hecht text is, then, a curious mixture of old and new, of simple and ornate, of formal and conversational language. Hecht manages to mix phrases like "drop dead" or "bite the dust" (or references to Ph.D.'s and Seconal) with high French diction. But this is a tricky poem to control, because it has also to risk juxtaposing melodrama and eighteenth-century syntax with passages that should move us. Otherwise the poem is a set-piece—which it is, and is not. Voltaire's tone itself, that playful sarcasm sliding at times into a sneer, makes it hard to know when to read seriously. The linguistic landscape of the poem shifts, as if itself from an earthquake: Voltaire can be pompous and wordy or write a pure, graceful line in the tradition of Racine; but since Voltaire, the philosopher, cared about the movements of the mind as much as Racinian passion, certain lines translated into English take on an uncannily modern air. "Poem upon the Lisbon Disaster" may intensify the ineluctable demands on the translator, who controls how a text will sound but who cannot control that mobile proportion of strangeness to familiarity which makes translation different.

Hecht must, and does, constantly play with the poem's discourse. He keeps a certain flexible economy in mind that we sense when we compare the English and French, but the exchange is never parallel and equal. Hecht removes some "I"'s, but he puts some in where they weren't before. Sometimes he downgrades Voltaire's rhetoric, and sometimes he inflates it to the point of seeming parody. Voltaire writes, for instance, this typical post-Racinian eighteenth-century sentence, rhetorical but not without its simplicity: "Mais je vis, mais je sens, mais mon coeur opprimé / Demande ses secours au Dieu qui l'a formé" ("But I live and feel and my oppressed heart / Asks help from God Who formed it"). And Hecht translates: "But I, who live and feel in wracked dismay, / Yearn for His aid Who made me out of clay." On the whole Hecht (and English) gives more energy and relief to the line, but this makes Voltaire sound more high-flown than he often is. (I'm cheating somewhat by giving such flat, literal translations, but Voltaire, screechy sometimes, also possesses his own elegant simplicity.) Voltaire writes: "All beings . . . / Live in pain, and die like me." Hecht gets in a good active verb, but alters the quietness: "All creatures . . . / Must ache through life, and end, like me, in death."

It is perhaps, finally, the case that Hecht and Voltaire, for all the grimness of their content, are having fun with the range of language they use. I noticed one instance in particular: Voltaire describes lowly man, fallen from the Platonic ideal: "Un faible composé de nerfs et d'ossements" ("A weak composite of nerves and bone-pieces"), and Hecht renders the epithet as follows: "A thin pastiche of nerves and ligaments." Voltaire's *composé* etymologically means a simple posing-together of disparate elements (although it has a scientific, even eighteenth-century, ring—from botany or chemistry: a composite flower, a chemical compound); just so, Hecht makes us read etymologically, for *pastiche* means hodgepodge, pasticcio, and derives from paste, pasta (noodles). Thus we have an uncannily accurate translation, which at the same time adds a more organic trope and "glue" to the geometrical image of the body. But Hecht activates a new dimension in the word I'm stressing here, as I think he does in the poem at large: in his very relish of the renderer's linguistic options, he stresses the issue of language itself and (the history of) literature, even if in his model those issues are hardly present.

There is another telling moment near the end of "Poem upon the Lisbon Disaster" when Hecht translates the substance of Voltaire but uses the mark of his own language. Images of shadow, not to be found in Voltaire's own lines, link the poem to that collection of Hecht's in which it finds itself:

> *Quelquefois dans nos jours consacrés aux douleurs,*
> *Par la main du plaisir nous essuyons nos pleurs.*
>
> (Sometimes in our days devoted to sorrows,
> With pleasure's hand we dry our tears.)
>
> Sometimes a glint of happiness appears
> Among the shadows of this vale of tears.

This swerve away from the original and toward Hecht's own oeuvre reminds us that the Lisbon poem disengages itself for him from its internal discourse so as to shed light, or dark, both backward and forward on his work as a whole. The poem becomes a variant of the larger night music, a hybrid of Voltaire and Dante, where night alternates with glints, stars, a shadowless light, a lull in the pain.

This night music is Voltairean by virtue of its connection to philosophical skepticism, to history, to a visceral indignation that flares whether the awful thing is predestined or criminal, grandiose or everyday, mass produced or engendered by one demagogue. The legendary image of Voltaire, as well as the specific commitment of Voltaire's work, oddly illuminates Hecht's personal poetic project. Voltaire's quirky tone combines a non-romantic eighteenth-century sensibility, a nagging, plucky vigilance for civil rights (much before its time), and the threat of inarticulateness in the face of horror.

It is patent—in his wayward progress from the "yellowish sperm of horror" in *The Hard Hours* to "the lees of the Venetian underworld"—that Hecht excels in infernos. Though he may seek to balance those hard hours with *très riches heures*, there's no denying that energy suffuses him when he's stoking his hells and abysses. The Voltaire poem provides a chance to sharpen his lexicon of the "category of woes." Wars, beatings, millions of cells that die in indifferent fallopian tubes, and the ever-present *Sturm-Abteilungs Kommandant* populate *Millions of Strange Shadows*, a volume that in many ways culminates in the trope of earthquake. Yes, Nazi atrocities remain both the concrete, historical scandal and the Ur-evil that generates Hecht's inquiry, rage, and silence; but all other examples in world history tie into it as if through some underground lava, and it becomes irrelevant, even petty, as he suggests *à travers* Voltaire, to argue a hierarchy of woes. Each has a specificity, but each unhinges the mind similarly.

Hecht's work quite understandably may set a natural disaster beside the death camps, may at once blur and distinguish their "evil." Perhaps we ought to recall (as I find myself forced by this writer to do) the paradox so common to nineteenth-century thinkers like Marx or Michelet: that man makes a history he can never know. "Fate" haunts the Voltaire translation and recalls the "Three Prompters" of *The Hard Hours*, those Parcae who arbitrarily measure and snip. Hecht's primitive, Greek destiny is a radical, unaccountable thing, and "responsibility" a mind-boggling issue. Unlike the eerie, outer limit of Stevens, fate for Hecht is always bloody and earth-groveling, and to the oppressed what difference does it make whether a faceless destiny (or "God") bears down on them, or a stormtrooper in uniform? Hecht is aware also how deliberate evil tries to confuse itself with facts of nature as if there were no historical origin for that evil nor possibility of its end.[3]

It is too simple to say that Voltaire/Hecht counters "optimism" with "pessimism." If facile optimism has often piqued Hecht ("It's all very well to dream of a dove," from "Birdwatchers of America"), the alternative to such optimism in Voltaire's poem and its rendering here is not a symmetrical pessimism but the less easily defined skepticism of a Pierre Bayle, whose seventeenth-century *Historical and Critical Dictionary* anticipated the eighteenth century's major contribution to the freedom of knowledge: the *Encyclopédie,* to which Voltaire was of course a most prominent contributor. Skepticism, when taken through the loops of its logic, portrays over and over its own limits, the limits of philosophy itself. It acknowledges not-understanding and lets the dense world of evil appear. It does not, like the rather self-forgiving view of the sophists, refuse to see evil and its own complicities in it. That's why the skeptic does not engage in philosophy without irony, without an openness to literature, an openness that in Voltaire's (and Hecht's?) case impelled at least one assay of that difficult, if not impossible, hybrid: the philosophical poem.[4]

It seems that Hecht may take extra time at the point in Voltaire's original where Bayle is introduced, not only so that an unfamiliar American public may see the importance of Bayle in Voltaire's poem and ideology but perhaps also to stress this difficulty of poem-as-philosophy, philosophy-as-poem. Voltaire needs but two lines—"Wise enough, great enough to be without system, / He destroyed them all, and fought [his own] himself"—where Hecht takes four:

> Rejecting all closed systems by sheer strength
> Of mind and command of stature, Bayle at length
> Has overthrown all systems, overthrown
> Even those bleak constructions of his own.

The emphasis here adds a modern note, bringing the unsystematic philosophical tradition from Erasmus and Bayle to Nietzsche and Kierkegaard—perhaps even (though surely not wittingly; rather by the ironic shift of language from fault to fault) to "deconstruction." At times Hecht's poetry of not-knowing takes a light satirical tone: "Even a Pyrrhonist / Would admit it's getting dark" ("A Lot of Night Music"). At other times it assumes a terrifying form, representing the apparently ignorant child behind whom "hopeless riddles" "knot" in the cold air ("Auguries of Innocence"). And at times, worst of all, this child is full of "apprehensions" that nearly drive him crazy: do I alone, he wonders, vibrate with this universal terror I do not understand but know is there?

The fears that bring history up close, hot and horrible, are unbearable and call forth their opposite: Hecht's equally distinctive voice devoted to praising the shadowless light, the "fine particulars" of the present, and images of timeless beauty and love. History, thick with suffering and unknowing, that provokes not only fear and rage but the acrid reactions of resentment and hatred, must be stopped for a while, even if it means shutting a part of the mind itself down. "Surely the mind in all its brave assays / Must put much thinking by" ("The Cost"). In "Green: An Epistle" the poet wrestles with his need for exile in the "cheap hotel" and turns upon himself the irony and critique of the Voltaire poem: "These days, with most of us at a safe distance...."

Later, in "The Venetian Vespers," the figure of Molière's Alceste, the misanthrope, is more appropriate for the poet than that of the young Voltaire sent packing off to England to escape the Bastille or racing to the border to avoid arrest by King Frederick I.[5] The narrator of "The Venetian Vespers" recognizes his desire for "a policied [as opposed to policed] exile from the human race, / a cultivated, earned misanthropy." This is flight "from all the anguish of this world," "an escape / From time, from history, from evolution...." The narrator is tempted to become, self-consciously, the kind of persona he reviled through Voltaire: the cool scholar, the detached poet, internally exiled. The Other turns out, as usual, to be part of the self. At this point, a concentration on poetic form, its craft and technique "governed by laws that stand for other laws" ("Peripeteia"), displaces if not resists the lawlessness or the incomprehensible law of history.

But when does such a focus on language repress history as well as revive it, or worse, become, despite the impression of neutrality and innocence, complicit with historical forms of repression? In "Poem upon the Lisbon Disaster," Hecht subtly veers the translation toward an accusation of language itself that is not present in the original. At the close of the "Drop dead . . ." passage, Voltaire's narrator explodes against such insensitive language: "A des infortunés quel horrible langage! / Cruels, à mes douleurs n'ajoutez point l'outrage" (literally: To these unfortunate ones, what a horrible language! / Cruel [optimists], don't add outrage to my sorrows). Hecht translates the exclamation and imperative in one of his clinching statements: "This were to heap some last, insulting stones / Of language on that monument of groans." By so doing, the American poet brings forth a concrete image where there is only its suggestion in the verb "to add (onto)." The Voltaire text implies simply that those are horrible words to use in this context of suffering. Hecht transforms the words into stones, and although he too appears to mean those preceding words in particular, language takes on an ambiguous generality and an unambiguous violence. The cruel speakers literally stone the gravestones with their hard words. Their indifferent, moralizing, pseudo-scientific or commercially crass discourses not only cover up the damage done by the natural earthquake but also add to the injury. They turn catastrophe into martyrdom, compound the original evil, drive it further into the ground. (Note that both the first and second persons drop out of the translations.)

Does poetic language escape all contamination from the destructive, compromising languages just adduced? Is language itself a paradoxical monument of speech that smothers its subjects, silences their cries and pain with a block of words? And what about Hecht's "Poem upon the Lisbon Disaster," in which the cry is set back more than two hundred and thirty years in a foreign country where a foreign poet is talking about another foreign country where he wasn't a witness to the suffering—and all this in translation? Do so many layers blunt the effect, or enhance it?

The oppositions that a study of Hecht's poetry calls up (generosity and palimpsest, passion and intertextuality, history and literary history) are, finally, ideological in nature. "Feeling and form" always interrelate paradoxically in our major poets. I might even say that the highest degree of poetic control elicits the most surprise, the most violent return of the repressed, the sharpest cry. That is the premise on which Hecht, Merrill, Howard, Wilbur, Bishop, and Auden work. (The reverse is also true. "Free" verse can be as definitely fixed: for example, late Celan, René Char, and Stevens, or more recently, Louise Gluck.) The tradition of Keats and Yeats demands a poetic object and language "at once fixed and free" as Hecht rewrites it in "Gladness of the Best." To continue the earthquake metaphor, Hecht builds his quakeproof house or poem over the continental fault, the shifting abyss of language. Like language, translation is both circulation and obstacle, cry and disguise; the poet doesn't always know which works where or when; and the slippery relationship is always changing. That's why pain and pastiche are not mutually exclusive.

NOTES

1. If I as a Southerner (however ambivalent) seize upon this satire of the North, I am also a part of that greater North plundering Central and South America. Hecht has always had a troubled relationship to "investment" (to be compared to Merrill's). Another long poem preceding the Lisbon poem in Hecht's book, "Apprehensions," expresses ever so discreetly that belated rage of the child-in-the-adult against "the market" that brought no fresh, healthy produce into the family but only destruction. These multivalent emotions are all rolled up in the one image of the sadistic Teutonic governess, goddess of the North and one of the typically ambiguous female figures in Hecht. In his dreams, she lured the poet like millions of others into a dark rendezvous.

2. Today I'm struck by how close that "Drop dead . . . " passage or the one "they deserved their fate" comes to the present, paranoid if not fascist reaction to AIDS victims. This, from a letter to the *Durham Morning Herald* (March 2, 1987): "54,000 will die in one year. . . . Indeed, what a price to pay for the immorality that has swept our land and may God in His grace and mercy somehow honor the prayers of those who are diligently keeping a vigil for the time when this country has had enough!" From here to vigilantes is only a step. One might even add, with all the sadness of radical skepticism, that AIDS too is ruining some and enriching others.

3. Fascism, to choose a relevant instance, took on a momentum of its own, in which Hitler himself held only symbolic power in a system (or "the

complete absence of system," as Hannah Arendt reminds us in *The Origins of Totalitarianism*) that went beyond him. On the other hand, natural disasters are not only exploited but also precipitated by determined social conditions and competing political states. Thus, the difference between the two kinds of disasters may often fade.

4. It is telling that that poem has had nowhere near the posterity of *Candide*, though each work is composed around the same themes and issues.

5. Voltaire does not dare to live in Paris when he writes his Lisbon poem and *Candide* in Switzerland, but he'll take his own advice from *Candide* after that and "cultivate [his] own garden." On the French border (Ferney), he organizes a little domain for himself where he holds the "court of Europe." His exile turns into a symbolic realm where he rules like a philosopher king. Is there a dialogue with Voltaire in Hecht's use of the Ruskin epigraph to "The Venetian Vespers"?—"We cannot all have our gardens now."

John Frederick Nims

"The Venetian Vespers":
Drenched in Fine Particulars

"The Venetian Vespers" is a fascinating poem; once into it, I may have overstayed my welcome, or even poked into a few closets I was not supposed to.

The form is that of a dramatic monologue in which an expatriate American, settled in Venice, reviews his life and its meaning. He never gives his name—his identity, age, and such details of selfhood are a burden he would consider it a mercy to escape from. To avoid elegant variations on "the child," "the young man," "the speaker," "the persona," and so on, suppose we call him "X."

There are several levels of interest in what he tells us: his life story, revealed gradually and piecemeal in the six sections of the poem and complicated by our not being certain how reliable a narrator he is; the analysis of his character and temperament as he interprets them; his general culture, with his opinions and theories about the reality, or the unreality, that he lives in. All three are engrossing.

Before we begin to read, we are likely to find ourselves meditating on the title and the two epigraphs. "The Venetian Vespers," a dark title, may remind us that Venice, in its long decline from glory, has for centuries been a vespertine city. As we read we learn that X has come there to let the evening of his life "peter out" in an atmosphere congenial to his melancholy.

We may also detect in the title what in Pound criticism has been called a subject rhyme. What it evokes is thought of the Sicilian Vespers, that massacre of the occupying French forces, including women and children, by the Sicilians in a revolt that began in a quarrel at vesper services in Palermo on the Easter Monday of 1282.

This is an ominous note in itself; though never stressed, it may be relevant to the bloody battlefield experiences X has been unsettled by.

But "vespers" also means evensong, the music of evening devotions. Likely enough it will remind us of what music meant to the Venetians, especially during the sixteenth and seventeenth centuries, when some of the best music in Europe was to be heard there. We may recall that Monteverdi, *maestro di capella* at St. Mark's from 1613 until his death thirty years later, composed "Christmas Vespers" and "Vespro della Beata Vergine," performances of which are in the record catalogs yet. Some of the most brilliant music of the year was to be heard at the Venetian vespers of the great holidays, particularly at the Incurabili (twice mentioned in our poem): the hospital, originally for syphilitics, so well known by 1605 that Ben Jonson, in far-off London, could refer to it in the last scene of *Volpone*, his own dark comedy of what the English saw as Venetian depravity. The Incurabili was one of the four charitable hospitals in Venice with conservatories that gave orphan girls, and some who could pay, what was probably the best musical training then available. Such visitors as Rousseau and Goethe lavished fascinated praise on the girl musicians. Many composers in Venice contributed such music as that of the vesper services: Vivaldi, the three Gabrieli, Albinoni, the brothers Marcello. Galuppi, about whom Browning wrote his Venetian poem, was choirmaster at St. Mark's and later musical director at the Incurabili.

"The Venetian Vespers," as title, is a three-word poem in itself, ominous and alluring. In the body of the poem, the poet speaks only through the persona of X, but in the choice of epigraphs we may expect his own aside on what occurs. The first of the two, from *Othello*, offers a caution we do well to keep in mind as we read. Iago, the Venetian villain, is the speaker. He is telling Othello, evil tongue in cheek, that perhaps his (Iago's) thoughts about Desdemona are "vile and false." For which of us, he asks rhetorically, has a mind so pure as not sometimes to entertain "foul things" and "uncleanly apprehensions"? Since the mind of the narrator is the only mind that expresses itself in "The Venetian Vespers," we may wonder if its integrity is being impugned by the epigraph. Is X telling us the truth about others or are his interpretations "foul" and "uncleanly," as he sometimes wonders? Is he possibly his own Iago?

The second epigraph is from "The Vestibule," the last chapter of Volume 1 of *The Stones of Venice*. After some thirty chapters of analysis of such architectural features as cornices, shafts, arches, apertures, and ornaments, Ruskin is about to introduce the reader to Venice itself, seen dimly across her lagoon. Before doing so, he has some further reflections on nature and art. The sentence I italicize is the second epigraph to our poem.

> We are forced, for the sake of accumulating our power and knowledge, to live in cities: but such advantage as we have in association with each other is in great part counterbalanced by our loss of fellowship with nature. *We cannot all have our gardens now, nor our pleasant fields to meditate in at eventide.* Then the function of our architecture is, as far as may be, to replace these; to tell us about nature; to possess us with memories of her quietness; to be solemn and full of tenderness, like her, and rich in portraitures of her; full of delicate imagery of the flowers we can no more gather, and of the living creatures now far away from us in their own solitude.

The sentence's application will grow apparent as we read. To some it may suggest no more than the platitude about life that is popularly expressed as "I never promised you a rose garden." Some may dally, perhaps otiosely, with reminiscences of another Venetian story, "The Aspern Papers," in which the "publishing scoundrel" who is its deceitful narrator uses his pretended passion for a garden in Venice as a way of gaining entry into the palace he hopes to despoil of the manuscripts he covets. The poet, in any case, has given us a good deal to think about before we have read a line of his poem.

As we begin to read, and as X takes us into his confidence, we find there are two epistemological levels in what he is reporting. First, there is what he knows "for sure." Then there is the more ambiguous material that he says "I learned, or else I dreamed." We can piece his life together, detective-fashion, as we read. Doing so is part of the absorption—or call it the fun—of reading the poem.

What he knows "for sure" and states as fact, or what we can deduce from his facts, is about as follows. Sometime between 1971 (he mentions Stravinsky's grave) and 1978, when the poem was published in *Poetry*, the narrator, in his fifties, is looking back on his life. He tells us how his uncle, a Latvian immigrant, settled in Lawrence, Massachusetts, where, by the early 1920s, he was prosperous enough as manager of an A&P to send for his three younger brothers. One, the future father of X, brought his wife of two months. The other two brothers are hardly mentioned again; references to "uncle" in our discussion will refer always to the oldest of the four. X is the only child in the family; it seems that just one of the brothers married. Figuring back from data given later about X's war service, we find he was born within a year or two of 1923—that happens to be the year of Hecht's own birth, so his narrative is set in a world contemporary with him. X, a shy asthmatic child, dreamy, fond of reading, spent his childhood in living quarters over the store and in the comfortable and colorful A&P itself, which he describes as lighted up in the evening like a theater, compared to the duller homes of his schoolmates. In school he was a champion speller, good at elocution and English assignments, an expert in such trivia as how many times the name of Lea and Perrins appears on the bottle (forty-eight times). There is little mention of other boyhood activities, though he is familiar enough with the Boy Scout salute to remember it decades later. Precocious and clever he was, but, as he tells us in the last line of the poem, in his final despondent appraisal of himself, he was "never . . . a wise child."

"I thought I was happy almost through my youth," he remembers. But when X was a year old, his father, feeling that profits from the store were strained in supporting the four brothers and the one wife and child, took off to make his fortune in the west. "We never heard from him again."

When he was six, his mother died after a long illness. The uncle appeared grief-stricken. By the time X was eighteen, he was living with the well-to-do uncle, who was always generous and supportive—"or so it seemed." It was then that the missing father made an appearance—but as a corpse brought back from the west in a boxcar. Again the uncle seemed overcome by grief. Immediately after the funeral, X enlisted in the army; refusing to bear arms, he served in the medical corps, often under fire, until two and a half years later he was mustered out as "mentally unsound."

What he did for the next thirty or so years we are not told—though it is clear that he acquired a considerable knowledge of literature and the arts—Hecht has, in fact, endowed him with some of his own wide culture. When X first appears, at the beginning of the poem, it is as the expatriate in Venice, living modestly on the annuity from his uncle, whose sole heir he was. He has never married. Living in a seedy albergo, he feels that his life has been a failure and that he is "an exile from the human race."

This is his *vita* as we can assemble it from the data he gives us. What else he tells us, the things "learned . . . or else dreamed," may be only the "uncleanly apprehensions" Iago would warn his victim against. X admits that they are known by "painful inference" alone and that he can no longer distinguish between fact and "the enfleshment of disembodied thought"—a phrase which may recall the words Shakespeare put in the mouth of Theseus to describe poetry. His suspicions may even be, says X, due to some "melanotic malevolence" of his own.

On the last page of the poem, he reveals explicitly what these suspicions are:

> my uncle,
> Who, my blood tells me on its nightly rounds,
> May perhaps be "a little more than kin,"
> Has paid the price for his unlawful grief
> And bloodless butchery by creating me
> His guilty legatee, the beneficiary
> Of his money and his crimes.

Hamlet's riddling aside—"a little more than kin, and less than kind"—is the key to what X has come to suspect: that his uncle has somehow been too close to the sister-in-law, X's mother, and may have been involved, like Claudius, in her husband's death. And, since the epigraph implies that all of us have our uncleanly apprehensions, should we go whole hog and think we are invited to complete the proverb the final line of the poem hints at? "Who was never even at one time a wise child." And, in completing it, say that X suspected his uncle was his real father? That would mean that he had seduced the young bride, new to the ways of Massachusetts, and then, like King David, had the legitimate spouse disposed of. Common sense seems against this, but if one is influenced by "melanotic malevolence"?—the phrase is close enough to the "motiveless malignity" that Coleridge ascribed to Iago to be disquieting. Or shall we content ourselves with saying that the uncle, out of embarrassment at having a brother (as we will see) in detention, and wishing to stand in well with the New Englanders on whom his prosperity depended, abandoned his brother to his fate, only to be tormented later by feelings of guilt and the need to make amends? Or did none of this happen?

Earlier in the poem we have been a witness to what X calls his uncle's "unlawful grief." Coming home in the school bus on a rainy evening, the six-year-old X found the store, usually so cheerfully lighted, almost in darkness. His uncle, soaked through, was on the steps waiting for him. Though the boy knew that "something was clearly up," he asked no questions as his uncle took him off to a movie. Blindly chosen, it turned out to be, with appropriate irony, a bedroom comedy, which his uncle wept all through. They then had dinner at a Chinese restaurant. It was not until the next day that the boy was told that the gloomy distractions of the night before had been because his mother had died. The uncle's grief hardly constitutes hard and fast evidence that he had been involved—perhaps in "noontide infidelities"—with the mother, who never appears in the poem. Nor is the uncle's solicitude for the child after her death any certain evidence that he is trying to make up for earlier wrongdoing. It may be that he is "forbearing and encouraging and kind" because that really is his nature. It may be that he makes X his heir out of natural family feeling, and not as any kind of atonement.

Evidence that the uncle is guilty of "bloodless butchery" is implied by the son's impression, when the father's body is brought home, that

> there was torture in my uncle's face
> Such as I did not even see in war.

That, by itself, does not establish guilt either. But there is also the something else that X says he "learned, or else . . . dreamed." It was this: his father, setting out for the west, had reached Toledo, where "late one night in a vacant parking lot / He was robbed, hit on the head with a quart bottle" by thugs who had just held up a liquor store. Without his wallet or other means of identification, and in his hysteria recalling little of the "dozen words of English" which he knew, he was sent to the State Mental Hospital. There he was kept for a year, until by chance a Lithuanian visitor recognized his Latvian speech. Since it was then determined that he was "in full possession of his faculties," the police wrote the uncle requesting that the money be sent to cover his transportation home. No answer, we are told, from the uncle. Two more letters also went unanswered. So the police apparently decided to forget about the matter, and about the strange vagrant from Massachusetts, who remained in confinement. At least we think he did; what happened to him for the next sixteen years we are not told.

A painful story. But is it true? "I learned, or else I dreamed. . . ." Unless the sanity of X is in question, he would not be likely to confuse, in so crucial a matter, reality and dream. Yet he says he does confuse them. It would seem that he knew perfectly well whether he was told these things, or had made them up either to justify an antipathy already felt toward the uncle or out of a natural morbidity of temperament.

Although this is not a detective story, and although the effect of the poem does not depend on the historicity of these events, yet the world Hecht has created is so beguiling that we do wonder about them. We wonder about such things as: from whom could X have learned about the affair in Toledo? Surely not the uncle. And if someone else knew about a victim unjustly confined in Toledo, why was nothing done about it?

The story is curious in other ways. Unless the mother of X was already pregnant when she got married, the father must have been working in the grocery store in Lawrence for close to two years— until the boy was a year old. Are we to believe that in those two years the father learned "no more than a dozen words of English"? And was unable to explain his situation to the Toledo police, or to the authorities in the mental institution for a year thereafter? And that for the next sixteen years he was equally unresourceful?

Yet the story does not sound like a dream—if we thought for a moment it was. It is too factual, too documentary: the vacant lot, the quart bottle, the Lithuanian visitor. It does not have the inconsequence and surrealist bedizening dreams are likely to have.

It seems we will never know. Perhaps that very puzzlement is an essential component of the poem. We are tempted, though, to try to construct a psychiatric history of X, since the poet has provided us with so many clues to that psyche.

That his mind is not at peace with itself is implied in the first two lines of the poem. As he leans his head against the cool glass of the window, he is thinking

> What's merciful is not knowing where you are,
> What time it is, or even your name or age,
> But merely a clean coolness at the temple.

We know that he was mustered out of the army as "mentally unsound," but this, we may feel, could happen to any but the staunchest or most stolid after two and a half years of gruesome battlefield experience handling "the wounded and the dead."

It may, however, have done psychic damage. In middle age, he describes himself as

> not very well,
> Subject to nightmares and to certain fevers
> The doctors cannot cure.

There were also early signs that X was a likely candidate for neurasthenia. A shy child, apparently much alone, he led a covert life, finding instead of real chums secret faces in the wallpaper that were his "agents in the field." When still young enough to play around "the legs of chairs" (like the little soul in "Animula") he sensed in the drift of motes "a tide of sadness . . . a dying fall." We might suspect that he, beginning with his childhood asthma, was susceptible to the kind of ailment thought of as psychogenic. As a child he seems to have overreacted to the routine unpleasantnesses of existence: the "disgusting" membrane that gathers on hot milk, the "unbearable" close-up of a wart with a bristle of hair, a ham hung "like a traitor's head" in a butcher shop, the "truncated snout" of a small bat, sunken in like a syphilitic face. Details others might find innocent or even pretty seem to have upset him: the way, for example, that waterdrops on a glossy black railing seem to be sucking in "some morbid nourishment" from its blackness.

When very young too he suffered from

> precocious hints of hell
> Those intuitions of living desolation
> That last a lifetime.

Most of the hints he tells us about seem not quite hellish: an abandoned boxcar in fierce summer heat, a row of deserted Victorian houses with one flapping windowshade, incontinent old men who urinate in viaducts, schoolboy jokes about bedpans. But to X they are hellish, and his graphic descriptions convince us he finds them so.

From such harrowing images it was "but a child's step . . . to the appalling world of dreams." All of his life X suffered from sleep disorders, like those that moved Macbeth to his famous complaint. When X wakes in the morning, his spirit comes from a world of "Piranesian *Carceri* and rat holes / Of its own deep contriving." He often has nightmares, and indeed sees his life as a nightmare, played out, like a film, "on the ceiling of my rented room," much as the sleepless girl in Eliot's "Preludes" sees the sordid images of her own life "flicker against the ceiling." It is not surprising that the painter he talks about the most is Henry Fuseli, whose nightmare paintings of demons squatting on a sleeper's breast are of psychiatric interest. Not only at night did the dreams disturb him; there was also the "obsessional daydream" that made him review his life like a film run in reverse, in the hope of undoing what had been done, as, in the film, the "wound" in water is healed when the diver emerges backward, miraculously dry, and soars easily to his serenity on the board.

As we will see, the vivid interest X has in perceiving *things* will give him what little escape and comfort he can expect. But, as we have seen, *things* also distress him. Together with his concern for them is what seems an indifference to people—a kind of anesthesia in their regard. Though he has refused to bear arms, and says he has tried not to hurt anyone, "A goal which, in the very nature of things, / Is ludicrous because impossible," still he does not have, in the poem, an affectionate word for any human being (or for dogs either). His father disappeared when X was a year old; not much basis for affection there. The most emotional detail he mentions, and then repeats, is "a casket lined with tufted tea-rose silk." The mother, though incapacitated by a long illness, was with him until he was six, but the only detail we have about her is the mention, at least three times, of the tiny bubbles—related to the glassblowing at Murano—that formed on the stems of the flowers in the room "somebody" died in. Toward his uncle he has little but suspicion. The only friend—if he was that—X mentions is a fellow soldier who escaped from the realities of the war by immersing himself in a book of etiquette by Emily Post. But he seems less a friend than a curiosity who "Haunts me here, that seeker after law / In a lawless world." It is always possible that the emotions X felt toward his parents and others were of an intensity he could not bring himself to reveal.

In speaking about his misanthropy, he says, "It wasn't always so." But at least the roots of it were there in childhood, and perhaps before childhood: "the origin of things / Lies elsewhere. Back in some genetic swamp." Perhaps an instability was inherited from his father, who himself drew it from the genetic swamp. When questioned by the police, we are told, the father's "hysterical anxiety" and "wild excitability" led authorities to suspect that he was deranged. In the years thereafter he seems to have shown a lack of decisiveness approaching abulia.

But not all of the troubles of X were genetic or subjective. His sense of "the anguish of the world," the loss of parents at an early age, the suspicion he felt about his uncle, the "inconceivable pain" he was close to for so many months as a medic, the hypocritical dishonesty he came to feel in a society that lived only for respectability, his own sense of worthlessness—all of these deepened the tendency toward gloom and depression that was his by nature. He came to regard himself with disgust for having truckled, in a "craven and repulsive" way, to an uncle he considered guilty. Corrupted by what he took to be the corruption around him—as Othello and Hamlet were—he felt that his sickness was in "the gross intestinal wormings of the brain." All of this self-accusation is not without self-pity, as he feels in himself "profoundly soiled, pointlessly hurt / And beyond cure."

As if a friendless and failing old age were not bad enough, he also fears he might end in insanity, in dying "at the top first," as Swift and Byron had feared before him:

> the mind
> Can scarcely cope with the world's sufferings,
> Must blinker itself to much or else go mad.

It is hardly surprising that so much despondency found relief in the thought of death. "One slides to it like a swoon," as one glides, by gondola, to the Venetian graveyard on its island. Such deliquescence he finds "delicious," though in a more nihilistic sense than Whitman did when he invoked lovely and soothing death.

X is, of course, not a person. He is a literary creation, a persona through whose hollowness can resonate only the voice of the poet who brought him into being. But a persona is believable only if he meets the criteria by which we judge the people around us. X, as I understand him, passes that test; he is real, convincingly and dismally real, throughout the poem. There are ambiguities in his attitudes and in his behavior, but no more so than in many people in the world we know. What we will probably never be sure of is whether the traumas of his life made him the somber misanthrope he says he is, or whether his own saturnine temperament led him to feel traumas where there were none. Or whether, as is more likely, a synergism of the two made him the X we see. The ambiguities by no means diminish the interest of the poem.

If we treat X as a free-standing figure, it is fair to look at the kind of culture with which the poet has endowed him. We find him to be a sensitive amateur, a connoisseur if not an expert, in many of the arts.

Music is referred to less frequently than the others. The play of sunlight on leaves reminds him of the "light chromatics" of Debussy; in St. Mark's he can rejoice in "the warm light of Gabrieli's horns." Cimarosa, Wagner, and Stravinsky are mentioned only because they died or were buried in Venice. But there are repetitions and harmonies of imagery in the poem that are like the use of themes in music. X is round enough as a character for us to feel that he would have much more to say about music if he had occasion to.

Though the great Venetian painters—Titian, the Bellini, Giorgione, Tintoretto, Veronese—are not mentioned, X seems to have looked long and carefully at painting and speaks of it with wit and discernment. In a brilliant description of the clouds over Venice, he praises a sky "determined to maintain / The reputation of Tiepolo." In speaking of our dream of paradise as an escape into "the blessed stasis of a painting," he has a savagely amusing description of typical palace art: the apotheosis of "some boorish-looking count" levitating toward heaven on quilts and comforters of downy cloud.

His own tastes, or the course of his reveries, lead him to a more somber art. Of the animated Carpaccio he mentions only the "terrifying boredom" in the faces of his heavy-eyed prostitutes. We have quoted before his reference to Piranesi's *Carceri*. Henry Fuseli, the "authority on nightmares," is more in harmony with his own moods. X has remembered, and can even quote, with touches of his own to make the diction more vivid, the description which Fuseli gave his pupils of his method of painting:

> "I first sits myself down.
> I then works myself up. Then I throws in
> My darks. And then I takes away my lights."[1]

He has read the art critics and remembers that Turner's visions of reality have been described (by Constable) as "tinted steam."

He is knowledgeable about the architecture of Venice and knows the story of its great churches. Looking across the Canal, he can refer allusively to San Giorgio Maggiore and Santa Maria della Salute as "Palladio's church . . . and the great church of Health." He has read *The Stones of Venice* and can draw upon it for a memorable phrase. Ruskin, describing the loungers outside St. Mark's, notices among them "unregarded children,—every heavy glance of their young eyes full of desperation and stony depravity" (vol. 2, chap. 4). Returning from the golden dusk of the interior of the piazza, X observes among the tourists

> Those dissolute young with heavy-lidded gazes
> Of cool, clear-eyed, stony depravity.

The rich description of the "aquarium dimness" of St. Mark's that preceded this observation shows that X is a student and appreciator of the exotic grandeurs of its architecture. His page or so on the interior is as keen an evocation of the feeling one has there as we get from Ruskin's many pages—X is far more lavish and imaginative, if less technical. As befits these "pavonine and lapidary walls," the language of X is more opulently incrusted than Ruskin permits himself:

> Patines
> And laminae, a vermeil shimmering
> Of fish-scaled, cataphracted golden plates.

X is not being highfalutin here; there is a craftsmanly exactness in his knowledge and perception of materials, just as there is when he describes how "the wobbled clarity of streams" shows a pattern of gravel so rich and intricate that it can be described, by someone with X's knowledge, as "tarsial, cosmatesque bespattering"—hardly a vocabulary available to the run-of-the-mill globe-trotter, who will not have come across the work of the Cosmati or be familiar enough with *tarsia* (or *intertarsia*) to coin an adjective from it.

But literature is the field in which he is most at home. We have noticed some of his allusions to literary passages; there are other reminiscences, some going back to the schoolroom classics he read as a boy.

Though professing himself a "twentieth century infidel," he quotes the Bible, both Old and New Testaments, more often than any other source. He seems to have read the King James version thoughtfully and not merely "as literature" for its quotable quotes. The passages he does refer us to are meaningful in the context he constructs, though he may not always give them the meaning the divine writers intended. Losing all thought of self as one contemplates a thunderstorm in Venice may not be exactly what Saint Matthew had in mind when he wrote down what X rewords as "One takes no thought whatever of tomorrow." But the quotation is significant where it occurs in the poem. When X seems to agree that

> As the writ saith:
> The fathers (and their brothers) shall eat grapes
> And the teeth of the children shall be set on edge

he may be forgetting that both Jeremiah and Ezekiel quote the proverb only to deny—given their new consciousness of personal responsibility—that it is any longer valid. But, in holding to a more primitive view, X is applying the proverb to his own situation.

For here and elsewhere he is no mere passive rememberer; his sensibility is creative, quick to take a familiar passage and remold it nearer, as he might put it, to his heart's desire. Another example of such artful change is in his reference to his "cultivated, earned misanthropy" as "after the fashion of the Miller of Dee." But the miller—in the old song that Isaac Bickerstaffe made famous in his "ballad opera" *Love in a Village* (1862)—was not really a misanthrope. He was a "jolly miller . . . No lark more blithe than he." He didn't really say, as the author has him say in a note:

> I care for nobody, no, not I,
> And nobody cares for me.

What he said was, "*If* nobody cares. . . ." No surly Timon, he is only a man who is sturdily independent. The old song is not misused in the poem; the change merely dramatizes the way in which X can artfully misremember or modify to suit his own purposes (as perhaps he does also when he thinks about his uncle's behavior).

We may wonder how X is supposed to have come across the Miller of Dee at all. But we are often surprised at the width of the reading from which his allusions come and at how his familiarity with them is such that he can suggest them with a word or two instead of parroting them by rote. When he describes, near the end of the poem, how

> Gradually, like the death of virtuous men,
> Streaks of electrum

underline the clouds at evening, we know that he wants us to think of the beginning of Donne's "A Valediction: Forbidding Mourning," which may have other sympathetic vibrations with his own thought. When he describes how bricks, clinkers, and old iron "Burn in their slow, invisible decay," he trusts that we will appreciate the contrast with the rural setting of Frost's "The Wood-Pile," which ends "With the slow smokeless burning of decay."

One of the richest textures of allusion is in section 2, which begins with X's remembering that Byron wrote how

> "Many a fine day
> I should have blown my brains out but for the thought
> Of the pleasure it would give my mother-in-law."

This reminds him of "Gerontion," in which the speaker has a certain resemblance to X:

> Thus virtues, it is said, are forced upon us
> By our own impudent crimes.

He then thinks of Byron's life at the Palazzo Mocenigo in Venice in 1818–19:

> With his consorts of whores and countesses
> Smelling of animal musk, lilac and garlic,
> A *ménage* that was in fact a menagerie,
> A fox, a wolf, a mastiff, birds and monkeys,
> Corbaccios and corvinos, *spintriae*,
> The lees of the Venetian underworld,
> A plague of iridescent flies.

We know about the whores, countesses, and the many animals from the letters and journals of Byron and those who visited him at the time. But "corbaccios" (ravens) and "corvinos" (crows)? These must come from X's reading of Ben Jonson's *Volpone* (the Fox), set in Venice. The names Corbaccio and Corvino occur together, in that order, in "The Persons of the Play," in which they are two of the avaricious schemers for Volpone's fortune—not unlike some of the hangers-on in Byron's ménage. *Spintriae* is the Latin plural, feminine in form, for "male prostitutes." The expatriate from Lawrence must have read widely and curiously to have come across the word—unless indeed he was at home with such writers as Tacitus and Suetonius. (Jonson anglicizes the word to "spintry" in his *Sejanus*.) "The plague of iridescent flies," which concludes the passage quoted, may be a reminiscence of a phrase used by Iago: in telling Roderigo that although Othello seems secure they can at least annoy him, he says, "though he in a fertile climate dwell, / Plague him with flies."

Thoughts of the corruption around Byron in Venice take him back to thoughts of wartime horrors, his father's casket, the humiliations of old age, and his own death sometime in the future "among the albergo's seedy furniture." Then his mind goes back again to Byron and his fear, like Swift's, of madness at the end. He thinks then of Fuseli, whom some called mad, and George III, who, gossips reported, was seen to shake hands with the branches of an oak that he took for the King of Prussia. Richly stored with such reminiscences, his mind moves aptly and easily among them.

So far we have talked about the content of "The Venetian Vespers," and have said little about why it works so well as a poem. We have dwelt on such matters as the verisimilitude of the narrative and the nature and credibility of its narrator; we have pondered how, with X, event has shaped personality and personality colored event. On first reading, our impression might be that story and storyteller were only the *ficelle* on which poetic events were to be strung. But a better term than *ficelle* is infrastructure, without which the poetic structure could not stand. Or, to see it in Venetian terms, we could liken it to the brickwork under the gorgeous interiors of St. Mark's. The builders might have left that brickwork of a puritan bareness, and then we would have a great dark hollow of dingy masonry, like a cinder-block warehouse. Similarly, the writer might simply have given us a biography and character sketch of X, and then we would have an interesting piece of informative prose. But hardly a poem.

What gives St. Mark's its glory and makes it one of the world's wonders is what Ruskin called its "incrustation," the richness of gold and colored stone and glass mosaic that make it seem alive with a play of light and color. Ruskin is at pains to show that he is using "incrustation" in no disparaging sense, as if it meant only something like superficial decoration. Given the materials the builders had to work with, he explains, there was no other way in which the cathedral could have been invested with its splendor. Provided we are aware of this legitimate and honorable meaning, we can apply the word "incrustation" to poetry; it refers to a richness and rightness of imagery, diction, sound, and rhythm investing the bare thought. It is what turns the brickwork of

That's the end of my peace and quiet, and
of the challenge and excitement of army life.
It's all spoiled for me now

into the incrustation of

Farewell the tranquil mind! farewell content!
Farewell the plumed troop, and the big wars
That make ambition virtue! O, farewell!
Farewell the neighing steed and the shrill trump,
The spirit-stirring drum, th' ear-piercing fife,
The royal banner, and all quality
Pride, pomp, and circumstance of glorious war! . . .
Farewell! Othello's occupation's gone.

If we appeal to Shakespeare's familiar formulation of the nature of poetry, we find that what produces it is the power of transforming abstractions, "airy nothings," which it "bodies forth" as the physical images and gives a "local habitation" to by molding them into words and rhythms through "the poet's pen."

The lunatic, the lover, and the poet,
Are of imagination all compact.

X is not a lover in the usual sense, unless we concede him a dubious right to that title because of the intensity of his attachment to the dense particulars of life. But Theseus might well include him among the lunatics, who see "more devils than vast hell can hold." And he is always the poet—or better, the persona through which a genuine poet speaks—turning "things unknown" to definite images and giving them names that localize them for our own imagination.

We have seen examples of how X can reshape, to poetic effect, the données of his experience and his reading. The thought of Byron and mortality bring back memories of battlefield horrors: of a soldier the top of whose head is sheared off, "like a soft-boiled egg," by machine-gun fire so that his brains are "spilled like sweetbreads." X thinks of "lights and livers," of how the body can turn suddenly into organic refuse and of the irony of our making the fuss we make over it. But he turns these feelings into imagery:

O that the soul should tie its shoes, the mind
Should wash its hands in a sink, that a small grain

Of immortality should fit itself
With dentures.

Thoughts of death in Venice provide another example of how fact can be remodeled into poetry. X imagines the mortuary gondolas on their way to the island cemetery of San Michele, passing the Incurabili and the Calle dei Morti on the way. To glide silently toward the cemetery by way of a hospital called the Incurables and then the Street of the Dead is a poetic way to get there; it is not the direct route. In actual Venice, one might run up quite a bill with the gondoliers, but as poetic cartography the route is rewarding.

There is a similar enhancing of fact when X is recalling how "those lawless two / Entrepreneurial Venetians" stole the body of St. Mark from Alexandria so that it could be entombed in Venice. He gives their names as "Buono and his sidekick Rustico," The Good Man and The Simple Man—names out of a morality play for the two who effected "the major heist of Christendom." But historians tell us there was a third body snatcher named Stauracio. It may not be good history to deep-six him, for it was Stauracio, and not The Good Man or the Simple Man, who was chosen chief dignitary of the monks attached to the cathedral where the holy heist was buried. But it is good poetry; the name Stauracio does not lend itself to allegory.

The literary genius of X is seen in the felt detail of his perceptions and the intensity with which his words convey them. The once familiar A&P emblazoning has never been so glorified as in his exalting of it:

> Where to begin? In a heaven of golden serifs
> Or smooth and rounded loaves of risen gold.
> Formed into formal Caslon capitals
> And graced with a pretzeled, sinuous ampersand
> Against a sanded ground of fire-truck red,
> Proclaiming to the world at large, "The Great
> Atlantic & Pacific Tea Co."?
> The period alone appeared to me
> An eighteen-karat doorknob beyond price.

The eerie ambience of an abandoned boxcar has never seemed more like one of those "hints of hell" he says it is than in his description:

> Here in the haywire weeds, concealed by wilds
> Of goldenrod and toadflax, lies a spur

With its one boxcar of brick-colored armor,
At noon, midsummer, fiercer than a kiln,
Rippling the thinness of the air around it
With visible distortions. Among the stones
Of the railbed, fragments of shattered amber
That held a pint of rye. The carapace
Of a dried beetle. A broken orange crate
Streaked with tobacco stains at the nailheads
In the gray, fractured slats. And over all
The dust of oblivion finer than milled flour.

Nor has the decay of once fashionable apartments, now deserted, ever seemed more desolate:

> late afternoon in autumn,
> The sunlight rusting on the western fronts
> Of a long block of Victorian brick houses,
> Untenanted, presumably condemned,
> Their brownstone grapes, their grand entablatures,
> Their straining caryatid muscle-men
> Rendered at once ridiculous and sad
> By the black scars of zigzag fire escapes
> That double themselves in isometric shadows.
> And all their vacancy is given voice
> By the endless flapping of one window-shade.

I wonder if Turner himself has given a better impression of weather in Venice than X does in his description of a thunderstorm there:

> I find peace
> In the arcaded dark of the piazza
> When a thunderstorm comes up. I watch the sky
> Cloud into tarnished zinc, to Quaker gray
> Drabness, its shrouded vaults, fog-bound crevasses
> Blinking with huddled lightning, and await
> The vast *son et lumière*. The city's lamps
> Faintly ignite in the gathered winter gloom.
> The rumbled thunder starts—an avalanche
> Rolling down polished corridors of sound,
> Rickety tumbrels blundering across
> A stone and empty cellarage. And then,
> Like a whisper of dry leaves, the rain begins.
> It stains the paving stones, forms a light mist
> Of brilliant crystals dulled with tones of lead
> Three inches off the ground. Blown shawls of rain

> Quiver and luff, veil the cathedral front
> In flailing laces while the street lamps hold
> Fixed globes of sparkled haze high in the air
> And the black pavement runs with wrinkled gold
> In pools and wet dispersions, fiery spills
> Of liquid copper, of squirming, molten brass.

Such perceptions as "Three inches off the ground" give us the exact but surprising detail, the detail we recognize as right but had not thought to notice ourselves. "Blown shawls," "quiver and luff," "flailing laces" are the exact but surprising words for what they describe. Throughout the poem the reader (this reader anyway) has been delighted by what Ammons has called "shenanigans . . . in the lingo"—the legerdemain with words that perform like a magic trick done deftly. I know that I have watched the bright behavior of ripples on the Grand Canal and elsewhere, but they have never seemed more like themselves in the world of words than when X describes them:

> These little crests and ripples promenade,
> Hurried and jocular and never bored,
> *Ils se promènent* like families of some means
> On Sundays in the *Bois*.

What pleasure X gets in life he gets from such perceptions: from losing himself in the fascinating sense-detail of the world, its "fine particulars"—for him nearly always visual—to such a degree that he is "for the moment cured of everything," the burden of the past, the fear of the future. Such absorption as he feels in watching the storm in Venice is

> a sort of blessedness. No room is left
> For antecedence, inference, nuance.
> One escapes from all the anguish of this world
> Into the refuge of the present tense.

But the cure is only for the moment; he knows he cannot "be saved simply by looking." For one thing, there are not only such sights as the dead corporal, "His brains wet in the chalice of his skull," but also such "hints of hell" as he feels in the abandoned boxcar and the row of deserted apartments. For another thing, "seeing is misbelieving"; he knows that what he sees, even when it makes him happy, is "composed / Of clouded, cataracted, darkened sight." Everything that we look at is mirage and illusion, as if seen through the distorting medium of water, or "Through crizzled and quarrelled panes of Bull's Eye Glass." Our happiness, it seems, consists in not seeing things as they are, in "Merciful blindnesses and ignorance." He quotes *Genesis* on the state of humanity after the Fall: "And the eyes of them both were opened, and they knew." Paradisal bliss, he thinks, is not compatible with open-eyed vision and the knowledge they can bring. Many readers would understand the biblical passage differently and might wonder if X had forgotten that it was another Venetian who said, "The devil can cite Scripture for his purpose."

It is like X to deny the reality of the only pleasure he knows. But although all lenses, including "the corneal tunic of the eye," can only "mislead us / With insubstantial visions," yet he seems to have spent a good deal of his life looking through glass. The poem opens with X, brow against a windowpane, finding something merciful in the feeling of "a clean coolness at the temple." And the poem closes as it comes full circle with X back at the window, "Its glass a cooling comfort to my temple." Often what he looks at through the window is rain or moving water. On the day his mother dies, there is rain on the window of the school bus; after he learns of her death he feels touched and assuaged as he watches the rain from his bedroom window. It seems to have been even earlier that he meditated on the mystic word SALADA seen in reverse from the inside of the grocery store window. This "early vigilance at windows," he thinks, may even explain why he came to regard life as a spectator sport, seen through the cool glass of his isolation.

It is appropriate then that the key image of the poem is glass—a fitting motif for a work of art set in Venice, itself somehow as insubstantial as the glass it is famous for. The key image is not always of window glass. A related figure is introduced, and at least twice repeated, in reference to his mother's death:

> . . .the roe of air bubbles,
> That tiny silver wampum along the stems,
> Yellowed and magnified, of aging flowers
> Caught in the lens of stale water and glass
> In the upstairs room when somebody had died.

A little later they are "underwater globes, / Mercury seedpearls." In the same key is another image of air bubbles, these fashioned by the glassblowers: "prisoned air-bubbles, / Breathless, enameled pearly vacancies." This later modulates into an image of St. Mark's (with its bubbled domes) as a "gigantic vacancy."

The "Murano furnaces," on the island off Venice where the glassworks are, have here something of the portentous symbolism they have in Joseph Losey's 1979 filming of *Don Giovanni*. There the lurid flames of Murano, with which the film opens, turn at the end into the hellfire into which Don Giovanni tumbles unrepentant. But for X their "glory holes" are for the liquidation and resurrection of all that is glassy in the refuse of Venice, where one is wakened not by birdsong or traffic noises, but by the "harsh smashing of glass" as the gondoliers compact it to make room for other trash. What the furnaces produce is the "silicate fragility" of their glassware, in gaudiness not unlike that of the evening clouds, "full of the splendor of the insubstantial," with which the poem closes: "clouds of muscatel / With pencilings of gold."

Imagery of glass links what might otherwise seem scattered elements in the poem. There are also incidental mentions of it that we can, if we wish, relate to the main use of the theme: the shattered amber of the pint of rye by the boxcar, the quart bottle that precipitates the father into his lifelong troubles, "grey bottled babies in formaldehyde."

The glass and bottle imagery culminates in the last section when X realizes that he himself has made a "fiasco" of his life. We know that a fiasco is a failure, and "a complete and ignominious" one, as the dictionary adds. We know that the literal meaning of the Italian word is flask or bottle, and that the colloquial *fare fiasco* (to make a bottle) means to fail badly.

Ho fatto un fiasco, which is to say,
I've made a sort of bottle of my life,
A frangible and transparent failure.

But although X is saying, in his way, that he is one of the hollow men of our time, the poem he figures in is anything but empty. He may be a fiasco, but the poem about him is a triumph. What he says may be dispiriting, but the way he says it is rich in splendors we can treasure. In the words of Hippolyta, after Theseus has given his little talk on poetry (and in a time when "admirable" meant "to be marveled at"), it is a work which "grows to something of great constancy, / But —howsoever—strange and admirable."

NOTE

1. Compare P. Tomory, *The Life and Art of Henry Fuseli* (Praeger, 1972), 25: "First I sits myself down. Then I work myself up. Then I throw in my darks. Then I pulls out my lights."

Part III: Anatomies

William Matthews

Horatian Hecht

"The true Horatian note is serenity," one of Horace's recent translators claims. Working backward from this reading of the work to the imagined life produces a familiar sketch:

> In 23 B.C., when he published the first three books of his lyrics, Horace was 42 years old, sure of his poetic gifts, secure in the favor of his emperor, Augustus, and living in ease and comfort on his Sabine Farm.... A worldly, high-spirited, cultivated man, Horace responds in his poetry to the myriad elements of Roman life he knew so well.[1]

Horace himself contributed mightily to this. "Go little book," he urges,

> say I was born in poverty of a father once a slave
> but stretched my wings far beyond that humble nest:
> what you subtract from my descent, add to my virtues;
> say that I pleased the greatest Romans, in war and peace;
> say I was small, and early grey, and loved hot sunshine,
> swift to anger and yet easy to pacify.[2]

According to Suetonius's *Vita Horatii,* Augustus used to call Horace, teasingly, a "chaste little dick" and "charming little fellow." After reading some of the *sermones,* Augustus complained that he wasn't mentioned in them. "Can you be afraid that your reputation will suffer in later times because you appear to be my friend?" Thus when Horace shortly afterward published a new and thin book of poems including some pieces specifically commissioned by Augustus, Augustus sent him a letter: "Onysius has brought me your little book, which I accept in good part, small as it is, as making your excuses. But you seem to fear that your books will be bigger than you are yourself, though it is height you lack, not bulk. You are therefore permitted to write on a pint pot, so that your volume may be pot-bellied like yourself."[3]

But what has this placid, modest, and chatty character to do with the author of the cruel and pessimistic *Epodes* or the melancholy sensualist ("chaste little dick," indeed) of the *Odes*?

In fact, what we conventionally value Horace for is least convincing in the poems. How threadbare his off-the-rack Epicureanism is, how dilatory the patriotism of the Roman odes, how donnish the *Ars Poetica* (*Epistles* 2.3). Horace's great and elusive subject is happiness, and in poetry, as in life, happiness can't be described so well as it can be embodied.

When Horace pictures Pindar as "the Theban swan" and himself as being

> just like a small bee
> sipping each sweet blossom of thyme and roving
> through the thick groves, over the slopes of Tiber
> rich with streams—so, cell upon cell, I labor
>   moulding my poems.[4]

he is generally thought to be exercising a charming modesty as well as comparing the stature of Greek to Latin poetry, but he is also describing the difference between a poet (Pindar) with a solid religious context and a subject matter, and a poet like himself, the diligent attendant of the ineffable. In his *Ars Poetica*, with what sadness he must have written "non satis est pulchra esse poemata" (it's not enough for poems to be beautiful). C. H. Sisson has wisely suggested that the most comparable modern text to the *Ars Poetica* is Pound's "A Stray Document," in *Make It New*. Pound, too, despaired that he could only make his poems beautiful, and that when he tried to stuff them with truths, they didn't cohere.

In his last years James Wright spoke frequently of his devotion to Horace and in an interview, referring to the first thirteen lines of the *Ars Poetica*, of "the ideal, what elsewhere I've called the Horatian ideal, the attempt finally to write a poem that will be put together so carefully that it does produce a single unifying effect. I still conceive of a poem as being a thing which one can make rather than as a matter of direct expression," that is, a way to embody what can't be directly said.[5]

Such an understanding of the poetic enterprise is naturally haunted by whether the unspeakable is truly unspeakable or merely a measurement of where a particular poet's courage and skill run out. This situation is like a lifetime of unanswered missives to the beloved, and thus a Horatian temperament is often drawn to the theme of art as a consolation, or at least as a steadying and leveling force, like lithium for manic depressives. Perhaps the melancholy to which the Horatian temperament is so susceptible is equivalent to the manic depressive's suspicion that the loss of extreme highs and lows is also a loss of vivacity and authenticity.

Anthony Hecht muses as steadily on such matters as any of our poets. A characteristic poem, "The Cost," begins *Millions of Strange Shadows* (1977).

> Instinct with joy, a young Italian banks
>   Smoothly around the base
> Of Trajan's column.

The young man is on a Vespa, "at one with him in a centaur's race." Hecht wants to allude here both to chariot races and to *Lear*: "But to the girdle do the gods inherit, / Beneath is all the fiend's." The young man has his girlfriend riding with him. The obduracy of lust and the rhyme of *lust* and *dust* are recurrent tropes in Hecht. The Vespa is circling Trajan's column, erected to celebrate the successful prosecution of the Dacian wars.

> And even Trajan, of his imperial peers
>   Accounted "the most just,"
>
> Honored by Dante, by Gregory the Great
>   Saved from eternal Hell,
> Swirls in the motes kicked up by the cough and spate
>   Of the Vespa's blue exhaust,
> And a voice whispers inwardly, "My soul,
>   It is the cost, the cost,"
>
> Like some unhinged Othello, who's just found out
>   That justice is no more,
> While Cassio, Desdemona, Iago shout
>   Like true Venetians all,
> "Go screw yourself; all's fair in love and war!"
>   And the bright standards fall.

> Better they should not hear that whispered phrase,
>> The young Italian couple;
> Surely the mind in all its brave assays
>> Must put much thinking by,
> To be, as Yeats would have it, free and supple
>> As a long-legged fly.
>
> Look at their slender purchase, how they list
>> Like a blown clipper, brought
> To the lively edge of peril, to the kissed
>> Lip, the victor's crown,
> The prize of life. Yet one unbodied thought
>> Could topple them, bring down
>
> The whole shebang. And why should they take thought
>> Of all that ancient pain,
> The Danube winters, the nameless young who fought,
>> The blood's uncertain lease?
> Or remember that that fifteen-year campaign
>> Won seven years of peace?

The allusive machinery of the poem is considerable. In parts of the poem I have not quoted he mentions Calder's mobiles and, alluding to *Lear* again, "samphire-tufted cliffs which, though unseen, / Are known." The effect is to shore against erosive costs of living the achieved poise of the arts, and the implicit result is the Pyrrhic ratio of fifteen to seven on which the poem ends.

Hecht's virtuosity was apparent from the beginning. *A Summoning of Stones* (1954), with its Orphic title, opens with a double sonnet and demonstrates a canny mastery of the period style—a poetry of sobered wit rooted in the metaphysical poets, allusive, skeptical, urbane. Given to religious, mythological, and historical occasions, these poems owe more, perhaps, to Allen Tate than to any of the other elder poets by whom Hecht might have been influenced. The intellectual tone is a warily resigned humanism; we see in these poems how much Hecht's generation grew up in the magnetic influence of Arnold's *Culture and Anarchy* and Eliot's essays. Of course Hecht was later to send up Arnold in his famous parody, "The Dover Bitch." And a close reading of *A Summoning of Stones* reveals a skepticism about what art can and cannot do that is at least partially at war with the tension-resolving period style Hecht was not so much working in as working his way through.

"A Poem for Julia," "The Gardens of the Villa d'Este," "A Roman Holiday," and "Alceste in the Wilderness" all bulge interestingly from their battles between an elegant style and a distrust of elegant art. In "Japan" the speaker tells how he thought of Japan as a child, during World War II, and afterward. Here's the second of the poem's seven stanzas:

> A child's quick sense of the ingenious stamped
> All their invention: toys I used to get
> At Christmastime, or the peculiar, cramped
>   Look of their alphabet.
>   Fragile and easily destroyed,
>   Those little boats of celluloid
> Driven by camphor round the bathroom sink,
> And delicate the folded paper prize
>   Which, dropped into a drink
> Of water, grew up right before your eyes.

In the poem the speaker, too, grows up right before your eyes. Here's the last stanza:

> Now the quaint early image of Japan
> That was so charming to me as a child
> Seems like a bright design upon a fan,
>   Of water rushing wild
>   On rocks that can be folded up,
>   A river which the wrist can stop
> With a neat flip, revealing merely sticks
> And silk of what had been a fan before,
>   And like such winning tricks,
> It shall be buried in excelsior.

In the long interval between *A Summoning of Stones* and *The Hard Hours* (1967), Hecht's style shifted significantly. In the words of Ted Hughes, "He did the most difficult thing of all: this most fastidious and elegant of poets shed every artifice and began to write with absolute raw simplicity and directness." I offer Hughes's words not because I concur wholly with them, but because they measure the surprise with which fellow poets met Hecht's long-awaited book.

Certainly Hecht's justly famous poem "A Hill," the first in *The Hard Hours*, signals a new tone in its opening lines.

> In Italy, where this sort of thing can occur,
> I had a vision once—though you understand
> It was nothing at all like Dante's, or the visions of saints,

> And perhaps not a vision at all. I was with some friends,
> Picking my way through a warm sunlit piazza
> In the early morning. A clear fretwork of shadows
> From huge umbrellas littered the pavement and made
> A sort of lucent shallows in which was moored
> A small navy of carts.

The elegance here is agreeably offhanded, and the passage allows Hecht to indulge to good effect his love of describing effects of light and shadow, of the effervescent.

>   Books, coins, old maps,
> Cheap landscapes and ugly religious prints
> Were all on sale. The colors and noise
> Like the flying hands were gestures of exultation,
> So that even the bargaining
> Rose to the ear like a voluble godliness.
> And then, when it happened, the noises suddenly stopped,
> And it got darker; pushcarts and people dissolved
> And even the great Farnese Palace itself
> Was gone, for all its marble; in its place
> Was a hill, mole-colored and bare. It was very cold,
> Close to freezing, with a promise of snow.
> The trees were like old ironwork gathered for scrap
> Outside a factory wall. There was no wind,
> And the only sound for a while was the little click
> Of ice as it broke in the mud under my feet.
> I saw a piece of ribbon snagged on a hedge,
> But no other sign of life. And then I heard
> What seemed the crack of a rifle. A hunter, I guessed;
> At least I was not alone. But just after that
> Came the soft and papery crash
> Of a great branch somewhere unseen falling to earth.

In contrast to the elaborately turned recurring stanza forms of *The Hard Hours*, "A Hill" pauses here for its first stanza break.

> And that was all, except for the cold and silence
> That promised to last forever, like the hill.

Another stanza break.

> Then prices came through, and fingers, and I was restored
> To the sunlight and my friends. But for more than a week

I was scared by the plain bitterness of what I had seen.
All this happened about ten years ago,
And it hasn't troubled me since, but at last, today,
I remembered that hill; it lies just to the left
Of the road north of Poughkeepsie; and as a boy
I stood before it for hours in wintertime.

Not the vain splendor of the Farnese Palace but the gesticulating fingers of vendors and the crying of prices bring the speaker back to daily life with its costs and pools of shadows. There is a palpable though not literal suggestion of his own fingers returning from frostbite at the start of the third stanza, and the plain bitterness of his vision is not something in the landscape, but something he sees in himself by means of the landscape.

Elsewhere in *The Hard Hours*, in poems like "Third Avenue in Sunlight" and "The End of the Weekend," when surfaces are peeled away or sundered, something that seems partly an implacable evil and partly a madness is revealed. "Lizards and Snakes" tells of two boys, related to the youngster recalled in "Japan," who torment an aunt with the lizards and snakes she hates and they are fascinated by. The poem is in three stanzas; I quote the last two.

> Aunt Martha had an unfair prejudice
>   Against them (as well as being cold
> Toward bats.) She was pretty inflexible in this,
>   Being a spinster and all, and old.
> So we used to slip them into her knitting box.
>   In the evening she'd bring in things to mend
> And a nice surprise would slide out from under the socks.
> It broadened her life, as Joe said. Joe was my friend.
>
> But we never did it again after the day
>   Of the big wind when you could hear the trees
> Creak like rockingchairs. She was looking away
>   Off, and kept saying, "Sweet Jesus, please
> Don't let him near me. He's as like as twins.
>   He can crack us like lice with his fingernail.
> I can see him plain as a pikestaff. Look how he grins
> And swinges the scaly horror of his folded tail."

Whatever the comparatively plain style Hecht perfected for *The Hard Hours* refers to in his experience is of course his business and not ours, but in the poems it seems to embody an unadorned peril from which the blandishments of art cannot so much restore as distract us.

Two poems poised against each other in *Millions of Strange Shadows* suggest a conflict that recapitulates the terms of Hecht's first two books. The first poem is "Dichtung und Wahrheit" and is dedicated to Cyrus Hoy, a colleague of Hecht's when he was teaching at the University of Rochester. The poem asks the old question: what does the study of humane letters mean? The diction and supple turns of the first stanza remind us of *A Summoning of Stones*, though of course "Dichtung und Wahrheit" is in Hecht's mature and not apprentice style.

> The Discus Thrower's marble heave,
>   Captured in mid-career,
> That polished poise, that Parian arm
>   Sleeved only in the air,
> Vesalian musculature, white
>   As the mid-winter moon—
> This, and the clumsy snapshot of
>   An infantry platoon,
> Those grubby and indifferent men,
>   Lounging in bivouac,
> Their rifles aimless in their laps,
>   Stop history in its tracks.

How can we invent a continuity of feeling with the past? Perhaps a certain linguistic sophistication helps, in which we might speak the dialects of different historical moments, so far as we are able. To know the names of the classical sculptors is a beginning, and to be able to reach without strain for the apt pun of "aimless."

The second half of the poem (I've quoted one of three stanzas in the first half) begins by assertion:

> We begin with the supreme donnée, the world,
> Upon which every text is commentary,
> And yet they play each other . . .

and the poem concludes, "We begin with the supreme donnée, the word."

The very next poem is "A Voice at a Seance."

> It is rather strange to be speaking, but I know you are there
> Wanting to know, as if it were worth knowing.

Nor is it important that I died in combat
In a good cause or an indifferent one.
Such things, it may surprise you, are not regarded.
Something too much of this.

You are bound to be disappointed,
Wanting to know, are there any trees?
It is all different from what you suppose,
And the darkness is not darkness exactly,
But patience, silence, withdrawal, the sad knowledge
That it was almost impossible not to hurt anyone
Whether by action or inaction.
At the beginning of course there was a sense of loss,
Not of one's own life, but of what seemed
The easy, desirable lives one might have led.
Fame or wealth are hard to achieve,
And goodness even harder;
But the cost of all of them is a familiar deformity
Such as everyone suffers from:
An allergy to certain foods, nausea at the sight of blood,
A slight impediment of speech, shame at one's own body,
A fear of heights or claustrophobia.
What you learn has nothing to do with joy,
Nor with sadness, either. You are mostly silent.
You come to a gentle indifference about being thought
Either a fool or someone with valuable secrets.
It may be that the ultimate wisdom
Lies in saying nothing.
I think I may already have said too much.

The identification of the speaker as a soldier and the use of the adjective "indifferent," also used in the first stanza of "Dichtung und Wahrheit," give us the eerie sense that the speaker of this poem might be one of the soldiers in the photograph from the preceding poem. In this poem, of course, we have no gift, no donnée, but cost. The poem adopts an old trick of science fiction that purports to describe a future but seems, unsettlingly enough, to describe a queasily familiar present. Perhaps we could perceive it without seance if it weren't for the beautiful distractions of art, like a procession of gorgeously confected clouds. Behind them, if we could but see, there might well be a hill, "mole-colored and bare." Of course there are no trees, for this is *paysage démoralisé.*

One of the epigraphs to *The Venetian Vespers* (1979) is from *Moby Dick*: "Though in many of its aspects this visible world seems formed in love, the invisible spheres were formed in fright." These frights are not only lizards and snakes but also far too much of our recent history. "Apprehensions" in *Millions of Strange Shadows* and "An Overview" in *The Venetian Vespers* eloquently embody, respectively, the haunting presences of the Holocaust and the Vietnam War.

The Horatian temperament has always poised against organized terrors as well as more private ones the virtues of personal civilization—work well done, love pursued as a benign sport, the good report of one's peers. So for Hecht to include in *The Venetian Vespers* two versions "freely adapted from Horace," as he identifies them, is quite germane to his ongoing meditation on the powers and impotences of art. The two poems Hecht adapts are both widely known: *Odes 1.1* and *1.5*.

Horace's first ode is addressed to Maecenas, his patron, whose interest in Horace's talents led to the Sabine Farm and a sinecure. Since Maecenas was also an intimate of Augustus, his patronage meant as secure a social position as volatile Rome could offer a poet and a lifetime to write. Such largesse required a stupendous thank-you letter, and Horace set jauntily to work: "Maecenas, descended from olden kings, / my rampart and sweet admiration...."[6] The poem goes on to list the various ways men seek their happiness: some race chariots, some strive in politics, some farm, some seek leisure and some battle, and so forth. But he just wishes a little honor for his verses, and, indeed, if Maecenas would bestow his approval on Horace, Horace would think himself singled out by Euterpe herself: "and should you list me among the lyric bards / I should nudge the stars with my lifted head."[7]

The nudged stars may well be a joke about Horace's height. There's a loose, banter-among-old-friends tone to Horace's original that's part of its relaxed, beguiling sophistication. After all, the favor the poem seems to be asking has in large measure already been granted, and so whatever element of submission there might be in application to Maecenas has already gone by the boards.

Here's Hecht's version, called "Application for a Grant."

> Noble executors of the munificent testament
> Of the late John Simon Guggenheim, distinguished bunch
> Of benefactors, there are certain kinds of men
> Who set their hearts on being bartenders,
> For whom a life upon duck-boards, among fifths,

Tapped kegs and lemon twists, crowded with lushes
Who can master neither their bladders nor consonants,
Is the only life, greatly to be desired.
There's the man who yearns for the White House, there to compose
Rhythmical lists of enemies, while someone else
Wants to be known to the *Tour d'Argent*'s headwaiter.
As the Sibyl of Cumae said: It takes all kinds.
Nothing could bribe your Timon, your charter member
Of the Fraternal Order of Grizzly Bears to love
His fellow, whereas it's just the opposite
With interior decorators; that's what makes horse races.
One man may have a sharp nose for tax shelters,
Screwing the IRS with mirth and profit;
Another devotes himself to his shell collection,
Deaf to his offspring, indifferent to the feats
With which his wife hopes to attract his notice.
Some at the Health Club sweating under bar bells
Labor away like grunting troglodytes,
Smelly and thick and inarticulate,
Their brains squeezed out through their pores by sheer exertion.
As for me, the prize for poets, the simple gift
For amphybrachs strewn by a kind Euterpe,
With perhaps a laurel crown of the evergreen
Imperishable of your fine endowment
Would supply my modest wants, who dream of nothing
But a pad on Eighth Street and your approbation.

This is a curious performance. The ostensible objects of satire here—drunks, Nixon, the muscle-bound pinheads at the Health Club—are fish in a barrel. The jibe about the Fraternal Order of Grizzly Bears smells as much of snobbery as the jibe about interior decorators does of homophobia. The level of wit is, for Hecht, unusually low; there's a rather ponderous money-does-too-grow-on-trees joke ("evergreen / imperishable of your fine endowment"), but mostly the tone is not only sour but curdled. The "pad on Eighth Street" is, I take it, a stock property of the feckless Bohemian's fantasy life, though Auden had a place there.

The reader can hear the engines of satire churning in this poem, but against whom is the satire directed? Surely not at all those easy targets, so it must be directed at the speaker.

Whereas in Horace's original the fiction is that the speaker and poet are the same, the opposite is surely true here. Hecht already had his Guggenheim—here's a parallel with the original. And by choosing to use his version of Horace in his own book, Hecht chose to further complicate the relationship of poet to speaker by adding translator to the cast of characters.

Well, then, whom does the speaker represent? Poets who like to feel superior to the middle class but in doing so betray a sensibility hopelessly middle class? That kind of satire uses one end of a snake to beat the other end to death. Bad poets? The proposition that all urge for recognition and ease in a life in the arts is fundamentally crass? Or is this the "plain bitterness" of "A Hill" projected on the blank screen of the world?

Hecht does far better with *Ode 1.5*. Horace's original begins:

> What slender youth besprinkled with fragrant oils
> now crowds you, Pyrrha, amid the roses
> in some convenient grotto?
> For whom do you dress that yellow hair?[8]

And the three remaining quatrains anticipate that Pyrrha's imagined current lover will, as the speaker once did, compare his time with Pyrrha to a close call at sea. There's an allusive metaphor at the end of the poem that's hard to translate without building a footnote into the translation, for it refers to the custom of hanging on a certain votive plaque to Neptune the damp clothes in which one escaped death at sea. Here's Hecht's version, called "An Old Malediction."

> What well-heeled knuckle-head, straight from the unisex
> Hairstylist and bathed in *Russian Leather*,
> Dallies with you these summer days, Pyrrha,
> In your expensive sublet? For whom do you
> Slip into something simple by, say, Gucci?
> The more fool he who has mapped out for himself
> The saline latitudes of incontinent grief.
> Dazzled though he be, poor dope, by the golden looks
> Your locks fetched up out of a bottle of *Clairol*,
> He will know that the wind changes, the smooth sailing
> Is done for, when the breakers wallop him broadside,
> When he's rudderless, dismasted, thoroughly swamped
> In that mindless rip-tide that got the best of me,
> Once, when I ventured on your deeps, Piranha.

Hecht has left Neptune's plaque out of his version and made other metaphorical use ("dismasted") of the storm. And since Hecht's version argues throughout the likelihood that Pyrrha is a shallow creature, the torque he puts on "deeps" in the last line is sly.

The metamorphosis of "Pyrrha" to "Piranha" glosses an element added to Horace by Hecht rather than freely adapted: bitterness. Except for "Clairol" and "Piranha" most of it is in the first five lines; one can perhaps feel the distasteful shudder strongest at "Russian Leather." It is all too easy, as it was almost throughout "An Application for a Grant." The convulsive brilliance of a line like "The saline latitudes of incontinent grief" may have been an attempt to wrench the translator away from his loathing so that he could, as Hecht did, perform a splendid job with what's left of Horace's poem.

As we have seen, the virtuoso style of Hecht's earliest poems has matured along with this remarkable poet. It is in eclipse for whole poems at a time in *The Hard Hours* and later books, while the poet gives his abilities over to embodying some brute and bare thing from which the lucent polish of a more embellished art might reflect and deflect our gaze. In his best poems the two styles and the two attitudes of mind they embody contest to achieve a balance—the Vespa-riding Italian youth in "The Cost" is one of Hecht's central figures for this balance—between, at one extreme, a merely pyrotechnical art and, at the other, an obdurate thing so powerful that it beggars not only art but also the will to speak at all ("I think I may already have said too much").

Of course one job of a poet is not to fall silent.

Hecht's formidable descriptive powers are at their happiest and best when working on the effervescent, "the splendor of the insubstantial." This love of what is ever-changing outside the self makes particularly poignant sense for a poet to whom the mysteries of the self, and thus the mysteries of the species in microcosm, can perhaps be figured by a bare, mole-colored hill.

And one senses in his best writing how little accommodation he has made with the conflict as well as how masterfully he has learned to embody that dilemma. I'll close this essay by quoting the concluding passage of "The Venetian Vespers." The speaker of the poem, who is of course not Hecht himself, is looking at the Venetian sky from a window.

> Against a diorama of palest blue
> Cloud-curds, cloud-stacks, cloud-bushes sun themselves.
> Giant confections, impossible meringues,
> Soft coral reefs and powdery tumuli
> Pass in august processions and calm herds.

Great stadiums, grandstands and amphitheaters,
The tufted, opulent litters of the gods
They seem; or laundered bunting, well-dressed wigs,
Harvests of milk-white, Chinese peonies
That visibly rebuke our stinginess.
For all their ghostly presences, they take on
A colorful nobility at evening.
Off to the east the sky begins to turn
Lilac so pale it seems a mood of gray,
Gradually, like the death of virtuous men.
Streaks of electrum richly underline
The slow, flat-bottomed hulls, those floated lobes
Between which quills and spokes of light fan out
Into carnelian reds and nectarines,
Nearing a citron brilliance at the center,
The searing furnace of the glory hole
That fires and fuses clouds of muscatel
With pencilings of gold. I look and look,
As though I could be saved simply by looking—
I, who have never earned my way, who am
No better than a viral parasite,
Or the lees of the Venetian underworld,
Foolish and muddled in my later years,
Who was never even at one time a wise child.

NOTES

1. *The Odes and Epistles of Horace*, trans. Joseph P. Clancy (Chicago: University of Chicago Press, 1960), "General Introduction," p. 1.
2. Gilbert Highet, *Poets in a Landscape* (New York: Knopf, 1967), p. 154.
3. Horace, *The Complete Odes and Epistles*, trans. W. G. Shepherd (London: Penguin Books, 1983), p. 196.
4. Highet, p. 118.
5. *The Pure Clear Word: Essays on the Poetry of James Wright*, ed. Dave Smith (Champaign: University of Illinois Press, 1982), p. 12.
6. Shepherd, p. 69.
7. Shepherd, p. 70.
8. Shepherd, p. 74.

Kenneth Gross

Anthony Hecht and the Imagination of Rage

Imagine the dark work of an unremitting eloquence. It must find out all false dreams of eloquence. It must face off the seductive ideals of plain speaking. It must refuse any easy claims to decorum or skill. It must know that no mere subject will redeem it, but it must not refuse any subject that might make a mockery of it. It must enchant and disenchant. A species of delight, it must become a question, a protest, a stance of embodied skepticism in the face of what is given. In the face of what is given, what is not our own, that eloquence must find out its own poison, its own poverty and injustice; it must know itself as a garment of Nessus, and yet keep faith with its own labor and mania. It must explore all phases of silence, confusion, and curse. It must animate what it can, and will see only what it animates (after Emerson). It must not explain itself; it must not settle itself; it must not ask for effects.

I raise the matter of "eloquence" only by way of introduction, since despite its impurities I think the word still speaks to the concerns of contemporary poets. It at least seems to me of use when looking at the work of a writer like Anthony Hecht—whose poetry is so often praised for its verbal beauty and formal mastery, but praised thus with little clear thought about what burdens such beauty and mastery might impose, about the ways in which the poet might suffer or struggle with his eloquence. My primary subject in this essay, however, is somewhat different: not the poet's eloquence but the rage that it voices, contains, or transfigures—rage against loss, against cruelty, against pain; rage that can be self-authenticating or self-destructive; rage that may expose charity or hatred. I want to examine the shifting objects or vehicles of that rage, what the poetry tells us about the subterfuges of rage itself, how it may force us to reimagine what rage looks like. Questions about the masks of rage, its election of objects or enemies, bear directly on the poet's mode of confronting the real and the imaginary. Rage is the foundation of much of the poet's humor, the affective fuel of much of his eloquence—though one soon realizes as well how much the expressive pathos of rage can be modulated or hedged in the poems, how often the rage can be implicitly directed at eloquence itself. In speaking of the imagination of rage we touch on some of the most central questions of poetic vocation in Hecht's work. But just because the rage of the poetry is so elusive, as intricately manifested as in any dreamtext, one must be both patient and shifty in bringing it to light.

I want to begin with a fairly recent poem, "The Deodand" from *The Venetian Vespers*, because in it the object and rationale of the poet's rage seems at first glance fairly definite. The poem directs itself, with considerable wit but also harsh intelligence, against a seductive cultural lie, one that interests the poet all the more urgently because it is so romantic, so "poetic" a lie. Still, the latter half of the poem may make us see the poet's rage against that object as more troubling than we had expected, not only because of the uncertain tone of the poet's own rhetoric but also because that rage seems to conjure up so unsettling an image that the reader cannot rest easily in any obvious position of moral condemnation. We are rather forced into an ambivalent confrontation with the paradoxes, the shifting fantasies, the violent and impure incarnations of rage—forced furthermore to question where it is we should locate the real interest or fascination of the poet himself.

A deodand, as Hecht explains in a note, is an expiatory offering, a gift offered to God, often (especially under English law) the forfeit of a creature who had caused the death of a human being. How literally we are to take this, how we are to apply the label, is, in a sense, the real problem of the poem. It begins with the poet asking questions, trying to make sense of a scene which we later learn is that of a painting by Renoir: "Parisians Dressed in Algerian Costume." "What are these women up to?" the speaker asks, why dressed in oriental robes, jewels, makeup—silks, kohl eye-shadow, bangles, and all those "soft sexual fetters"? Why the set-up of a seraglio? Whence such contrived and secret fantasies of seductiveness and vassalage, imitated from, say, Ingres or Delacroix, and hidden behind drapes in a darkened, airless room, where a scent of "animal strength" hints at "violations, swooning lubricities and lassitudes"? The slow, hovering description of the scene is itself rather voyeuristic, as Hecht himself admits, but the text's querulous, indulgent brooding yields about halfway through to a different tone. What we see, the poet tells us, is no innocent retreat, no localized nostalgia or decadence, nor even a vision of women unwittingly playing out the repressive fantasies of a patriarch. It is instead a kind of perverse cultural theft, one strangely implicated in a larger history of colonial exploitation:

> What is all this but crude imperial pride,
> Feminized, scented, and attenuated,
> The exploitation of the primitive,
> Homages of romantic self-deception,
> Mimes of submission glamorized as lust?

The breaking forth of so direct, condemnatory a tone is rare enough in Hecht that one may wonder whether it is not protesting a trifle too much. (The poet is for the most part more charitable toward the ambivalent seductions of the aesthetic, or at least more subtly ironic about them.) The anger, the slightly defensive scorn aimed at such "romantic self-deception," however, only makes full sense when seen against what follows from it. The poet moves swiftly from this sort of direct criticism of bourgeois orientalism to a phase of more violently prophetic irony (and prophetic literalism)—placing against the painted scene a competing picture, one which seems both a grotesque parody of and a hideous revenge against so self-indulgent an act of fanciful disguising. Untaught (he observes) by the spectacle of an earlier revolution against aristocratic excess, the women shall find that

> for this little spiritual debauch . . .
> Exactions shall be made, an expiation,
> A forfeiture. Though it take ninety years,
> All the retributive iron of Racine
> Shall answer from the raging heat of the desert.

Whereupon the poem silently closes with this tableau:

> In the final months of the Algerian war
> They captured a very young French Legionnaire.
> They shaved his head, decked him in a blonde wig,

> Carmined his lips grotesquely, fitted him out
> With long, theatrical false eyelashes
> And a bright, loose-fitting skirt of calico,
> And cut off all the fingers of both hands.
> He had to eat from a fork held by his captors.
> Thus costumed, he was taken from town to town,
> Encampment to encampment, on a leash,
> And forced to beg for his food with a special verse
> Sung to a popular show tune of those days:
> "*Donnez moi à manger de vos mains
> Car c'est pour vous que je fais ma petite danse;
> Car je suis Madeleine, la putain,
> Et je m'en vais le lendemain matin,
> Car je suis La Belle France.*"
>
> (Let me be given nourishment at your hands
> Since it's for you I perform my little dance.
> For I am the street-walker, Magdelen,
> And come the dawn I'll be on my way again,
> The beauty queen, Miss France.)
>   (Hecht's translation)

In the dressed-up, mocked, and mutilated youth, an image of the victimizer victimized, we are invited to see an emblem of a historically emergent, tragic justice. The picture is indeed taken as a nightmarish peeling back of something hidden in the painting by Renoir (even the painting's own nightmare) such that the merely discursive warning of the earlier lines is now written in violent anger on the innocent body of the young soldier caught up by the mechanisms of war.[1] Let us say that in this image of compelled transvestism, dismemberment, and mocking ventriloquism (much more like something from Genet's *The Screens* than a drama of Racine, by the way) we see the victims of colonial tyranny staging a dark political satire, a farce that co-opts for their own vengeful satisfaction the prophetic image of the oppressor as whore or seductress. So physically and conceptually violent a turn faces Hecht with something that haunted earlier poets like Shelley or Blake: the fact of the inevitable tyranny or counter-terror of revolution, a terror with which the innocent Parisian women are nonetheless secretly complicitous. (Auden will sum the situation up in his rueful commonplace, "Those to whom evil is done / Do evil in return," though he knew how obvious and evasive such wisdom could be.) But even to derive from the poem so finely ironic a lesson about the workings of rage in history is not quite enough, for it tends to rationalize the description; it lets us keep our distance from the "terror," lets us imagine the poet as keeping his distance as well, when the very thing that needs to be brooded upon is the dark, infectious fascination of the final picture.

The kind of ironic matching or juxtaposing of images that we find in "The Deodand" is a recurrent feature of Hecht's poetry. Very often past and present, real and imagined pictures are balanced against one another in a strange, skeptical, or indulgent reverie. It is a kind of lyrical archaeology or Proustian slide show, one in which the past may emerge as a warning to the present, a daunting or fantastic dream, or a plain picture of blank, intractable origins (a picture whose bitterness or terror we will know a lot better than its truth). Such a strategy is developed most fully in the hermetic architecture of the recent long poems—for example, in the recollections of youthful mortification, sacramental farce, and awkward miracle that haunt the reveries of the heroine of "The Short End," or the stories of lost paternity and bloody war that break in upon the meditations of the retired speaker in "The Venetian Vespers." The past may also become a kind of alien or frozen idol, a trouble to thought, as in the lyric "Dichtung und Wahrheit," where the poet regards at one moment, side by side, a "clumsy snapshot" of himself as an infantry soldier in World War II and the ancient statue of a discus thrower (a figure which, as Hecht knows, also caught the fantasies of Adolf Hitler) and wonders what can be made of such different forms of stillness and opacity. It is the work of the poet, the (Emersonian) scholar, he tells us, to make "such fixture speak to us," to trace the hidden sense of the old imagery, to restore to some manner of life the "wan homunculus" of memory (and to save us at the same time from our own self-indulgent fatalism). This kind of labor has its dimensions of anxiety as well as delight, but the important point here is that the sorts of connections which Hecht's lyrics propose between such past and present images—or between images of different pasts—are ordinarily left extremely virtual, tentative, the moral lesson withheld. Given this, it is just the strident tone of condemnation in "The Deodand," its holding up of the present as a death's head or Gorgon's head to terrorize the not-so-innocent past and expose its darker motivations, that seems oddly out of key. The mask of prophetic cop, policing the painted fools of history and arranging their punishments, is indeed one I think Hecht dons for a moment in the middle of the poem just to show how badly it fits. And we can see this not only because we may be put off by the speaker's hyperbolic, melodramatic claims about historical/tragical justice, but because such claims serve only partially to account for the strange lure of the final image itself.

One does not normally think of Hecht as a political poet, even of the reticent sort that Auden tried to be. And indeed, even if one grants the force of both the poem's judgment and its externalized image, the description of the young legionnaire—terrifying not just in its nightmarish details of androgyny and castration but in its picture of a tortured, lyrical performance—shows its full resonance only if we see that it bears back in a more hidden or personal way upon the situation of the poet himself. This is not to say that this complexly placed historical image is simply the mirror of some private, archaic fantasy (unless we are talking about the fantasies of the torturer as much as those of the poet, though in both cases this might get us into a vulgarly Freudian interpretation). What I would insist on, however, is that the dancing youth must be recognized as at least in part a figure of the poet—not only object but also mirror, a piece of dark self-romance—though a romance that is more chastening than self-indulgent. It is an image whose placement exposes something crucial about the poet's mingled sense of pain, sympathy, complicity and terror in confronting the human and inhuman ironies of history; it is a way of making sense of what it means to witness such things, to write about them as lyricist or satirist, to try to combine charity and justice, in full awareness of how corrupt both the anger and pity of the would-be prophet can become.

The youth is a picture of the fate of the poet. Indeed, though the likeness is somewhat hidden, we might think of the picture as one modern reimagining of the crucial Romantic image of the poet we find at the end of Coleridge's "Kubla Khan"—a poet with "flashing eyes" and "floating hair," a poet likewise haunted by the seductive image of an oriental maiden and an artificial pleasure dome, by ghostly wails from the chasm below it as well as by "ancestral voices prophesying war"; a poet surrounded by an audience that is terrified by his song, that shuts its eyes and encloses his fearful but sacred presence within a magic circle. However covert the resemblance, Hecht's dancing, singing youth, ringed by tormentors, decked in a wig and false eyelashes, his lips horribly reddened, is a descendant of Coleridge's figure. But he is now no charmed visionary, however misconstrued; he has become at once seducer, oppressor, and victim, terrorized by his audience in the guise of courting it, chanting in a voice that is not his own, a *poète maudit* who can only announce his own imminent departure, his own meretricious beauty and real need. He is a poet burdened more darkly by the recollection of an oriental maid and caught by something more than shadowy prophesies of war. What might have seemed a piece of sensational journalism offers no obvious "lesson" nor any call to action; rather the business of coming to "know" or "understand" history through watching its horrific images is short-circuited to the degree that the historical object, the picture of victimage, turns back upon and victimizes the contemplative subject. The poet becomes what he beholds. In a strange transformation of the historical irony which Hecht has described, the image that the poet tries to colonize for his own explicit moral argument turns around in order vengefully to colonize, transform, and terrorize him.

There is a complex and self-wounding identification at work in "The Deodand," as well as an ambivalent kind of fetishizing of the final image (one that parallels the confusing fetishisms of the Parisian women). To say that this is the poet's narcissism or bad faith—given one's plain responsibility to history—is somewhat to miss the point. That the poet absorbs such an image to himself does not impugn his obviously profound interest in accurately making sense of the historical facts of victimage or of the fantasies that sustain such victimage. Hecht, more than most contemporary poets (at least in America), is a close watcher of the theater of cruelty. Thus, for example, in recent essays on *Othello* and *The Merchant of Venice* he struggles to define as carefully as he can Shakespeare's use of and fundamental adherence to the European tradition's parodic images of Moor and Jew, as if any kinder, apologetic attempt to make the dramatist seem more liberal, more secretly sympathetic than he must have been could only beget a subtler kind of blindness.[2] Likewise, in a poem like "The Feast of Stephen," the poet coldly watches boyish rituals of strength or male narcissism fade into scenes of secret cruelty, murder, and martyrdom. And yet such acts of attention, if that is what we should call them, carry no single moral valence. Hecht's poetry knows that it is no easy matter to find the right stance toward incidents of cruelty and revenge, no simple thing even to accuse those whom one may think of as false accusers or to understand *their* imagination of the enemy. A poem like "The Deodand," especially in its closing picture, suggests how intricate are the motivations and fantasies that sustain our moral criticism, how ambivalent our identifications with suffering. The poems contemplate horror and yet can also confess that "the contemplation of horror is not edifying, / Neither does it strengthen the soul." Pictures of martyrdom may do as much to bewilder and shame us, make us fear more ourselves than others: "Fear of our imperfections, / Fear learned and inherited, / Fear shapes itself in dreams / Not more fantastic than brute fact"—dreams that may breed not only terror but also further violence in the attempts to push them away.

"Who indeed knows how best to think about victims?" asks the political philosopher Judith Shklar, since they are so very likely to be regarded untruthfully, to be made to serve the onlooker's pleasure and anxiety.[3] It is a question crucial to a poetry so haunted by the fact, the memory and spectacle of the Holocaust. So one might observe that even in a poem like "Rites and Ceremonies," Hecht's one extended work on the subject (from which the above quotations are taken), there is a deep resistance to moralization or melodrama, even to gestures of mourning. To witness, even to relive, are acts that require of the writer a discipline of both plainness and surprise:

> In the camps, one can look through a huge square
> Window, like an aquarium, upon a room
> The size of my livingroom filled with human hair.
>
> I am there, I am there, I am pushed through
> With others into the strange room
> Without windows; whitewashed walls, cement floor . . .
> Are the vents in the ceiling, Father, to let the spirit depart?

What there is of prayer is elegiac, uncertain of response, always rehearsing the blank inquisitions of Job, the Psalmist, or the prophets (though echoing also their blank utterances of promise: "He shall come down like rain upon mown grass"). And here as elsewhere, one must add, the poetry refuses to posit some "huge psychopathic god," some monstrous or mechanical other, as if the effort so to locate an enemy or cause might itself be a danger for the poet, a temptation to bad theology or evasive mythmaking. Indeed, if the victims in Hecht's poetry tend often to be virtual, voiceless—seen in the coldest of lights, at the margins of visibility, their images mixed with a tangle of other memories—the enemy too is elusive, hidden, like the invisible Algerian rebels who ring that dancing soldier, an audience in whose midst we may seem ourselves to stand.

In Hecht, not only the watching of victims but also the search for the enemy bears back continually on the condition of the poet who engages in that search. So in an early lyric like "Christmas Is Coming," the rifleman who is "wandering the hills at night, / Gunning for enemies," finds the aim of his quest in an intensified consciousness of his own passage over frozen earth, his own isolation and pain, while the "enemy" becomes as abstract and evasive (but also as edifying) as the "nothing" that fills the landscape of Stevens's "The Snow Man":

> Where is the pain? The sense has frozen up,
> And fingers cannot recognize the grass,
> Cannot distinguish their own character,
> Being blind with cold, being stiffened by the cold;
> Must find out thistles to remember pain.
> Must keep to the frozen ground or else be killed.
> . . . .
> . . . And still we crawl to learn
> Where pain was lost, how to recover pain.
> Reach for the brambles, crawl to them and reach,
> Clutching for thorns, search carefully to feel
> The point of thorns, life's crown, *the Old Man's hat.*
> Yet quietly. Do not disturb the brambles.
> Winter has taught the air to clarify
> All noises, and the enemy can hear
> Perfectly in the cold.

In yet another poem from *A Summoning of Stones*, "Halloween," the poet is like Edgar/Mad Tom on the heath, watching the ghosts, demons, and death's heads that pursue him reveal themselves not as alien tormentors but as his own starving, demanding children—phantasms who cry for charity even as their songs drive one mad, "kiss the daft ones into their disease." The poetry gets written from both inside and outside this madness; it is a watching of one's own imagination as well as the world; it is an attempt both to animate and to call back one's projections, which are also the projections one shares with the world.

Let me return to the image of the caught youth in a wig. If, as I said, it recalls Coleridge, it also calls up memories of two central figures or alternative selves from *A Summoning of Stones*. The first of these is the noble, modestly ascetic hero of a modestly ascetic but brilliant lyric, "Samuel Sewall":

> Samuel Sewall, in a world of wigs,
> Flouted opinion in his personal hair.
> For foppery he gave not any figs,
> But in his right and honor took the air.

This is a character, let us recall, who finally rejects a somewhat preachy paramour who bids him "suffer a peruke." He is a rather Stevensian hero (not unlike the helmetless "Pastor Caballero"), Hecht's answer as well to the unbonneted Whitman or Ginsberg. It is his darker double that I want to focus on, however, the exiled misanthrope of "Alceste in the Wilderness," who at the close of that lyric returns chastened but no purer to the courtly life of Versailles, "*Peruked* and stately for the final act" (my emphasis). The shared wig image is perhaps insufficient reason to enter at this point into an analysis of the piece (although an essay on the theory of wigs in Hecht would scarcely be superficial), but the poem happens to offer more comprehensive connections with the issues I've raised so far. It is, like "The Deodand," a poem about the burdens of withdrawal and confrontation, about one's response to the perception of decadence and disguise; it is likewise a poem about being horrified by the world.

Hecht, varying a strategy that Auden used in *The Sea and the Mirror*, envisions Alceste in the afterworld of Molière's comedy. He is discovered (without a wig, one assumes) in that offstage, imagined place ("wild, trackless, solitary") into which he had unsuccessfully tried to bear the resistant Célimène—in order, as he had said in the comedy, to keep the world away, and to remove his "present horror" of his duplicitous, mocking paramour. In Hecht's lyric Alceste is caught there alone. The place is the scene of the skeptic's or satirist's withdrawal from the contaminations of human life. Yet as Hecht's writing often suggests, attempts at withdrawal (whether into "purity" or "indulgence") never quite work since, however tempting, they leave one haunted or threatened all the more strangely by what one had tried to flee. Hence those Parisian women (followed by the absorbed eye of the poet), screening out the world, wrapping themselves up in the clothing of an oriental idyll, are suddenly, vengefully confronted with an ironic mirror that speaks out of "the raging heat of the desert." Alceste's desert offers likewise an answering utterance.

The poem begins on an "evening clogged with gnats," filled with the "gold and copper screams" of exotic birds whose tails are sought for fashionable dresses and hats—as if the wilderness were itself supplying the vanities Alceste had left. He carries a snuffbox ornamented with some pastoral enamel, an image of Daphnis "touching love's defeat," but this only manages to "call up the color of her underthings." The wilderness itself is no pure, inhuman place but the site of human heat, of a kind of ruinous generation and decay that is more than merely natural:

> One day he found, topped with a smutty grin,
> The small corpse of a monkey, partly eaten.
> Force of the sun had split the bluish skin,
> Which, by their questioning and entering in,
> A swarm of bees had been concerned to sweeten.
>
> He could distill no essence out of this.
> That yellow majesty and molten light
> Should bless this carcass with a sticky kiss
> Argued a brute and filthy emphasis.
> The half-moons of the fingernails were white,
>
> And where the nostrils opened on the skies,
> Issuing to the sinus, where the ant
> Crawled swiftly down to undermine the eyes
> Of cloudy aspic, nothing could disguise
> How terribly the thing looked like Philinte.
>
> Will-o'-the-wisp, on the scum-laden water,
> Burns in the night, a gaseous deceiver,
> In the pale shade of France's foremost daughter.
> Heat gives his thinking cavity no quarter,
> For he is burning with the monkey's fever.

Alceste has withdrawn into the ambivalently motivated dream of his own purity, but instead of providing a kind of "critical distance," this strange wilderness/jungle only presents him with an ironic relic or corpse, a grotesque dream-image that is at once mirror and mockery. We might first suppose that the rotted, honey-combed, ant-ridden monkey is the satirist's vision of the rotted body of the world, a fantasy produced by that rage for perfection, that ideal of love as criticism, which "finds its perfect consummation / In ecstasies of rage and reprobation."[4] It would likewise be a vision of the intractable contradictions in human action or discourse which Alceste always construes as a reflection of hypocrisy, hence his nastiest vision of his friend and enemy, Philinte. But the clouded and undermined eye of the monkey looks terribly back at him like an accuser, for he is not only Alceste's victim but also his double—an image of his haughty, self-indulgent disgust, an image of the sickness he shares with (and projects onto) the world from which he divides himself. Most profoundly, perhaps, the creature is an image of the rotting, feverish body which his reason tries to sweeten but cannot escape.[5]

In the introduction to his translation of *The Misanthrope* (published in the same year as *A Summoning of Stones*), Richard Wilbur notes that in Molière's play "the advocate of true feeling and honest intercourse is the one character most artificial, most out-of-touch, most in danger of that nonentity and solitude which all, in the chattery, hollow world of this play, are fleeing," and further that Alceste's blind, jealous criticism and indignation, despite a certain spiritual grandeur, seems after all "in great part instrumental, a desperate means of counterfeiting an identity."[6] This judgment fits Hecht's version of Alceste to a degree, but the poem points to something more than Alceste's subjective emptiness or existential solitude. Its real focus is on Alceste's confrontation with that half-human, grotesquely smiling, eviscerated and generative corpse—not so much an image of the "physical" or "sexual" in some abstract sense as an image of the horrible, mocking thing that the body becomes when we place it in a divided, brutal, and intractable relation to the honeyed, questioning, ideally critical faculty of reason. The Blakean irony recurs: Alceste becomes what he beholds—the odd, scary corpse is his own specter, a vision of himself as the victim of his own satiric puritanism. What is most remarkable here is that Hecht manages to conjure up something which not only Alceste but Molière himself, for all his subtle turns of ironic recognition, scarcely pays attention to: the jealous, desiring body that so entangles or gives form to the motions of our minds, the scandalous thing whose near invisibility in Molière's comedy is perhaps one of the things that makes it so hard for us to fix the play's moral and satirical stakes.

It is Célimène who tells Alceste, early in the play, that "none but yourself shall make a monkey of you."[7] Alceste in the wilderness is caught by another *ignis fatuus*; he cannot quite see the monkey he was, or has become. The poem projects his confused, fascinated, disgusted regard of the thing, his odd romance with the corpse (something brought out, for example, in the splendid rhyming of "ant" and "Philinte"), but along with great irony there is a perverse kind of lyric success in the scene, as if the real failure would be to turn away one's gaze too quickly. I say this because the poem reserves its subtlest, least-voiced disdain not for the critic in the jungle but for the "edified" returnee:

> Before the bees have diagrammed their comb
> Within the skull, before summer has cracked
> The back of Daphnis, naked, polychrome,
> Versailles shall see the tempered exile home,
> Peruked and stately for the final act.

The last line suggests that the social or satirical "theater" might resume on Alceste's return, might find a better way of ending itself than a retreat into the wilderness. And yet the "act" that Hecht anticipates (rhyming as it does with the "cracked back" of the plaster, pastoral lover Daphnis) is one which unavoidably crosses the theatrical with the sexual, as if the hypocrisy Alceste has fled will now return with a vengeance.

What deepens the moral and erotic bitterness in the poem is, as I've suggested, that it articulates what amounts to an anatomy of the poet as satirist, a kind of cost accounting of Alceste's illusions and his divided impulses (though an accounting that is more thoroughly distanced than in a poem like "The Deodand").[8] Indeed, one might suggest that the image of the satirist (as opposed to the prophet) caught in the wilderness defines a kind of archetype for Hecht. For the voice, tone, or stance of the satirist returns upon Hecht almost obsessively through his work, often with a kind of alienation or uneasiness. The "Alceste" element emerges, for instance, in an elusive tone of distance or distaste one finds in some poems, an anxious, mocking regard for both his own words and the things they would describe, or a sense of defiled artificiality (abetted by subtly modulated excesses or apparent lapses of diction) that emerges even in some of his more forthrightly romantic meditations, though usually complicated by a more elegiac tone. It comes out most directly, of course, in the poet's translations of satire, invective, or comic curse from writers like Horace, Ronsard, du Bellay, or Voltaire.[9] Such brilliant, liberating rehearsals of scorn and neoclassical irony should be seen, however, as acts of both appropriation and distancing; they explore a tone that draws the poet and that he yet does not want totally to possess him. One is tempted to regard such formal imitations as instances of rage at play, as if their venom were weirdly "pure." And yet, if for no other reason than that such texts are scattered in the collections among others whose modal or generic character is less circumscribed, they may as we read them take on a more uncertain coloring. And in general, even in those of Hecht's "original" lyrics where the satirical tone predominates, it may be inordinately hard to separate out any clear sense of a satirical mask or persona, or to know exactly where and how the poet's ironic regard is fixed. The irony of the poet's voice is unstable partly because the bearers of that irony are so unstable, or because it wanders in so many directions. This does not mean, of course, that the voice has no inflection. The combined intensity and diffuseness of the "Alceste" tone indeed often translates into a maddening, weightless kind of nastiness (however morally charged) that hovers through many of the poems. But like Baudelaire's poetical "spleen," this is not so much direct "expression" as an intricate rhetorical achievement in its own right, obviously the product of some imaginative struggle. Now tonal ambivalence or opacity (as distinguished from some ideal of a transparent "voice") is as frequent an object of modern poets as imagistic or metaphoric compression—it is, among other things, a deeply figurative way of keeping silent. But in Hecht's case we must at least try to connect the tonal complexities to a broader characterization of his work. The studied ambivalence or shiftiness of the poet's tone reflects a peculiar double burden: the poetry takes upon itself the Horatian or Juvenalian mantle, marks out a stance of stern, bitter, satiric regard, knows its constitutive opposition to enemies like cruelty, vanity, rationalization and hypocrisy, yet not only does the poet brood over the inevitable excesses of such a stance but also traces with great rigor and gentleness the strange relation that its rage bears to what we like to think are the "better" motives of love, wonder, charity, or art. Hecht's are the poems of a slightly wiser Alceste who has remained in the wilderness.

I have been talking about the imagination of rage as something manifest in the figures of victimage or the tone of satire in Hecht's poetry. As a closing text, I turn to a remarkable long poem from *Millions of Strange Shadows*, "Green: An Epistle," a text that takes as its explicit "subject" "the forbidden topic / We by a truce have never touched upon, / Resentment, malice, hatred." It is a poem that offers an account, a laying bare, of the elusive animus whose expression and objects I have been tracing. And yet personal, even intimate as the feeling of the poem is, it is no obvious exercise in confession or self-expression. "Green" in fact generates one of the poet's most complexly buried pictures of rage, a picture that forces us to reconceptualize both our own notions of rage and our idea of the self that speaks it. The poem is a quest, not so much for the origins or causes of rage within the self as for the origins of the self *in* rage, the picture of a self constituted but also fissured by rage.

The "we" in the opening lines quoted above is rather chilling in context, since it marks a past complicity with the speaker's self-censorship, a gap in a long-standing conversation, before we even know who the speaker is. The poem is, formally speaking, the letter writer's account of the character or psychic history of another, the "you" to whom he writes—the story of that person's hidden battles, his secret fears, his repressions and evasions. But what gives this account its eeriness and claustrophobia is that not only do we have no glimpse of that "you" outside of the probing, slyly malicious descriptions of the poem's speaker but also that as we read the very possibility of making a clear distinction between the speaker and his object continually breaks down. It is as if the "you" were wholly saturated in the other's projections, or nothing more than a split-off and alienated mirror of the speaker's "I." That elusive "you" might seem in some ways comparable to the generalized "one" of Wallace Stevens's poems (perhaps even to the "Other I am" of Walt Whitman), save that in "Green" the gesture of setting the self at a distance seems more defensive as well as oddly symptomatic of the very shifts of mind that the speaker is eager to diagnose in his subject. The locating of that self whose history is unfolded in the poem is made all the harder insofar as the poet—rather than exposing that history through what seem like human, personal memories, however fragmentary or dreamlike these might be (as he does in "The Venetian Vespers")—plots the course of the subject's character and the history of his motives by means of a strangely abstracted, nearly allegorical phantasmagoria, a narrative in which even the rhetorical illusion of an "ego" or continuous personal identity is largely scattered.

In this mock-epistle to the self we are not wholly denied circumstantial detail. The speaker tells us, for instance, that he is writing his letter from a situation of troubled retirement, in a "grubby border town" where nobody knows him. (The tone here sounds a bit like that of Nabokov's Kinbote.) What he is in flight from we do not know, only that he seems to have a story to tell to a friend. He speaks as if they had been childhood companions and begins by making fun of their shared tendency to act "like bad philosophers" who "go back and stay forever in the dark," like that of an old cinema, amidst comforting pictures of heroism and romance, absolute good and absolute evil. But when he suddenly turns to peeling back what is hidden, all particularity, all anecdotal context drops away. We cannot quite tell now what state of the self, what presence or habit of mind the speaker is describing:

> It began, I suppose, as a color, a yellow-green,
> The tincture of spring willows, not so much color
> As the sensation of color, haze that took shape
> As a light scum, a doily of minutiae
> On the smooth pool and surface of your mind.
> A founding colony, Pilgrim amoebas
> Descended from the gaseous flux.

From this surmise the poet does move to what might seem the specific recollection of a child's glimpse through a microscope, but this turns out to be primarily a metonymy for the act of memory or self-analysis itself. Staring at the "contents" of a drop of vinegar, peering down into a liquid "clear as your early mind," evading the shadows of the eye that will otherwise appear on the slide, in parody of Genesis, "as a darkness on the face of the first waters"—one sees only

> long, thin, darting, shapes, the flagellates,
> Rat-tailed, ambitious, lash themselves along—
> Those humble, floating ones, those simple cells
> Content to be borne on whatever tide.

Such pilgrim flagellates are, we are told,

> the frail unlikely origins,
> Scarcely perceived, of all you shall become.
>
> pale beginnings, lace endeavours
> That with advancing ages shall mature
> Into sea lettuce, beard the rocky shore
> With a light green of soft and tidal hair.

The description that follows is complex enough that I must quote at length:

> Vascular tissue, conduit filaments
> Learn how to feed the outposts of that small

Emerald principate. Now there are roots,
The filmy gills of toadstools, crested fern,
Quillworts, and foxtail mosses, and at last
Snapweed, loment, trillium, grass, herb Robert.
How soundlessly, shyly this came about,
One thinks today. But that is not the truth.
It was, from the first, an everlasting war
Conducted as always, at gigantic cost.
Think of the droughts, the shifts of wind and weather,
The many seeds washed to some salt conclusion
Or brought to rest at last on barren ground.
Think of some inching tendrils worming down
In hope of water, blind and white as death.
. . . .
Yet, for all that, it clearly was a triumph,
Considering, as one must, what was to come.
And, even by themselves, those fields of clover,
Cattails, marsh bracken, water-lily pads
Stirred by the lightest airs, pliant, submissive—
Who could have called their slow creation *rage*?

What, after all, are we looking at? Of what is this a picture? Should we say that this is what childhood looks like? (And if so, what is it in the speaker or his subject that wishes childhood to look like this?) In its shifting vision of seeds and cells, of a self beginning in a surface scum, a drift of bits which move through odd, inconsequential phases of quest and conflict, action and suffering, exile and colonization, it offers a kind of Genesis myth, one that is read through vaguely Darwinian surmises about the origins and proliferation of organic life.[10] It is a story about the fate of words, perhaps, a revision of the parable of the sower. The visionary space glimpsed through the microscope is also a kind of Hechtian Garden of Adonis—not, like Spenser's allegory, the vision of a fixed cycle of creation, but similar in being an attempt to revise our pictures of genesis, providing the picture of an early Eden which internalizes rather than pushes away the trials of birth, death, time, and entropy. Other analogues come to mind as well: Hans Castorp's quasi-Goethean meditations on the inorganic origins of human life in *The Magic Mountain*, or Freud's picture of that threatened, single-celled creature in *Beyond the Pleasure Principle*, in whose response to internal and external threats he traces (half-allegorically) the origins of a psychic entity caught between the drives of eros and thanatos, between the urge to construct more complex wholes and the urge to destroy, the urge to return to a state of quiescence or inertia. Farfetched as this last analogue may seem, it fits the case of Hecht's poem both as Freud too grounds his picture of the course of human life on so seemingly inhuman, so minimal a story, and as that story challenges our sentimental pictures of what "growth," "life," or "progress" must look like.

Hecht takes the epigraph to his poem from Roethke: "This urge, wrestle, resurrection of dry sticks, / Cut stems struggling to put down feet, / What saint strained so much, / Rose on such lopped limbs to a new life?" The quotation, it seems to me, bears a kind of ironic weight (unless Roethke himself is being more ironic than I understand him to be). Hecht's poem does not echo the obvious pathos of such lines and regards somewhat less indulgently the romance of martyrdom and resurrection. Throughout his poetry, in fact, Hecht is more coldly dark, delicate and troubling in his pictures of "generation," and he never lapses into what can, in Roethke, sound like a kind of mindless, vegetable vitalism. Hecht makes his poetic gardens places of ruin, decay, and conflict but also places of strange artifice, places where restless energy or tragic burden meets with both delicate craft and mindless accident, where we see things that are ours but that we scarcely possess, things whose miraculousness is half a terror.[11] (Even when the poet does unveil for us tentative versions of what, following Auden, he might call "visions of Dame Kind"—visions of the "given" world made candid, fresh, related, or half-human, as by some special grace—the scene tends to be marred or emptied, taken as strangely self-indulgent, as in "Ostia Antica" [from *The Hard Hours*], where an ultimately inhuman idyll is broken in upon by one bearing "the heavy articles of blood.") "Green" in particular shows Hecht dismantling some of our more sentimental figurations of the color green. We get no "hopeful green stuff" as in Whitman, nor even the calmly elegiac "green light which lingers in the West" of Coleridge's "Dejection: An Ode." If the poem gives us "green thoughts in a green shade," then the shade is darker, with a more grotesque and bitter populace than anything we find in Marvell's garden. Reading Hecht's description, we might think of the aggressive, darkening, nearly apocalyptic growth of "summer woods" in Frost's "Spring Pools," but Hecht's gene pool offers us no vision of a possible innocence as starkly suspended as that of Frost's reflective "flowery waters." Hecht's green is, of course, more like the self-wounding green of envy (the rage against lost objects or blocked desire), but it is crucial to see that the poem tries to strain and develop even that clear iconic color, to see what it would look like, after all, to see the green of envy as also the green of a possible growth.

Although allegedly a description of origins, of what is deepest and most fundamental in the self, the "narrative" of "Green" is saturated with the sense of a self evaded or fragmented, as if the poem were both confessing and fending off confession, both exploring and guarding the self. Like all good allegory, this one works by putting pressure on our ways of picturing an idea—in this case by trying to remove the account of "rage" or "malice" from any easy melodrama, any obvious tones, objects, or moral justifications, any rationalized "causes." "Rage" becomes at once inescapable and opaque, while the self, "this foundling of an infected past," emerges without easily pictured ends or beginnings, as close to chaos as the poem can make it. The self is a precipitate of malice or envy, perhaps, but the occasions or causes of malice are invisible, and the account of it is suspended in such a way that we cannot tell to what degree the poet means to be monitory or celebratory, self-dramatizing or self-mocking. Hence the question about recognition with which he closes the above passage must, I think, be taken as more real than rhetorical: "Who could have called their slow creation *rage*?" And I take it that he is inquiring as much about the "creation" of a poem as about the creation of a person.

I have pointed so far to some biblical echoes, parallels in Spenser, Darwin, and Freud; various other "sources" may crowd into a reader's mind as well.[12] But there is at least one text that Hecht is playing against in an especially crucial way: Walt Whitman's "As I ebb'd with the ocean of life." Granting that allusion-hunting can become a rather academic exercise, I think that it is by seeing "Green" as a troubled commentary on Whitman's piece that we can best understand the logic and the stakes of Hecht's parable of origins.

On the most basic level, Hecht's view into a primeval, microscopic soup is filled with a thoroughly Whitmanian imagery of detitrus, of drowned or watery growth, of the half-organic, half-human stuff which drifts through the friable, ironic garden world of the estuary: "The rim, the sediment that stands for all the water and all the land of the globe . . . these slender windrows, / Chaff, straw, splinters of wood, weeds, and the sea-gluten, / Scum, scales from shining rocks, leaves of salt lettuce, left by the tide."[13] In Whitman, however, these fragments that he glimpses along the shore of Paumanok become a place where the self traces the present end rather than the past origins of its life and poetry; the estuary is a stage of failure, more a waste heap than a seedbed. That space in which the poet might have gathered the traces or answering projections of a self now faces him as alien; it offers evidence only of his own scatteredness, of the withdrawal of the "real Me." The given world that might have once been for him nourishment, mirror, or lover offers at best a mock and a reproach; it becomes a threatening questioner, laughing "at every word I have written." The quest for the evidences of the self, of its power of relation, the very attempt to sing the self, seems in "As I ebb'd" to wring the self apart; indeed, it elicits a confession that, after all, the self was always thus scattered. Whitman does try, for a moment, to imagine himself as an invisible Odysseus, wrestling with the endlessly metamorphosed shore-god Proteus, trying to make him hold a fixed form. But even so ambivalent a father figure deserts him. He manages not even the most tentative figure of regathering. Directionless, fatherless, the poet ends with a desperate act of identification with the "measureless float" and with the endless wash that "leaves little wrecks" upon the shore. If the poem does close on a note of uncanny calm and resolve, it is through an acceptance, a strange wooing of the fragmentary. Whitman stands, the most delicate and courtly of mourners, in the company of his own lost, phantomlike self, tending to his own corpse, attending upon the hoarse, angry maternal sea (the "you" of what follows):

> I mean tenderly by you and all,
> I gather for myself and for this phantom looking down where we
>   lead, and following me and mine.
> Me and mine, loose windrows, little corpses,
> Froth, snowy white, and bubbles,
> (See, from my dead lips the ooze exuding at last,
> See, the prismatic colors glistening and rolling),
> Tufts of straw, sands, fragments,
> Buoy'd hither from many moods, one contradicting another,
> From the storm, the long calm, the darkness, the swell,
> Musing, pondering, a breath, a briny tear, a dab of liquid or soil,
> Up just as much out of fathomless workings fermented and thrown,
> A limp blossom or two, torn, just as much over waves
>   Floating, drifted at random.
> . . . .
> We, capricious, brought hither we know not whence, spread out
>   before you.[14]

Hecht will not allow himself so uncanny a form of closure. Indeed, despite its strong parallels, the aim of the speaker's story in "Green" is largely to undo the earlier poet's suspended accommodations by making what for Whitman is the occasion of redemptive elegy into the scene of a catastrophic genesis. The present estuary becomes a space of past memory, and its vision of flux, we are to be persuaded, shows us not a place of entropy but of evolution. Yet it is an evolution whose motive and telos is something called rage; it is a place of innocence as well, but one in which the "heraldic hue of envy" appears in "pre-lapsarian disguise." In its weird refusal of mourning, in its desperate attempt to map a more progressive narrative shape onto the imagery of scattering and loss, the poem achieves a coldly parodic correction of Whitman, one whose goal is more subtly negative and troubling than anything in the earlier poet (as if Darwinian science provided at best a kind of Mephistophelian aid here). We may feel less strongly the "gigantic cost" of what Hecht's speaker calls "an everlasting war." For despite one's sense that the poet's densely worked description speaks of the history of a self as well as of cells—though that self is a chaos of sensations, acts, fantasies, an entity at once divided and created by events that seem both "internal" and "external"—Hecht shows us nothing like the picture of Whitman watching his own body being scattered, lost, or turned against him. Unless, of course, part of the cost is that the losses now seem as obscure as the gains, that the site of the war remains so painfully difficult to locate that one doesn't know where to look for either casualties or survivors.

One other "cost" of the war, perhaps, is to have so fully emerged from the self's early, subterranean history—since in the latter part of the text the poet's suggestive, or subtly implicit, allegory blossoms, or rather freezes into maturity, into more explicit forms of personification, an evolution not into chaos but into fixity, into the darker arbitrariness of the conventional:

> Consider, as one must, what was to come.
> Great, towering conifers, deciduous,
> Rib-vaulted elms, the banyan, oak, and palm,
> Sequoia forests of vindictiveness
> That also would go down on the death list
> And, buried slowly darken into lakes of coal
> And then under exquisite pressure turn
> Into tiny diamonds of pure hate.
> The delicate fingers of the clematis
> Feeling their way along a face of shale

With all the ingenuity of spite.
The indigestible thistle of revenge.
And your most late accomplishment, the rose.

That last emblem, left without any label, of course being "love," assuming that we could pronounce that word with sufficient bitterness. (Here again, the poet's extreme manipulations of tonality are essential to the text's power.) Brilliant as they are, the sudden access of these lines to such an array of abstract names makes them surprisingly hard to get a grasp on. One wants to know even more urgently: Whose history are we reading? To whom does this stratigraphy belong? How much exactly is being revealed in this allegory of burial and transformation? And what do we make of the arch tone of courteous and scholarly regard? The speaker is talking about the development of "emotions," yet the lines also suggest a half-articulated image of poetic creation, its burdened evolutions and crystallizations. But if so, the lines even in their intense delicacy suggest that the poet is making mock of his own creative ingenuity, his refined tracing out of conceits in the service of a hieratic, emblematic pedagogy. (It is the *writing* here that possesses "all the ingenuity of spite.") If he is speaking of poetry, it is a poetry that can only give an account of its "forbidden subject" by keeping it at a distance, resolving it into frigid, almost opaque names, generalizations that seem also terrifying evasions. It is a manner of speaking about the self that neither confesses any sins nor lifts any repressions, one in which no absolution is either asked or possible.

The poem does not stop at this point, however; it goes on to speak of unhoped-for respites, "moments almost of bliss, / A sort of recompense in which your mood / Sorts with the peach endowments of late sunlight"—moments that are nevertheless only gained at the expense of the past, by forgetting the "ages" of effort and disappointment, of motives twisted beyond recognition. They are moments when, he says with the most kindly of ambiguities, "you scarcely know yourself." This closing movement offers a return to a more circumstantial or mimetic framework, as if (with maturity?) we could get a clearer glimpse of that separate "you" whom the speaker wishes to address and criticize. And yet such a clearing culminates in a moment that only leaves the nature of the speaker's investments, and his authority, more fully problematic. For in this sketch of his subject's "final peace," what gets revealed is strangely enough the speaker's own latent paranoia about the subject's hidden aggression, a sense that his story will only bounce off the "you" and stick to himself. At the end, a "me" suddenly emerges, but in a context where any strong distinction between "me" and "you" seems again to dissolve and along with it any chance of getting a purchase on the speaker's relation to a world outside himself, leaving us within what seems a sealed, if internally fissured, sphere of paranoid self-reflection, projection, and méconnaissance:

> You sometimes contemplate a single image,
> Utterly silent, utterly at rest.
> It is of someone, a stranger, quite unknown,
> Sitting alone in a foreign-looking room,
> Gravely intent at a table propped with matchbooks,
> Writing this very poem—about me.

The poem as a whole, however, is no blank mirror. A few lines before those quoted above the speaker had asked, "Who could have hoped for this eventual peace," echoing the previous query, "Who could have called this slow creation *rage*?" Both questions seem ingenuous (though not quite rhetorical), and yet much of what we make of the poem (and I think of Hecht's work in general) hangs on what we make of those questions, how we weigh them, what further questions or stories we might offer in response. We have a question about how we recognize or name something, in particular something called "rage," and a question about the substance of things hoped for, in particular "peace"—and the pairing of the two suggests that our conclusions about peace and rage may bear on each other in unforeseen ways.

"Green" is after all not so much a "myth of origins" (which sounds rather too portentous) as a poem about growing up: about hidden trials, frenzies, accidents, "hair-breadth scapes," and "casual slaughters"; about half-remembered epiphanies; about presences so uncompassable they might be absences; about the memory of rage and the rage against memory; about maturing into oblivion, into false rather than fallen innocence; about inescapable and indulgent self-distancings, the gift and trouble of "scarcely knowing yourself"; about regarding the possibility of recompense or grace. That the bulk of this history, however much it grips us, remains nevertheless so abstract; that there are no anecdotes or dreams about authority figures, object choices, wounds, losses; that it so sharply allegorizes the affective movements which are its subject—this may after all have a lot to do with what the piece is telling us about the "poetics" of telling a life story, even a common one. It gets something very right, suggests a confession of something, not just a hiding. Still, remarkable and even experimental as "Green" is, I wonder whether the poet himself may not have felt that he had taken its mode of rarefied phantasmagoria (however much framed as dramatic monologue) to its aesthetic or formal limit, or perhaps felt it proper only to the particular "type" of paranoia that is his subject there. In any case, the fact is that Hecht attempts nothing quite so extreme in more recent long poems such as "The Venetian Vespers" or "The Short End," texts that continue to trace out the lineaments of selves divided from or burdened by their past histories, but which do so through more fully midrashic and dramatic narratives. If "Green" seems nonetheless a rehearsal for these efforts, the one thing it might remind us of is how elusive and uncanny the logic of the later pieces is likely to be, how uneasily suspended the anecdotal reveries, how obscure the trajectory of their anger and regret, how confessedly parabolic and violent the attempts to trace out origins, how hard and yet how necessary it may be to see in their stories the reflections of "a war conducted, as always, at gigantic cost."[15]

One of Hecht's most moving short poems, "The Man Who Married Magdalene: Variation on a Theme by Louis Simpson," carries an epigraph from the Book of Jonah: "Then said the Lord, dost thou well to be angry?" In its original context the question is part of a complex comedy whose theme is the nature of the prophetic wrath—the zealous wrath against sin; the wrath that promises sublime violence; the frustrated, self-destructive wrath of a prophet against a god who is free to change his mind; wrath held out as a form of pity, a wrath against the wanton destruction of things and creatures; wrath divided, projected, abstracted. In Hecht the question is addressed to a speaker caught in confused remorse over the death of his wife and the jealousy that occasioned it but whose utterances consist mostly of mocking slurs against a world which either disregards him or holds him responsible, a world in which love and faith are poisoned and in which his only glimpse of divine justice is a dream of farcical, leering angels with metal feathers making jokes about God's pity for the weak:

> "Such as once went to Gehenna
> Now dance among the blessed.
> But Mary Magdalena,
> She had it the best."

It is a world in which he can live only drunk or mad. The scene of the poem is that of a barroom confession, its hidden problem that of what kind of story one can tell about one's life, what "reward" looks like, where one can locate or find a voice for one's anger and pain, how one might answer anger's imaginative demands. The art of the piece, given its lyric compression, is to have invented a voice whose scorn is so plain and yet so ambivalent, so pitiable and so scary. Now it would take some time to explicate the moving "wit" of the displaced quotation from Jonah, especially in the case of the poem where the speaker's own iterations of biblical phraseology are so chilling. The main thing to say, however, is that the anger of which Hecht speaks has now become a more purely human anger, though it is no less ambiguous and no less burdened. What had originally been the challenging and ultimately ironic question of a deity turns into one that can only be asked by the poet, and in a fashion that makes the question both more direct and considerably harder to answer. The one thing to add is that it is a question which Hecht asks himself throughout his work.

NOTES

1. Speaking of Oedipus, in the voice of the fate Lachesis, Hecht has written:

> What the intelligence
> Works out in pure delight
> The body must learn in pain.
> He has solved the Sphinx's riddle
> In his own ligaments.

2. See Anthony Hecht, "*Othello* and *The Merchant of Venice*: A Venture in Hermeneutics," in *Obbligati: Essays in Criticism* (New York: Atheneum, 1986), 51–84 and 140–239, respectively.

3. See Judith Shklar, "Putting Cruelty First," in *Ordinary Vices* (Cambridge: Harvard University Press, 1984), 17.

4. The words are Célimène's, quoted from the translation of Molière's *The Misanthrope* by Richard Wilbur (New York: Harcourt, Brace, and World, 1954), 68.

5. The poem also recalls the image of a lion's carcass filled with a honeycomb that is the answer to Samson's riddle about how "out of the eater came forth meat, and out of the strong came forth sweetness" (Judges 14:14).

6. Richard Wilbur, Introduction to *The Misanthrope*, 8.

7. Molière, *The Misanthrope*, 52.

8. It may support my contention that the poet discovers projections of himself in the symbolic scene (however fragmentary or ironic) to observe

that the focus on the images of "ants" and "honey" seems in Spenserian fashion to literalize by false etymology the phonic components of the poet's first name. By a slightly different logic, we could link "Hecht" to the heckling or hectoring of Alceste, though that satirist might prefer to adduce the German *echt*, "true," even as he could uneasily recall that the German phrase *feiner hecht*, "sharp pike," is idiomatic for "fop" or "dandy." The poet is scarcely a stranger to such onomastic play, and in some recent verses on translation published in *Poetry* he suggests that the inhabitants of the netherworld might come to address him as "Signor Hecate."

9. See, for example, "Poem upon the Lisbon Disaster, or, An Inquiry into the Adage, 'All Is for the Best'" (after Voltaire) in *Millions of Strange Shadows*, or "Invective Against Denise, a Witch" (after Ronsard) and 'An Old Malediction" (after Horace) in *The Venetian Vespers*. From these one might turn to an explicitly comic piece like "The Dover Bitch: A Criticism of Life" or to an exercise in grotesque, sadistic, and satiric devotion like "To a Madonna" (after Baudelaire), both in *The Hard Hours*.

10. The "evolutionary" conceit worked out in such obscure detail in "Green" returns throughout Hecht's poetry as a more purely occasional or suggestive figure, as for example in the following lines from "The Venetian Vespers." After measuring his life against the "viscid, contaminate, dynastic wastes" of the city's canals, the speaker describes his own monastic half-life and its cut-off-ness from the past by ruminating on the fate of cells:

> A virus's life-span is twenty minutes.
> Think of its evolutionary zeal,
> Like the hyper-active balance-wheel of a watch,
> Busy with swift mutations, trundling through
> Its own Silurian epochs in a week;
> By fierce ambition and Darwinian wit
> Acquiring its immunities against
> Our warfares and our plagues of medication.
> Blessed be the unseen micro-organisms,
> For without doubt they shall inherit the earth.
> Their generations shall be as the sands of the sea.
> I am the dying host by which they live;
> In me they dwell and thrive and have their being.
> I am the tapered end of a long line,
> The thin and febrile phylum of my family.

Leonard Baskin's strange, egg- or skull-shaped drawing of a visionary, primeval swamp-garden, which appears on the cover of the British edition of *Millions of Strange Shadows* (full of insects, bats, and monitory birds, as well as trailing plants, weeds, and flowers), picks up on this imagery in Hecht's poetry. Indeed, the drawing itself might be taken as an "illustration" for "Green."

11. See, for example, "La Condition Botanique," from *A Summoning of Stones*, a text which can be read in part as an answer to some of Roethke's

"greenhouse" poems, though it is much more than that. Shelley's "The Sensitive Plant" or Swinburne's "Garden of Proserpina," among texts, should also be looked at for the sake of comparison.

12. Hecht himself, in a letter to the author, has suggested a parallel between "Green" and Auden's early poem "Since you are going to begin today" (of which, though, he was unconscious at the time of composition). There are, in fact, some striking resemblances between the two poems in both image and tone, the latter being a monologue, spoken in the voice of a monitory but still affectionate and maternal figure (we could call it Fate or Anangke), who describes to an undefined listener the web of contingencies, failures, and injustices that have shaped his development. Interestingly, however, the English poet seems comfortable in projecting his wise "other"; it possesses, that is to say, a kind of rhetorical security, even though we understand it as a mask. Hecht on the other hand—and this makes his text more American, or at least less neoclassical in its irony—leaves the wisdom or authority of his speaker much less stable, as if the dramatic or motivational logic of such a projection were questionable, such that (again) the speaker and the "you" seem always liable to collapse together.

13. Walt Whitman, *The Complete Poems*, ed. Francis Murphy (New York: Penguin, 1975), 281–82.

14. Ibid., 283–84.

15. As he begins to narrate one crucial portion of his early history, the story of a father's death, the speaker in "The Venetian Vespers" warns us:

> The story I have to tell is only my story
> By courtesy of painful inference.
> So far as I can tell it, it is true,
> Though it has comprised the body of such dreams,
> Such broken remnant furnishings of the mind
> That my unwilling suspension of disbelief
> No longer can distinguish between fact
> As something outward, independent, given,
> And the enfleshment of disembodied thought,
> Some melanotic malevolence of my own.

J. D. McClatchy

Anatomies of Melancholy

> *Then praise was for a kind of art*
> *Whereof there is no school;*
> *There the unlettered instinct rides*
> *In all its bodily skill.*
> —Hecht, "Speech"

At one point in a poem about his childhood, Anthony Hecht takes a small inventory. It is a poet's inventory, whereby gift is symbol, image conjures image, and a present predicts the future.

>   Here is the microscope one had as a child,
> The Christmas gift of some forgotten uncle.
> Here is the slide with a drop of cider vinegar
> As clear as gin, clear as your early mind.
> Look down, being most careful not to see
> Your own eye in the mirror underneath,
> Which will appear, unless your view is right,
> As a darkness on the face of the first waters.
> When all is silvery and brilliant, look:
> The long, thin, darting shapes, the flagellates,
> Rat-tailed, ambitious, lash themselves along—
> Those humble, floating ones, those simple cells
> Content to be borne on whatever tide,
> Trustful, the very image of consent—
> These are the frail, unlikely origins,
> Scarcely perceived, of all you shall become.

The kind of research that goes on here is twofold. The poem these lines are part of, the astonishing "Green: An Epistle," is itself a *recherche*, a finely detailed Proustian recovery of lost time, both a historical project and a personal obsession. And the passage also describes a literal research that peers into a world that makes itself manifest in the shapes and colors and rhythms of words. In fact, these lines comprise a miniature allegory of origins—of any lyric poet's "unlikely origins." But it is how this allegory is fractioned, into a darkness and two impulses, that most intrigues me, because it goes to the heart of Hecht's work. That primal darkness, first of all. That it is the very image of the poet's own eye echoes Emerson: "The blank we see in Nature is in our own eye." And it is crucial to remember how often Hecht takes this darkness as his subject. Few contemporary poets have so persistently and so strikingly come to terms with evil and violence in history, or what we literally call *human nature*. And throughout his four collections are occasions of madness, paranoia, catatonia, hallucination, and dream; there are exile, plague, miscarriage, murder, genocide. Indeed, the intricate trelliswork of his stanzas—some of them feats of engineering not seen since the seventeenth century—and the grandiloquent diction that are the hallmarks of Hecht's style seem at odds with such subjects: too composed.

"In each art," Richard Wilbur once wrote (Hecht quotes the sentence in his 1966 essay "On the Methods and Ambitions of Poetry"), "the difficulty of the form is a substitute for the difficulty of direct apprehension and expression of the object." Elaborate schemes, then, substitute for painstaking analysis. And in general that is true of Hecht. It is true as well that he seeks to dramatize both the difficulty and the apprehension by means of his style. Sharply contrasting tones of voice—lambent figures and Latinate turns suddenly give way to slang—are used not just to color his poems but to structure them. His poems continually favor such sorts of doubleness—paired perspectives, sentiment cut with cynicism, moral standards undercut by doubt. Some poems depend on abruptly juxtaposed points of view. Others work with the dynamics of motion and stasis. "The Cost" is one: a young Italian couple race on their Vespa around Trajan's Column. Theirs is a world—or a moment in the world—of "weight and speed," "risks and tilts," "the spin / And dazzled rinse of air," "their headlong lurch and flatulent racket." What they circle is, in a sense, the image in stone of themselves: the spiraling bas-relief of the emperor's troops, long since motes of dust like those the latter-day motor scooter kicks up. The couple's very motion depends on their *not* thinking of the difference. Self-consciousness, or what Hecht here calls "unbodied thought," is entropy.

Or, to return to the terms in the allegory I began with, we have two shapes, two forms of stylistic life, two modes of being—the flagellates and the simple cells. I want in this essay to look through the other end of the microscope, to look back at Hecht's work through these contrasting impulses and find the eye of the poet in the darkness visible. And, though I want to make connections with other poems of his, I want to take one poem as my "slide"—one of Hecht's most familiar and successful poems, "A Hill," first published in the *New Yorker* in February 1964 and collected in *The Hard Hours*.

> In Italy, where this sort of thing can occur,
> I had a vision once—though you understand
> It was nothing at all like Dante's, or the visions of saints,
> And perhaps not a vision at all. I was with some friends,
> Picking my way through a warm sunlit piazza
> In the early morning. A clear fretwork of shadows
> From huge umbrellas littered the pavement and made
> A sort of lucent shallows in which was moored
> A small navy of carts. Books, coins, old maps,
> Cheap landscapes and ugly religious prints
> Were all on sale. The colors and noise
> Like the flying hands were gestures of exultation,
> So that even the bargaining
> Rose to the ear like a voluble godliness.
> And then, when it happened, the noises suddenly stopped,
> And it got darker; pushcarts and people dissolved
> And even the great Farnese Palace itself
> Was gone, for all its marble; in its place
> Was a hill, mole-colored and bare. It was very cold,
> Close to freezing, with a promise of snow.
> The trees were like old ironwork gathered for scrap
> Outside a factory wall. There was no wind,
> And the only sound for a while was the little click
> Of ice as it broke in the mud under my feet.
> I saw a piece of ribbon snagged on a hedge,
> But no other sign of life. And then I heard
> What seemed like the crack of a rifle. A hunter, I guessed;
> At least I was not alone. But just after that
> Came the soft and papery crash
> Of a great branch somewhere unseen falling to earth.
>
> And that was all, except for the cold and silence
> That promised to last forever, like the hill.
>
> Then prices came through, and fingers, and I was restored
> To the sunlight and my friends. But for more than a week

I was scared by the plain bitterness of what I had seen.
All this happened about ten years ago,
And it hasn't troubled me since, but at last, today,
I remembered that hill; it lies just to the left
Of the road north of Poughkeepsie; and as a boy
I stood before it for hours in wintertime.

The poem is animated—urged, structured, and colored—by all of the contrasts I have mentioned and by the "painful doubleness" its displacements enact. It stands with a group of poems central to Hecht's achievement—among them "Coming Home," "Apprehensions," "The Grapes," "The Short End," and "The Venetian Vespers"—that are essentially anatomies of melancholy. They are poems richer in incident and memory than others. They seem to cast a wider net and into deeper waters. But their purpose is peculiar. That purpose can be seen all the more clearly when a poem with the opposite motive—"Peripeteia" would be my example—is placed beside this group. *Peripeteia* is Aristotle's term for the reversal of fortune or intention on which the action in the drama turns, and in Hecht's poem it is an extraordinary turn of events. The poet is alone—that is, he feels a "mild relief that no one there knows me"—in a theater that is filling with people before a play. He is, he says, "a connoisseur of loneliness," and his "cool, drawn-out anticipation" this night is less for the play to be performed than for a long-running "stillness" before the curtain rises. Even without knowing that the play is to be *The Tempest*, we might have guessed this poet to be a sort of Prospero (or Shakespeare) in contented exile (or retirement), en-isled in loneliness, his island (or "isolation") his work, his muse a miraculous daughter:

Each of us is miraculously alone
In calm, invulnerable isolation,
Neither a neighbor nor a fellow but,
As at the beginning and end, a single soul,
With all the sweet and sour of loneliness.
I, as a connoisseur of loneliness,
Savor it richly, and set it down
In an endless umber landscape, a stubble field
Under a lilac, electric, storm-flushed sky,
Where, in companionship with worthless stones,
Mica-flecked, or at best some rusty quartz,
I stood in childhood, waiting for things to mend.
A useful discipline, perhaps. One that might lead

> To solitary, self-denying work
> That issues in something harmless, like a poem,
> Governed by laws that stand for other laws,
> Both of which aim, through kindred disciplines,
> At the soul's knowledge and habiliment.

The image of the child standing, waiting, alone in an empty field—as the man he became is waiting in the theater—will bring at once to mind the child in "A Hill." But whereas the latter poem ends with the forlorn child, "Peripeteia" starts there, with some complacency, and then with an astonishing turn of the poem's fortunes moves on to quite another stage of "self-granted freedom." The play begins, unfolds its plot. By a sly and implicit irony, Hecht may mean for us to understand that his speaker has gradually fallen asleep and that the play resumes in his dream. But no matter. The see-through magic of theater or dreams or desire itself comes to the same thing, as suddenly

> Leaving a stunned and gap-mouthed Ferdinand,
> Father and faery pageant, she, and even she,
> Miraculous Miranda, steps from the stage,
> Moves up the aisle to my seat, where she stops,
> Smiles gently, seriously, and takes my hand
> And leads me out of the theatre, into a night
> As luminous as noon, more deeply real,
> Simply because of her hand, than any dream
> Shakespeare or I or anyone ever dreamed.

The eyes widen. The lush rhetoric, the sweetness at once improbable and inevitable, the whole panoply of redemption and enchantment have a truly Shakespearean resonance in Hecht's redaction. But, as I say, this is an unusual gesture. The group of poems of which I take "A Hill" to be representative does the work of disenchantment.

I want to start at the most literal level of reading: the biographical. All of these anatomies of melancholy seem the most autobiographical of Hecht's poems, even when they include the added displacement of characterized voices and plots. That might just make them the more identifiable as dreams. Like "Peripeteia," "A Hill" calls itself a vision or dream. And it seems more of a private poem than a personal one. Its juxtaposition of images—piazza and hill—is evidently charged with private associations and meant to operate both within the poem and on the reader as dream-work will. The images are not superimposed, but displaced, the one by the other, the later by the earlier—and both recalled, as if by an analysand, a decade later. The poem cannot be read as any simple alternation of manifest and latent meanings. The action here is the emergence of suppressed memory. The poem itself does not offer any elaboration or explanation. But the reader who remembers a bit of Hecht's biography may have some clues. The Roman setting, for instance. During World War II, Hecht served in the army in both Europe and Japan and returned home to a slow and difficult period of readjustment. "Like most others who saw any combat at all," he writes, "I experienced a very pronounced and fully conscious sense of guilt at surviving when others, including friends, had not." Then, in 1951, he was awarded the first Prix de Rome writing fellowship ever granted by the American Academy in Rome, and he returned to Europe. Rome, then, carried for the poet a sense of triumph and guilt. And it is not just the burden of history or of artistic tradition (mention of the Farnese Palace focuses that) that presses on the poet until, like Dante, he faints at the intensity of his own imagining, but the fact that Rome is where he has been *sent*, as if in luxurious exile, that makes it appropriate as a scene of instruction.

And what of the hill, the infernal landscape? Poughkeepsie? Perhaps. A state of soul? More likely. And with its factory wall and hunter, it is a landscape out of Auden as well. Let us say it is actual and literary, psychological and metaphysical. And with only slightly altered topography it recurs in several other poems. It serves an overtly symbolic function in such poems as "Exile," which is dedicated to Joseph Brodsky:

> Vacant parade ground swept by the winter wind,
> A pile of worn-out tires crowning a knoll,
> The purplish clinkers near the cinder blocks
> That support the steps of an abandoned church
> Still moored to a telephone pole, this sullen place
> Is *terra deserta*, Joseph, this is Egypt.

Or, in his nasty, brutal, long poem "The Short End," when Shirley turns away from the Live Entombment and faces another kind of death-in-life:

> A grizzled landscape, burdock and thistle-choked,
> A snarled, barbed-wire barricade of brambles,

> All thorn and needle-sharp hostility,
> The dead weeds wicker-brittle, raffia-pale,
> The curled oak leaves a deep tobacco brown,
> The sad rouge of old bricks, chips of cement
> From broken masonry, a stubble field
> Like a mangy lion's pelt of withered grass.
> Off in the distance a thoroughly dead tree,
> Peeled of its bark, sapless, an armature
> Of well-groomed, military, silver-gray.
> And other leafless trees, their smallest twigs
> Incising a sky the color of a bruise.

It is the same bleakness, out of Kafka or Beckett, and its props grow familiar: the ruined building, the tree, the military echo. The apparent sound of a rifle shot (what he first thinks he hears is more important than what it turns out to be—a dead and no golden bough) in "A Hill" brings to mind other allusions to World War II. The execution in "More Light! More Light!" The soldier-orphan in part 3 of "The Venetian Vespers." Or in "Still Life," where the exquisitely rendered natural detail of a misted landscape before dawn gives way to light—and to a sudden memory:

> As in a water-surface I behold
>   The first, soft, peach decree
> Of light, its pale, inaudible commands.
> I stand beneath a pine-tree in the cold,
> Just before dawn, somewhere in Germany,
> A cold, wet, Garand rifle in my hands.

Such memories hover over the landscape of "A Hill." But for Hecht himself, though he rigorously excluded them from the poem, there are specific personal associations. In a letter to me, he once explained:

> As for "A Hill," it is the nearest I was able to come in that early book to what Eliot somewhere describes as an obsessive image or symbol—something from deep in our psychic life that carries a special burden of meaning and feeling for us. In my poem I am really writing about a pronounced feeling of loneliness and abandonment in childhood, which I associate with a cold and unpeopled landscape. My childhood was doubtless much better than that of many, but my brother was born epileptic when I was just over two, and from then on all attention was, very properly, focused on him. I have always

felt that desolation, that hell itself, is most powerfully expressed in an uninhabited natural landscape at its bleakest.

The most direct poetic version of these same events is "Apprehensions." (The title alone indicates the poem's mix of fear and guilt, understanding and arrest, and a dreaded anticipation of the future.) The poem recounts his brother's "grave and secret malady," its effect and that of the stockmarket crash on his family and his father's attempted suicide (a double failure which is linked, by a stolen barbiturate, with the brother's illness). But those events, convulsive in themselves, seem the background to the primary relationship in the poem, that between the young Hecht and his Fräulein, "a Teutonic governess / Replete with the curious thumb-print of her race, / That special relish for inflicted pain." The world of this childhood, this poem, is one "made of violent oppositions" that the child could placate only by "mute docility." The pain inflicted is linked, finally, to the Holocaust and the war; even more eerily, during the dream reunion at the poem's end, Hecht associates himself with this figure, a witch out of Grimm, a foster mother. In fact, through the whole poem in some strange way this menacing Fräulein stands in for the child's mother, who is barely mentioned. The sense of abandonment, loneliness, and cruelty in the child's home life is balanced—or compensated for—in the poem by two gifts, two modes of apprehensions, a book and a vision, both of them associated with the creative imagination and thereby with the poet's later vocation. *The Book of Knowledge* gave him encyclopedic access to the treasure of the world's stories; a minutely detailed vision out the apartment window—whereby a taxicab, and then the street, and the city, and then the continent are held and transfigured in the transfiguring eye of the artist—gave him a sense of some other available power. In a young life marked by what he calls "elisions," these experiences are fulfilling.

But they are compensatory: fugitive, fragmentary, the stuff of romance, in every sense imaginary. To put this poem side by side with "A Hill" is to be struck with the similarity between *The Book of Knowledge* and the Farnese Palace, the Manhattan avenue and the Roman piazza—a world of figures apprehended there. The child standing alone in the front of the open window is a type of the solipsist, the artist; he is "superbly happy" because he is alone. (Freud defined melancholia as regressive narcissism.) But this is a rare indulgence of Hecht's and not altogether to be trusted. It is most likely a screen memory. The child standing alone in front of the hill is perhaps a screen memory too. A hill, a mound or barrow, may be a tomb, and this poem's genre is less the dream-vision than the elegy, perhaps an elegy for the self. A hill is also traditionally a symbol of the mother. It is where the dead abide and entrance to the otherworld, the matrix. My guess is that the mother is the unspoken, unacknowledged but looming presence in "A Hill," or at least in the second part of the poem—its landscape the mother's body—where a primal world supplants the busy, bright masculine Roman scene. And I suspect the figure of the mother is the focus of those feelings of fear and guilt, abandonment and loneliness in so many of Hecht's poems. His own account substitutes his brother, but he is the occasion, not the cause. The opening of "The Venetian Vespers," a poem set in a water-borne city, connects "the stale water and glass / In the upstairs room when somebody had died" (the somebody, it soon emerges, is the child's mother) with

> those first precocious hints of hell,
> Those intuitions of living desolation
> That last a lifetime. They were never, for me,
> Some desert place that humans had avoided
> In which I could get lost, to which I might
> In dreams condemn myself—a wilderness
> Natural but alien and unpitying.
> They were instead those derelict waste places
> Abandoned by mankind as of no worth,
> Frequented, if at all, by the dispossessed,
> Nocturnal shapes, the crippled and the shamed.

In fact, some lines later, the speaker associates his mother's death with the image of "underwater globes, / Mercury seedpearls"—Mercury the hermetic psychopomp to the dead. Another poem, "The Grapes," makes a similar association. The speaker now is a no-longer young chambermaid, an antitype to the Fräulein. (In this poem has Hecht cast himself, under the name of Marc-Antoine, as her neglectful lover?) Her experience of the vision-of-the-hill is a daydream, an image generated by a magazine article, the image of a sole survivor of a crash, adrift in a rubber boat in mid-Pacific, "that blank / Untroubled waste." And her disenchantment comes when she happens to be gazing,

> Gazing down at a crystal bowl of grapes
> In ice-water. They were green grapes, or, rather,

> They were a sort of pure, unblemished jade,
> Like turbulent ocean water, with misted skins,
> Their own pale, smoky sweat, or tiny frost.

Again, the underwater globes; something—a whole world—drowned and distant. The maid in "The Grapes" is mourning her own life, but the pattern persists, poem to poem. The most frightening appearance of the mother in all of Hecht's books comes in "Behold the Lilies of the Field," where, from the couch in a psychiatrist's office, the speaker relates a vivid fantasy of having attended at the flaying of a Roman emperor by his barbarian captors:

> When they were done, hours later,
> The skin was turned over to one of their saddle-makers
> To be tanned and stuffed and sewn. And for what?
> A hideous life-sized doll, filled out with straw,
> In the skin of the Roman Emperor, Valerian,
> With blanks of mother-of-pearl under the eyelids,
> And painted shells that had been prepared beforehand
> For the fingernails and toenails,
> Roughly cross-stitched on the inseam of the legs
> And up the back to the center of the head,
> Swung in the wind on a rope from the palace flag-pole;
> And young girls were brought there by their mothers
> To be told about the male anatomy.
> His death had taken hours.
> They were very patient.
> And with him passed away the honor of Rome.
>
> In the end, I was ransomed. Mother paid for me.

This nasty little Oedipal fantasy and its erotic violence—an impulse that fascinates and horrifies this poet—stand at one extreme of the group of poems I am discussing. "A Hill" stands at the other. Neither poem, nor any of those between, can be reduced to a textbook formula. I do not mean to solve the poem, to pluck the heart out of its mystery, but only to suggest that its mysterious force derives in part from such pressures. Besides, when I invoke the word *mother*, I mean it to stand in for the source of light and life, as well as the Queen of the Night. She is the preconscious. She is memory. She is the muse. The sense of abandonment makes the poet invert her sustaining warmth into a lifeless cold, the pit of hell. In other poems it is a grave for Jews. In "The Short End," whose remote, admonitory parent-figures are George Rose and Miss McIntosh, it is a coffin for George Rose, whose "other-worldliness" leads to a lesson that love and bitterness are the same. None of these anatomies of melancholy offers the reader—as distinct from their protagonists—any easy lesson. Indeed, what I suggest is the probing complex of emotions—the controlled disorder, painful doubleness—that drives the poem and is pursued through an intertexture of images that touches, obscurely or overtly, most of the major poems in Hecht's work.

Melancholy is Hecht's keynote, especially in *The Hard Hours*, whose first poem is "A Hill" and whose epigraph is *"Al that joye is went away."* Darkness and suffering suffuse the book. Its ironies curdle into cynicism; its wrenching horrors are dwelt upon. I wonder if the book's many victims aren't projections of the poet himself; if the sufferings of wartime Europe don't find their subjective correlative in the poet's own. There are also references in the book that puzzle. "Adam," for instance, is a poem addressed to one of his sons by his first marriage. It is a poem with the book's title in it ("Adam, there will be / Many hard hours, / As an old poem says, / Hours of loneliness"). Its concluding stanza is peculiar, except in the usual metaphoric way:

> Think of the summer rain
> Or seedpearls of the mist;
> Seeing the beaded leaf,
> Try to remember me.
> From far away
> I send my blessing out
> To circle the great globe.
> It shall reach you yet.

(Watery seedpearls, globe—already the central cluster of images has been invoked.) Likewise, "A Letter" ends ominously:

> There is not much else to tell.
> One tries one's best to continue as before,
> Doing some little good.
> But I would have you know that all is not well
> With a man dead set to ignore
> The endless repetitions of his own murmurous blood.

I have asked the poet what lay behind such lines—behind the entire book, really—and he answered me in a letter that I quote now with his permission:

At the termination of five-and-a-half years of a painfully unhappy and unsuccessful marriage, a separation settlement was made, followed by a divorce, which required of my ex-wife that she live within 150 miles of New York City, so that I should be able to see the children on a regular basis. I must add that, while the marriage had been an unhappy one virtually from the start, its failure was a terrible blow to my self-esteem, and it was not I who sought to terminate it. When it was over I invested all my frustrated familial feelings on the two boys whom I saw, like most divorced fathers, on weekends, making those days unhealthily emotional, and completely without any ease or naturalness. In a way, I resented this arrangement: I had a job to perform during the week (teaching at Bard in those years) and such spare time as I had was devoted entirely to the children, who were pretty young in those days, the younger one still in diapers when all this began. So I had no private life of my own, and consequently invested too much emotional capital in the children. I was the more inclined to do so because I knew their mother to be completely irresponsible with regard to them. Then one day she told me, as I was delivering the children to her at the end of a weekend, that she had fallen in love with a Belgian, and that while I could legally prevent her from moving to Europe, as this man wished her to do, if she were forced to stay in this country she would be very unhappy, and if she were very unhappy, the children would be very unhappy. There was, of course, no argument to counter this. I had asked my lawyer, before the separation papers were drawn up, whether it would be possible for me to obtain custody of the children. He told me that it was virtually impossible, and in those days he was right. So she took the children off to Belgium, and I sank into a very deep depression. I felt no incentive even to get out of bed in the morning. I don't believe I thought in terms of suicide, but neither did life seem to hold out any attractions whatever. My doctor was worried about me, and suggested that I commit myself to a hospital, chiefly, he said, for the administration of medication. It was thorazine, and some other drug the name of which I no longer recall. I was there for three months, toward the end of which time I was allowed to go out during the days. Lowell was particularly kind to me during this period. The hospital was called Gracie Square Hospital, and there were some public pay phones on my floor, on which incoming calls to patients would be carried. Anyone could pick up a phone when it rang, and then page in a loud shout whoever the call was for. It was the custom of the patients to announce, in a loud and cheerful voice, on picking up the phone: "Crazy Square." Many of the patients were on electric shock; it had been agreed before I went in that I would be treated solely with medication, and this was observed. And the medication did indeed control the depression. What would have been a grim three months was, while by no means cheerful, yet remarkably endurable. The only thing I remember complaining about—it was pointless, of course, to complain about the food or routine—was the pictures. The plain bare walls were occasionally "enlivened" by framed pieces of cloth with arbitrary patterns on them, things that might have been drapes or upholstery. The chief point about them was that they were non-representational, and would not remind any patient of anything that carried an emotional burden.

This memoir is all the more moving for its dispassionate and at times even witty tone. The "frustrated familial feelings" should by now be familiar ones. Hecht's own childhood feelings of abandonment are first recklessly overcompensated for and then sadly reinforced when his own children are taken away. The subsequent breakdown is as marked a contrast to his frenetic life before the children left as is the contrast of moods in "A Hill." And the symptoms of his resulting depression have also made their way into later poems. But there are just two details in this letter that I want to draw particular attention to. One is that pun, "Crazy Square." Even when drugged and confined, the poet's ear is attuned to the incongruous, to the play of words—as if, even when sliding around, language could still hold its meanings together. The other is his complaint about the hospital "art." The very words he uses here recall phrases in "A Hill"—"the plain bare walls" echoing "a hill, mole-colored and bare" and "I was scared by the plain bitterness of what I had seen." I suggest that what he is looking at has a great deal to do with "A Hill" and ask a reader to keep in mind this letter's memory of Hecht's complaint about those nonpicturing pictures. Ironically, their "function"—not to stir any old emotional burdens in a patient—had the effect of rousing Hecht. The burden they may have carried to him is a factor of their resemblance to the hill in his poem.

In his essay "On the Methods and Ambitions of Poetry," Hecht talks about the homage a poem pays to "the natural world, from which it derives and which it strives to imitate. And there is in nature a superfluity, an excess of texture which plays no necessary part in the natural economy." *Excess of texture* neatly defines that aspect of Hecht's own style we register as baroque. I say an aspect because he turns to it—turns it on, even—usually as a deliberate thematic maneuver. There are swags of it in "The Venetian Vespers," for instance. The poem's speaker, like the child in "Apprehensions," is looking out his window:

> Here is a sky determined to maintain
> The reputation of Tiepolo,
> A moving vision of a shapely mist,
> Full of the splendor of the insubstantial.
> Against a diorama of palest blue
> Cloud-curds, cloud-stacks, cloud-bushes sun themselves.
> Giant confections, impossible meringues,
> Soft coral reefs and powdery tumuli
> Pass in august processions and calm herds.
> Great stadiums, grandstands and amphitheaters,
> The tufted, opulent litters of the gods
> They seem; or laundered bunting, well-dressed wigs,
> Harvests of milk-white, Chinese peonies
> That visibly rebuke our stinginess.
> For all their ghostly presences, they take on
> A colorful nobility at evening.
> Off to the east the sky begins to turn
> Lilac so pale it seems a mood of gray,
> Gradually, like the death of virtuous men.
> Streaks of electrum richly underline
> The slow, flat-bottomed hulls, those floated lobes
> Between which quills and spokes of light fan out
> Into carnelian reds and nectarines,
> Nearing a citron brilliance at the center,
> The searing furnace of the glory hole
> That fires and fuses clouds of muscatel
> With pencilings of gold. I look and look,
> As though I could be saved simply by looking.

And of course he cannot be saved: the grandeur is a delusion, and its excess a measure of his own inabilities. Everywhere is *seems* and *like*. Left behind, but behind it all, is thin air. The empurpled passage stands as both tribute to and accusation of the imagination. Trope is a contrivance, a twisting, a turning aside.

Readers in the past have missed Hecht's canny relationship to such gold pencilings. "Somebody's Life," a pair of unrhymed sonnets, is a sly satire on this impulse of art. A poet sits atop a cliff overlooking the sea and rocks. In an attitude of sublimity he "Felt himself claimed by such rash opulence: / There were the lofty figures of his soul." The poem then goes on to ask a more serious question, "Was this the secret / Gaudery of self-love, or a blood-bidden, / Involuntary homage to the world?" (That last phrase an involuntary allusion to the essay published eleven years earlier?) In any case, the poem avoids a direct answer, as if thereby to acknowledge there is none, and instead juxtaposes the actual and the figurative:

> As it happens, he was doomed never to know.
> At times in darkened rooms he thought he heard
> The soft ruckus of patiently torn paper,
> The sea's own noise, the elderly slop and suck
> Of hopeless glottals. Once, in a bad dream,
> He saw himself stranded on the wet flats,
> As limp as kelp, among putrescent crabs.
> But to the very finish he remembered
> The flash and force, the crests, the heraldry,
> Those casual épergnes towering up
> Like Easter trinkets of the tzarevitch.

Again the notion of salvation; "épergne," or glass serving dish, is from a French word meaning "to save," and the mention of "Easter trinkets" hints at resurrection, though the tzarevitch, like the poet in his own dream, is doomed.

The extravagance of the high style in a Hecht poem should signal some unknowing desperation, some pride before a fall. It often verges toward a Latinate diction, and the added syllables give a kind of tumbling motion to the rhythm. Or appositional phrases and clauses are heaped up for momentum's sake. There is a brilliantly colored blur, a manic rush. One hears it, sees it, at the beginning of "A Hill":

> A clear fretwork of shadows
> From huge umbrellas littered the pavement and made
> A sort of lucent shallows in which was moored
> A small navy of carts. Books, coins, old maps,
> Cheap landscapes and ugly religious prints
> Were all on sale. The colors and noise
> Like the flying hands were gestures of exultation,
> So that even the bargaining
> Rose to the ear like a voluble godliness.

The language here is loaded with emptiness: "shallows," "gestures," the bogus art. At this pitch of exultation, the vision occurs. It is, first of all, a transformation scene, the world's flapping backdrops revealed as *teatrum mundi*. When Hecht says the "pushcarts and people dissolved / And even the great Farnese Palace itself / Was gone, for all its marble," certainly we are meant to hear the echo of Prospero's lines:

> And, like the baseless fabric of this vision,
> The cloud-capp'd towers, the gorgeous palaces,
> The solemn temples, the great globe itself,
> Yea, all which it inherit, shall dissolve
> And like this insubstantial pageant faded,
> Leave not a rack behind. We are such stuff
> As dreams are made on, and our little life
> Is rounded with a sleep. Sir, I am vex'd,—
> Bear with my weakness—my old brain is troubled.

What at the start is proposed as "real," the Italian setting, is described in language charged with metaphor, color, allusion, artifice. The "vision" that intrudes is described as starkly, as naturalistically as possible. A shred of ribbon, a distant crack—these are all that remain. And a whole series of contrasts is stressed: palace and hill, Rome and Poughkeepsie, commotion and stillness, warmth and cold, adult and child, lucent shallows and dark depths, sensual consciousness and numbed instinctual memory. The plain style of the poem's second half befits the stillness, the "cold and silence." And what is crucial to understand is that this deflation or disenchantment that works to mock the high style and reveal the insubstantiality of metaphor in fact accords with Hecht's own sense of the true art of poetry. In the essay I've already quoted from, he begins by asserting that "art serves to arrest action rather than promote it, and to invite instead a state of aesthetic contemplation." Twice in this poem its action is arrested, first by the scarifying vision, and a decade later by a sudden memory. And the poem then ends abruptly, even melodramatically, as if further to arrest the action of interpretation. The speaker reverts to childhood, and stands—as, in a sense, the reader does too—before the hill in winter, blank as a page. The clarification and connections we might expect to follow are omitted. But the point of the poem, what the reader is invited to contemplate, is not really the explication of personal experience, but an understanding of the competing forces of experience itself—forces that are embodied in the poem's contrasting styles. The poem ends with an image, not a moral. The tense of the last line could as well have been changed from the historical past to the present indicative—"It is winter. I am standing, for hours, before it."—to underscore the fact that he is describing a condition rather than an occurrence. Hecht's essay on poetic methods concludes with what may as well be the final word on "A Hill": "in allowing us to contemplate, even within a single poem, such diversity of experience, both the good and the bad, brought into tenuous balance through all the manifold devices of art, the spirit is set at ease by a kind of katharsis, in which we are brought to acknowledge that this is the way things are."

That last catch phrase, by which Rolfe Humphries called his translation of Lucretius's *De Rerum Natura*, brings me to a final observation about Hecht's anatomies of melancholy. Though his imposing rhetoric often belies it, Hecht is by temperament closer to Frost than Stevens, and like Frost, a poet in the line of Lucretius, who wrote, as he says at the head of book 4 of his epic, "clear verse about dark things." Lucretius was a poet of violence and profound melancholy, of intellectual rigor and imaginative grandeur. He searched in his poem the ground and limits of human life, the instability and monotony, and celebrated its mechanism—those principles of Strife and Love by which nature decays and regenerates, unraveling by night what was woven by day, and out of which we make our ideas (like Death Wish and Life Force), and gods (like Mars and Venus Genetrix), our fantasies and our metaphors. In *Three Philosophical Poets*, from which Hecht drew the epigraph and orphic title of his first book, *A Summoning of Stones*, George Santayana summarizes Lucretius's philosophical perspective and his poetic method:

> Naturalism is a philosophy of observation, and of an imagination that extends the observable; all the sights and sounds of nature enter into it, and lend it their directness, pungency, and coercive stress. At the same time, naturalism is an intellectual philosophy; it divines substance behind appearance, continuity behind change, law behind fortune. It therefore attaches all those sights and sounds to a hidden background that connects and explains them. So understood, nature has a depth as well as surface, force and necessity as well as sensuous variety.... Unapproachably vivid, relentless, direct in detail, he is unflinchingly grand and serious in his grouping of the facts. It is the truth that absorbs him and carries him along. He wishes us to be convinced and sobered by the fact, by the overwhelming evidence of thing after thing, raining down upon us, all bearing witness with one voice to the nature of the world.

That description comes as close to Hecht's purposes too as any critic can. He is a contemplative rather than a lyrical poet. A steady contemplation of things in their order and worth—the facts of his own life, the course of history, the archive of myth and belief—is his goal. And it is, in Santayana's phrase, the truth that absorbs him and carries him along: a wary, circumscribed but certain knowledge on which are erected love's monuments, and hope's ideal cities, and all the bright, revolving orders of the imagination. But he indulges their excesses precisely in order to test and often to undermine them. They are his rough magic, and he will abjure them.

Appendix

CHRONOLOGY

1923	Born (16 January) in New York City
1940	Enters Bard College
1943	Called up for military service
1944	B.A. in absentia, Bard College
1946	Discharged from Army
1947	Instructor, Bard College
1948	Instructor, New York University
1950	M.A., Columbia University
1950–54	Instructor, Bard College
1956–59	Instructor, Assistant Professor, Smith College
1961–67	Associate Professor, Professor, Bard College
1967–68	Associate Professor, University of Rochester
1968–85	John H. Deane Professor of Rhetoric and Poetry, University of Rochester
1971	Hurst Professor, Washington University
1973	Visiting Professor, Harvard University
1977	Visiting Professor, Yale University
1982–84	Consultant in Poetry, United States Library of Congress
1985–	University Professor, Georgetown University

AWARDS AND DISTINCTIONS

1951	Prix de Rome
1954, 1959	John Simon Guggenheim Memorial Foundation Fellowships
1960	Ford Fellowship
1967	Rockefeller Fellowship
1968	Pulitzer Prize; Russell Loines Award for *The Hard Hours*

1969   Honorary Fellow, Academy of American Poets
1970   Member, National Institute of Arts and Letters
1975   Fellow, American Academy of Arts and Sciences
1971–95 Chancellor, Academy of American Poets
1982–84 Consultant in Poetry, United States Library of Congress
1983   Bollingen Prize
1984   Eugenio Montale Award for Poetry

Honorary doctorates from Bard College, Georgetown University, Towson State University, and the University of Rochester.

Bibliography

WORKS BY ANTHONY HECHT

Books

A Summoning of Stones. New York: Macmillan, 1954.
The Seven Deadly Sins. Northampton, Mass.: Gehenna Press, 1958. With wood engravings by Leonard Baskin.
Aesopic. Northampton, Mass.: Gehenna Press, 1967. Twenty-four couplets by Anthony Hecht accompany the Thomas Bewick wood engravings for select fables. With an afterword on the blocks by Philip Hofer.
The Hard Hours. New York: Atheneum, 1968.
Aeschylus: Seven Against Thebes. Translated by Anthony Hecht and Helen Bacon. New York: Oxford University Press, 1973.
Millions of Strange Shadows. New York: Atheneum, 1977.
Voltaire's Poème sur le désastre de Lisbonne/Poem upon the Lisbon Disaster. Translated from the French by Anthony Hecht. Lincoln, Mass.: Penmaen Press, 1977. With six wood engravings by Lynd Ward and an introduction by Arthur Wilson.
The Venetian Vespers. New York: Atheneum, 1979.
A Love for Four Voices: Homage to Franz Joseph Haydn. Great Barrington, Mass.: Penmaen Press, 1983.
Jiggery Pokery: A Compendium of Double Dactyls. Edited by Anthony Hecht and John Hollander. New York: Atheneum, 1984.
Obbligati: Essays in Criticism. New York: Atheneum, 1986.

Articles, Essays, and Introductions

"Poets and Peasants." *Hudson Review* 10 (Winter 1957–58): 606–13.

"A Few Green Leaves." *Sewanee Review* 67 (Autumn 1959): 568–71. (On Allen Tate.)
"Shades of Keats and Marvell." *Hudson Review* 15 (Spring 1962): 50–71.
"On the Methods and Ambitions of Poetry." *Hudson Review* 18 (1965): 489–505.
"Double Dactyl." *Esquire* 65 (June 1966): 109+. With examples of poems.
"I Hear America Singing Slightly Off-Key." *Esquire* 66 (September 1966): 164–67. With examples of poems.
"Discovering Auden." *Harvard Advocate* 108 (1975): 48–50.
"Dichtung und Wahrheit." *American Scholar* 46 (Winter 1976): 56–58.
"The Motions of the Mind." *Times Literary Supplement* 3, no. 923 (May 20, 1977): 602. Review of Richard Wilbur's *The Mind Reader*.
"Awful But Cheerful." *Times Literary Supplement* 3, no. 937 (August 26, 1977): 1024. Review of Elizabeth Bishop's *Geography III*.
"The Riddles of Emily Dickinson." *New England Review* 1 (1978): 1–24.
"On W. H. Auden's 'In Praise of Limestone.'" *New England Review* 2 (1979): 65–84.
"John Crowe Ransom." *American Scholar* 49 (Summer 1980): 379–83.
"Masters of Unpleasantness: The Making of a Writer." *New York Times Book Review* 87 (February 7, 1982): 3+.
"My Most Obnoxious Writer." *New York Times Book Review* 87 (August 29, 1982): 7+. Various authors, including Hecht, comment on writers they consider to have had nasty personalities.
"Books That Gave Me Pleasure." *New York Times Book Review* 87 (December 5, 1982): 9+. Famous people, including Hecht, discuss favorite books.
"Le Byron de nos Jours." *Grand Street* 2 (Spring 1983): 32–48. On Ian Hamilton's *Robert Lowell*.
Introduction. *The Morrow Anthology of Younger American Poets*. New York: Morrow Quill, 1985.
"Symposium of Poets on T. S. Eliot." *Southern Review* 21 (Autumn 1985): 1138–63. With Hecht, Stephen Berg, Louise Gluck, Donald Hall, Howard Moss, Lisel Mueller, Carol Muske, Robert Pinsky, and Theodore Weiss.

SECONDARY WORKS

"American Editions." *Times Literary Supplement* 3, no. 430 (November 23, 1967): 1106. Unsigned review of *The Hard Hours.*

Atlas, James. "New Voices in American Poetry." *New York Times Magazine* 129 (February 3, 1980): 1–6.

Bogan, Louise. Review of *A Summoning of Stones. New Yorker* 30 (June 5, 1954): 134.

Brown, Ashley. "The Poetry of Anthony Hecht." *Ploughshares* 4, no. 3 (1978): 9–24.

Cole, William. "Trade Winds: Lighter-Than-Air-Craft." Review of *Light Year '85. Saturday Review* 10 (December 1984): 90.

Davie, Donald. "The Twain Not Meeting." *Parnassus* 8, no. 1 (1980): 84–91. Review of article on J. Miles and Hecht.

Dostert, Candyce. Review of *Obbligati: Essays in Criticism. Wilson Library Bulletin* 61 (December 1986): 71.

Ehrenpreis, Irvin. "At the Poles of Poetry." *New York Review of Books* 25 (August 17, 1978): 48–49.

Elliott, George P. "The Freshness of Text." *Times Literary Supplement* 3, no. 921 (May 6, 1977): 548. Review of *Millions of Strange Shadows.*

Fraser, G. S. "Some Younger American Poets." *Commentary* 23 (May 1957): 462.

Garfitt, Roger. "Contrary Attractions." *Times Literary Supplement* (May 30, 1980): 623. Review of *The Venetian Vespers.*

Gerber, Philip L., and Robert J. Gemmets, eds. "An Interview with Anthony Hecht." *Mediterranean Review* 1, no. 3 (1971): 3–9.

German, H. Norman. "'What Do We Know of Lasting?': Renewal of Perception and Reanimation of the World in the Works of Anthony Hecht." *Dissertation Abstracts International* 44 (August 1983): 489A.

Gross, John. "Double Dactyls and Other Wonders." Review of *Jiggery Pokery. New York Times Book Review* 89 (January 29, 1984): 8.

Guillory, Daniel L. Review of *Obbligati: Essays in Criticism. Library Journal* 3 (August 1986): 151.

Hemphill, George. "Anthony Hecht's Nunnery of Art." *Person* 12 (1962): 163–71.

Hoffman, D. "Poetry of Anguish." *Reporter* 38 (February 22, 1968): 52–54.

Howard, Richard. "Anthony Hecht." In *Alone with America: Essays on the Art of Poetry in the United States Since 1950,* 164–73. New York: Atheneum, 1969.

———. "Shadows." Review of *Millions of Strange Shadows. Poetry* 131 (November 1977): 103–6.

Jacobsen, Eric. "'Look Here upon This Picture and on This': Reflections on

Some Modern Picture Poems." *Papers from the First Nordic Conference for English Studies*, ed. Stig Johansson and Bjorn Tysdahl. Oslo: Institute of English Studies, University of Oslo, 1981. Study examples are Philip Larkin's "Lines on a Young Lady's Photography Album," Ted Hughes's "Six Young Men," and Hecht's "Dichtung und Wahrheit" and "Auguries of Innocence."

Jerome, Judson. "Page Turners." *Writer's Digest* 64 (August 1984): 10.

Jost, Nicholas. "Hecht's 'Ostia Antica.'" *The Explicator* 20 (October 1961): 14.

Madoff, Steven. "The Poet at Cross Purposes." *The Nation* 225 (September 3, 1977): 188+.

Menard, Louis. "A Metaphor Is a Terrible Thing to Waste." Review of *Obbligati: Essays in Criticism*. *New York Times Book Review* 74 (September 7, 1986): 19+.

Miller, Stephen. "A Poem by Anthony Hecht." *Spirit* 39, no. 1 (1971): 8–11.

Motion, Andrew. "Veils and Veins." Review of *Venetian Vespers*. *New Statesman* 99 (May 1980): 717.

Nelson, Dale. "Bollingen Back at LC." Column (Dateline Washington) in *Wilson Library Bulletin* 57 (April 1983): 684–85.

Review of *Obbligati: Essays in Criticism*. *Publisher's Weekly* 229 (June 13, 1986): 64.

Perloff, Marjorie. "Anthony Hecht, *The Hard Hours*." *The Far Point* (University of Manitoba) 2 (1969): 45–51. Review.

Pettingell, P. "Anthony Hecht's Transmutations." Review of *Venetian Vespers*. *New Leader* 62 (December 17, 1979): 22.

Plath, Sylvia. "Poets on Campus." *Mademoiselle* 37 (August 1953): 290.

Pritchard, William H. "Formal Measures." Review of *Obbligati: Essays in Criticism*. *New Republic* 195 (December 15, 1986): 37–38.

Ricks, Christopher. "Poets Who Have Learned Their Trade." Review of *Venetian Vespers*. *New York Times Book Review* 84 (December 2, 1979): 1.

Rowe, Portis. Review of *Millions of Strange Shadows*. *Library Journal* 102 (March 1, 1977): 611.

Shetley, Vernon. "Take But Degree Away." Review of *Venetian Vespers*. *Poetry* 137 (February 1981): 297.

Smith, Wendy. "An Interview with Anthony and Helen Hecht." *Publisher's Weekly* 230 (July 18, 1986): 70+.

Contributors

JOSEPH BRODSKY won the Nobel Prize for literature in 1987.

ASHLEY BROWN, a professor of English at the University of South Carolina, has edited several books, most recently *The Poetry Reviews of Allen Tate, 1924–1944*. He has contributed many essays, translations, and reviews to journals in the United States and England.

KENNETH GROSS teaches English at the University of Rochester. He is the author of *Spenserian Poetics: Idolatry, Iconoclasm, and Magic* and of various essays on the poetry of Dante, Milton, and Marvell.

EDWARD HIRSCH is the author of three books of poems: *For the Sleepwalkers*, *Wild Gratitude*, and *Testimony*. He teaches at the University of Houston.

DANIEL HOFFMAN is the author of *Hang-Gliding from Helicon: New and Selected Poems, 1948–1988* and of several critical studies, among them *Poe Poe Poe Poe Poe Poe Poe*. A former consultant in poetry for the Library of Congress, he is poet in residence and Schelling Professor of English at the University of Pennsylvania.

BRAD LEITHAUSER, a MacArthur Fellow, is the author of a novel and two books of verse, the most recent *Cats of the Temple*.

J. D. MCCLATCHY is the author of two collections of poems, *Scenes from Another Life* and *Stars Principal*. He has edited several books and his essays and reviews appear regularly in such magazines as *Poetry*, the *New York Times Book Review*, and the *New Republic*. He has taught at Yale and Princeton and is poetry editor of the *Yale Review*.

WILLIAM MATTHEWS is the author of seven books of poems, most recently *Foreseeable Futures*, and is a professor of English at City College in New York. He has held fellowships from the National Endowment for the Arts, the Ingram Merrill Foundation, and the Guggenheim Foundation and is the author of a book of essays, *Curiosities*.

Contributors

JOHN FREDERICK NIMS's most recent books of poetry are *The Kiss: A Jambalaya* and *Selected Poems*, both published in 1982, the year in which he was awarded a fellowship from the Academy of American Poets. He was the recipient of a Guggenheim Fellowship for poetry in 1986–87.

LINDA ORR is the author of *Jules Michelet: Nature, History, and Language* and *A Certain X*, a book of poems. Her translations from the French have appeared in *Antaeus, Seneca Review,* and *Paris Review*. She teaches French literature at Duke University.

ALICIA OSTRIKER is a poet and critic who teaches at Rutgers University and has a longstanding interest in matters prosodic. She edited *Complete Poems of William Blake* and is the author of *Stealing the Language: The Emergence of Women's Poetry in America*. Her most recent book of poems, *The Imaginary Lover*, won the William Carlos Williams Award of the Poetry Society of America.

PETER SACKS is the author of *In These Mountains*, a collection of poems, and *The English Elegy: Studies in the Genre from Spenser to Yeats*. He is associate professor in the Writing Seminars and English Department at Johns Hopkins University.

NORMAN WILLIAMS is an attorney and a poet in North Ferrisburgh, Vermont. His first book, *The Unlovely Child*, was published in 1985. He won the Amy Lowell Traveling Fellowship in 1979–80 and the Lavan Award from the Academy of American Poets in 1987.

CPSIA information can be obtained
at www.ICGtesting.com
Printed in the USA
FFOW02n1950080216
21231FF